Cloud Computing
and
Virtualization

Cloud Computing and Virtualization

Dr. R. Rajeswara Rao
Associate Professor of CSE
JNTUK-UCEV, Vizianagaram

V. Subba Ramaiah
Sr. Assistant Professor
Mahatma Gandhi Institute of Technology
C.B Post, Gandipet, Hyderabad.

BS Publications

A unit of **BSP Books Pvt. Ltd.**
4-4-309/316, Giriraj Lane, Sultan Bazar,
Hyderabad - 500 095
Phone : 040 - 23445605, 23445688

Published by

 **BS Publications**

A unit of **BSP Books Pvt. Ltd.**

4-4-309/316, Giriraj Lane, Sultan Bazar,

Hyderabad - 500 095

Phone : 040 - 23445605, 23445688

e-mail : info@bspbooks.net

ISBN: 978-93-85433-60-3 (HB)

Preface

This book was motivated by my experience in teaching the course "Cloud Computing" to the undergraduate and post graduate students of computer science and engineering courses.

Cloud computing is an emerging technology in today's world. Clouds provide access to inexpensive hardware and storage resources through very simple APIs, and are based on a pay-per-use model, so that renting these resources is usually much cheaper than acquiring dedicated new ones. Moreover, people are becoming comfortable with storing their data remotely in a cloud environment. Therefore, clouds are being increasingly used by scientists, small and medium sized enterprises, and casual users.

Virtualization enables cloud computing, providing the ability to run legacy applications on older operating systems, creation of a single system image starting from an heterogeneous collection of machines such as those traditionally found in grid environments, and faster job migration within different virtual machines running on the same hardware. For grid and cloud computing, virtualization is the key for provisioning and fair resource allocation. From the security point of view, since virtual machines run isolated in their sandboxes, this provides an additional protection against malicious or faulty codes.

An attempt has been made to write this book in a simple and lucid language with neat and self-explanatory diagram, which could be easily understood by all the students. The brief content of the book is as follows:

Chapter 1 Evolution of Cloud Computing

Chapter 2 Introduction Cloud Computing

Chapter 3 Services Delivered from the Cloud

Chapter 4 Building Cloud Networks

Chapter 5 Virtualization in cloud

Chapter 6 Security in Cloud

Chapter 7 Common Standards in Cloud Computing

Chapter 8 End User Access to Cloud Computing

Chapter 9 Cloud Architecture Defining the Clouds for the Enterprise

Chapter 10 Disaster Recovery and Security

This book is uniquely different from many other books in a number of ways. Some of the salient features of the book are as under:

- Each chapter contains an extensive list of exercises.
- Lucid, simple, and conversational language.
- Systematic and sequential arrangement of different topics.
- Concise and to-the-point description of all the topics.
- Eminently suitable for self-study.

Finally, the receipt of suggestions, comments and error reports for further improvement of the book would be welcomed and duly acknowledged.

-Authors

Acknowledgement

In the course of Publication, we received help from friends, colleagues and BS Publications.

We express our sincere gratitude to all of them.

We especially thanks the editorial and technical team of BSP, which is headed by director Anil Shah, Vasudeva Rao and Naresh for their kind support during preparation of the manuscript. Their encouragement was the greatest motivational factor for us in the completion of this assignment.

We would like to thank and express our appreciation to our parents and family members for their patients and encouragement in bringing out this book.

Finally, we would like to thank the staff at BSP for their enthusiastic support and guidance during the preparation of this book.

We hope that this edition of the book will prove useful to all students as well as teachers. Any suggestions for the improvement of the book are welcome and will be gratefully acknowledged.

Any Suggestions can be mailed to: raob4u@yahoo.com and subbubdl@gmail.com.

-Authors

Contents

Chapter 1

EVOLUTION OF CLOUD COMPUTING

Chapter 2

INTRODUCTION TO CLOUD COMPUTING

Chapter 3

SERVICES DELIVERED FROM THE CLOUD

Chapter 4

BUILDING CLOUD NETWORKS

Chapter 5

VIRTUALIZATION IN CLOUD

Chapter 6

SECURITY IN CLOUD

Chapter 7

COMMON STANDARDS IN CLOUD COMPUTING

Chapter 8

END USER ACCESS TO CLOUD COMPUTING

CHAPTER 9

CLOUD ARCHITECTURE DEFINING THE CLOUDS FOR THE ENTERPRISE

Chapter 10

DISASTER RECOVERY AND SECURITY

AJAX	Asynchronous JavaScript
AM I	Amazon Machine Image
Amazon EBS	Amazon Elastic Block Store
Amazon SQS	Amazon Simple Queue Service
Amazon S3	Amazon Simple Storage Service
API	Application Programming Interface
APP	Atom and Atom Publishing Protocol
ASP	Application Service Provider
AWS	Amazon Web Service
BIA	Business Impact Analysis
CSP	Cloud service providers
CaaS	Communication-as-a-Service
CORBA	Common Object Requesting Broker Architecture
CDN	Content Delivery Network
CD-ROM	Compact Disc read-only-memory
CPU	Central Processing Unit
DEC	Digital Equipment Corporation
DCOM	Distributed Component Object Model
DMTF	Distributed Management Task Force
DNS	Domain Name Service
DVD	Digital Versatile Disc
EC2	Elastic Compute Cloud
EA	Enterprise Architecture
FTP	File Transfer Protocol
GUI	Graphical User Interface
GPU	Graphic Processing Unit
HA	High Availability
HPC	High Performance Computing

RPO	Recovery Point Objective
RSS	Really Simple Syndication
RR	Round Robin
RTO	Recovery Time Objective
SAML	Security Assertion Markup Language
SETI	Search for Extraterrestrial Intelligence
SOA	service oriented architecture
SaaS	Software-as-a-Service
SOC	Security Operations Center
SIMPLE	Session Initiation Protocol for Instant Messaging and Presence Leveraging Extensions
SLA	Service Level Agreement
SMTP	Simple Mail Transfer Protocol
SOAP	Simple Object Access Protocol
SMP	Symmetric Multiprocessing Systems
SDLC	systems development life cycle
SSL	Secure Socket Layer
SVG	Scalable Vector Graphics
TCO	Total Cost of Ownership
TLS	Transport Layer Security
UNICOS	UNIX Cray Operating System
VDI	Virtual Disk Image
VM	Virtual Machine
VMDK	Virtual Machine DisK
VMM	Virtual Machine Monitor
WAN	Wide Area Network
XaaS	X-as-a-Service
XML	Extensible Markup Language
XMPP	Extensible Messaging and Presence Protocol

CHAPTER 1

EVOLUTION OF CLOUD COMPUTING

1.1 CHAPTER OVERVIEW

In this chapter we will examine some of the evolution technologies such as distributed system, distributed computing, server virtualization, parallel processing, vector processing, symmetric multiprocessing, and massively parallel processing has fueled radical change. Let's take a look at how this happened, so we can begin to understand more about the distributed system.

1.2 DISTRIBUTED SYSTEM

A distributed system consists of a collection of autonomous computers, connected through a network and distribution middleware, which enables computers to coordinate their activities and to share the resources of the system, so that users perceive the system as a single, integrated computing facility.

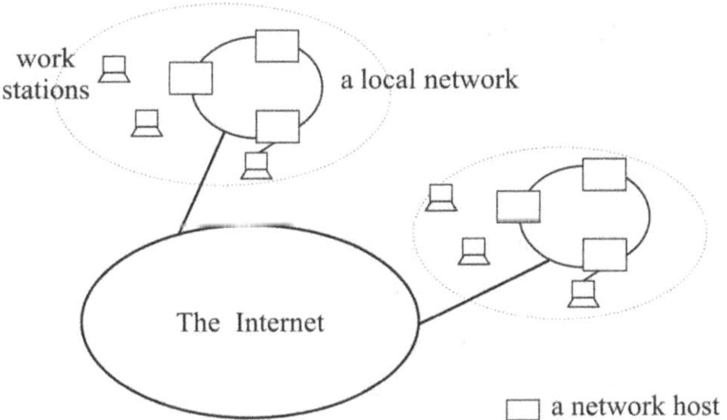

Figure 1.1 Distributed system

1.2.1   Examples of Distributed Systems

Probably the simplest and most well known example of a distributed system is the collection of Web servers—or more precisely, servers implementing the HTTP protocol—that jointly provide the distributed database of hypertext and multimedia documents that we know as the World-Wide Web. Other examples include the computers of a local network that provide a uniform view of a distributed file system and the collection of computers on the Internet that implement the Domain Name Service (DNS).

A rather sophisticated version of a distributed system is the XT3 (and XT4) series of parallel computers by Cray. These are high-performance machines consisting of a collection of computing nodes that are linked by a high-speed low-latency network. The operating system, UNICOS, presents users with a standard Linux environment upon login, but transparently schedules login sessions over a number of available login nodes. However, the implementation of parallel computing jobs on the XT3 and XT4 generally requires the programmer to explicitly manage a collection of compute nodes within the application code using XT3-specific versions of common parallel programming libraries.

Despite the fact that the systems in these examples are all similar (because they fulfill the definition of a distributed system), there are also many differences between them. The World-Wide Web and DNS, for example, both operate on a global scale. The distributed file system, on the other hand, operates on the scale of a LAN, while the Cray supercomputer operates on an even smaller scale making use of a specially designed high speed network to connect all of its nodes.

1.3   DISTRIBUTED COMPUTING

Early computing was performed on a single processor. Uni-processor computing can be called centralized computing.

Distributed computing is computing performed in a distributed system. Distributed computing has become increasingly common due to advances that have made both machines and networks cheaper and faster.

Computing performed among multiple network-connected computers, each of which has its own processors or other resources. A user, using a workstation, has a full set of resources on the local computer to which its workstation is connected.

Example: World Wide Web

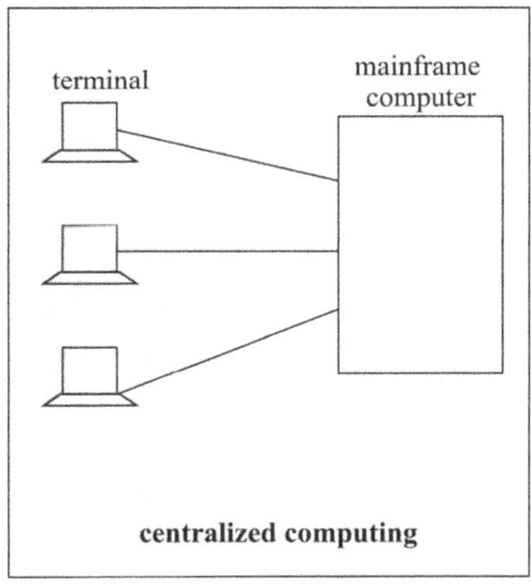

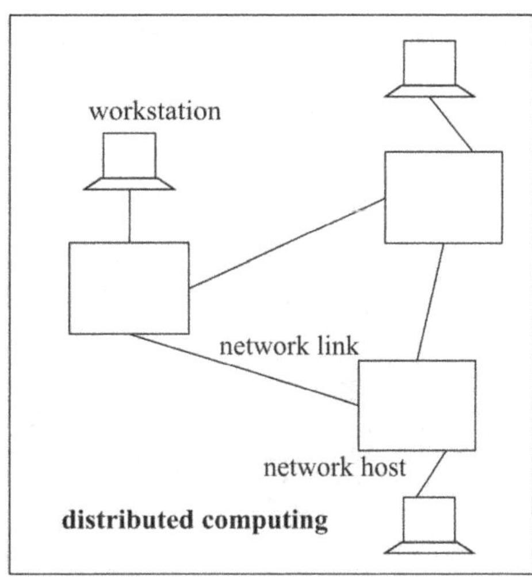

Figure 1.2(a)&(b) Centralized computing, Distributed computing

1.3.1 The Strengths and Weaknesses of Distributed Computing

The Strengths of distributed computing:

- The affordability of computers and availability of network access.

- *Reliability:* It is more reliable than a single system. If one machine from system crashes, the rest of the computers remain unaffected and the system can survive as a whole.

- *Resource sharing:* Shared data is required to many applications such as banking, reservation system and computer-supported cooperative work. As data or resources are shared in distributed system, it is essential for various applications.

- *Scalability:* Resources such as processing and storage capacity can be increased incrementally.

- Fault Tolerance.

The Weaknesses of distributed computing:

- *Multiple points of failures:* The failure of one or more participating computers, or one or more network links, can spell trouble.

- *Security:* The easy distributed access in distributed computing system which increases the risk of security. The sharing of data creates the problem of data security.

- *Programming difficulty:* Complex APIs, many issues that have to be handled at the same time.

1.4   PARALLEL COMPUTING ARCHITECTURES

In the simplest sense, parallel computing is the simultaneous use of multiple compute resources to solve a computational problem.

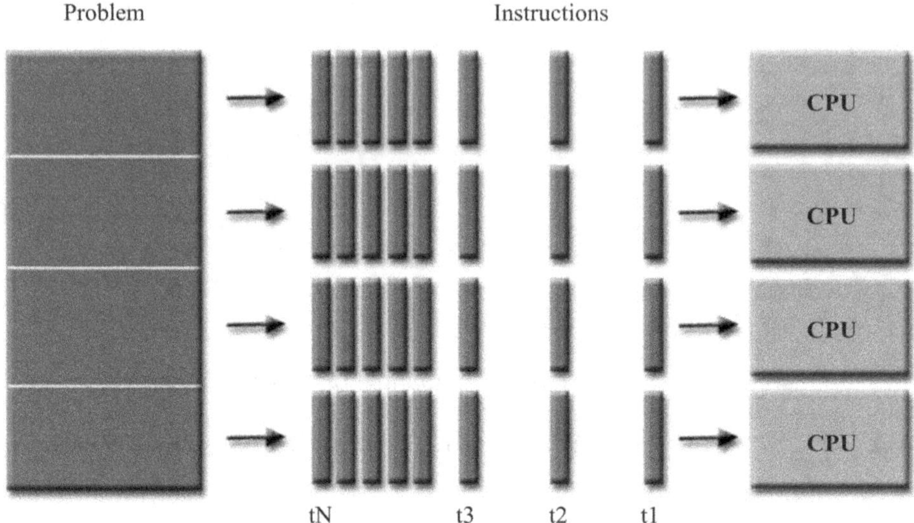

Figure 1.3 Parallel computing

Parallel processing is performed by the simultaneous execution of program instructions that have been allocated across multiple processors with the objective of running a program in less time. On the earliest computers, a user could run only one program at a time. This being the case, a computation-intensive program that took X minutes to run, using a tape system for data I/O that took Y minutes to run, would take a total of X + Y minutes to execute. To improve performance, the ability to perform CPU and I/O operation is the fundamental aspects of a computer system.

The next advancement in parallel processing was multiprogramming. In a multiprogramming system, multiple programs submitted by users are each allowed to use the processor for a short time, each taking turns and having exclusive time with the processor in order to execute instructions. This approach is known as "round-robin scheduling" (RR scheduling). It is one of the oldest, simplest, fairest, and most widely used scheduling algorithms, designed especially for time-sharing systems.

In RR scheduling, a small unit of time called a time slice (or quantum) is defined. All executable processes are held in a circular queue. The time slice is defined based on the number of executable processes that are in the queue. For example, if there are five user processes held in the queue and the time slice allocated for the queue to execute in total is 1 second, each user process is allocated 200 milliseconds of process execution time on the CPU before the scheduler begins moving to the next process in the queue. The CPU scheduler manages this queue, allocating the CPU to each process for a time interval of one time slice. New processes are always added to the end of the queue. The CPU scheduler picks the first process from the queue, sets its timer to interrupt the process after the expiration of the timer, and then dispatches the next process in the queue. The process whose time has expired is placed at the end of the queue. If a process is still running at the end of a time slice, the CPU is interrupted and the process goes to the end of the queue. If the process finishes before the end of the time-slice, it releases the CPU voluntarily. In either case, the CPU scheduler assigns the CPU to the next process in the queue. Every time a process is granted the CPU, a context switch occurs, which adds overhead to the process execution time. To users it appears that all of the programs are executing at the same time.

Resource contention problems often arose in these early systems. Explicit requests for resources led to a condition known as deadlock. Competition for resources on machines with no tie-breaking instructions led to the critical section routine. Contention occurs when several processes request access to the same resource. In order to detect deadlock situations, a counter for each processor keeps track of the number of consecutive requests from a process that have been rejected. Once that number reaches a predetermined threshold, a state machine that inhibits other processes from making requests to the main store is initiated until the deadlocked process is successful in gaining access to the resource.

1.4.1   Vector Processing

The next step in the evolution of parallel processing was the introduction of multiprocessing. Here, two or more processors share a common workload. The earliest versions of multiprocessing were designed as a master/slave model, where one processor (the master) was responsible for all of the tasks to be performed and it only off-loaded tasks to the other processor (the slave) when the master processor determined, based on a predetermined threshold, that work could be shifted to increase performance. This arrangement was necessary because it was not then understood how to program the machines so they could cooperate in managing the resources of the system. Vector processing was developed to increase processing performance by operating in a multitasking manner. Matrix operations were added to computers to allow a single instruction to manipulate two arrays of numbers performing arithmetic operations. This was valuable in certain types of applications in which data occurred in the form of vectors or matrices. In applications with less well-formed data, vector processing was less valuable.

Vector processors have high-level operations that work on linear arrays of numbers: "vectors"

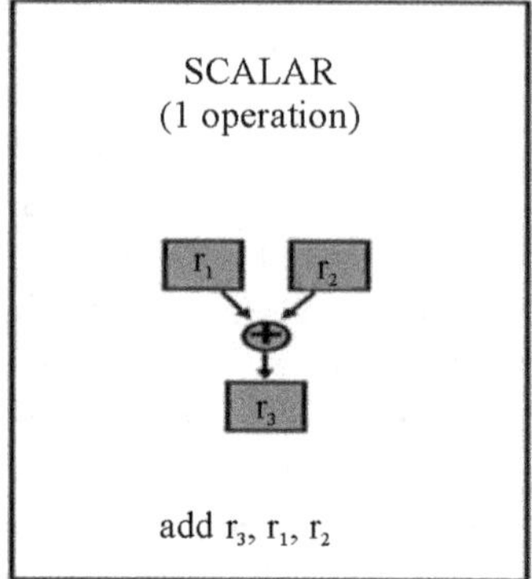

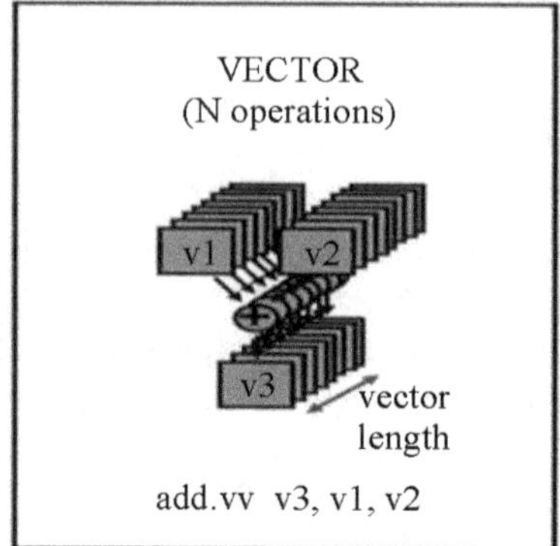

Figure 1.4(a)&(b) Scalar processing, vector processing

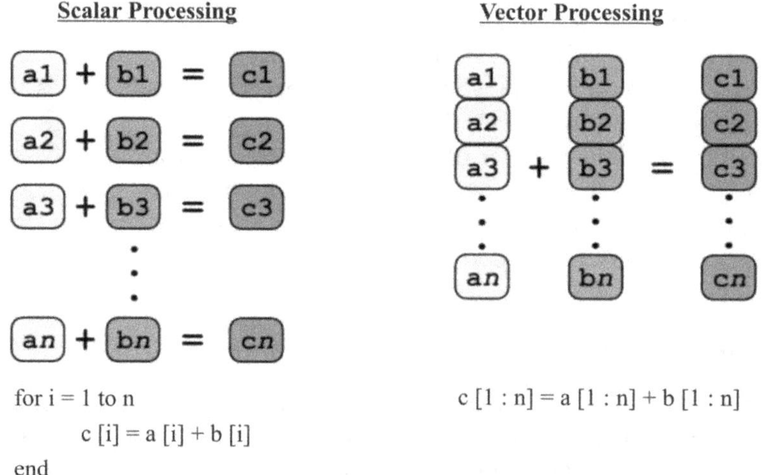

Figure 1.5 Example of a scalar and vector processing

1.4.2   Symmetric Multiprocessing Systems

The next advancement was the development of symmetric multiprocessing systems (SMP) to address the problem of resource management in master/slave models. SMP is a multiprocessing architecture in which multiple CPUs, residing in one cabinet, share the same memory. SMP systems provide scalability. As business increases, additional CPUs can be added to absorb the increased transaction volume.

SMP systems range from two to as many as 32 or more processors. However, if one CPU fails, the entire SMP system is down. Clusters of two or more SMP systems can be used to provide high availability (fault resilience). If one SMP system fails, the others continue to operate.

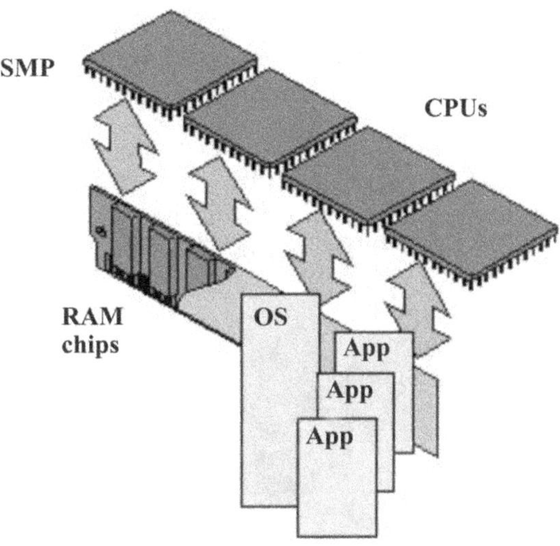

Figure 1.6 Symmetric multiprocessing systems

1.4.2.1 A Pool of Resources

One of the CPUs boots the system and loads the SMP operating system, which brings the other CPUs online. There is only one instance of the operating system and one instance of the application in memory. The operating system uses the CPUs as a pool of processing resources, all executing simultaneously, and either processing data or in an idle loop waiting to do something.

1.4.2.2 Whatever can be Overlapped

SMP speeds up whatever processes can be overlapped. For example, in a desktop computer, it would speed up the running of multiple applications simultaneously. If an application is multithreaded, which allows for concurrent operations within the application itself, then SMP will improve the performance of that single application.

1.4.3 Massively Parallel Processing Systems

Massive parallel processing (MPP) is a term used in computer architecture to refer to a computer system with many independent arithmetic units or entire microprocessors that run in parallel. The term "Massive" connotes hundreds if not thousands of such units. In this form of computing, all the processing elements are interconnected to act as one very large computer. This approach is in contrast to a distributed computing model, where massive numbers of separate computers are used to solve a single problem (such as in the SETI project). Early examples of MPP systems were the Distributed Array Processor, the Goodyear MPP, the Connection Machine, and the Ultra-computer. In data mining, there is a need to perform multiple searches of a static database. The earliest massively parallel processing systems all used serial computers as individual processing elements, in order to achieve the maximum number of independent units for a given size and cost.

The implementation of massively parallel processor arrays are becoming cost effective, and finding particular application in high performance embedded systems applications such as video compression. Examples include chips from Ambric, picoChip, and Tilera.

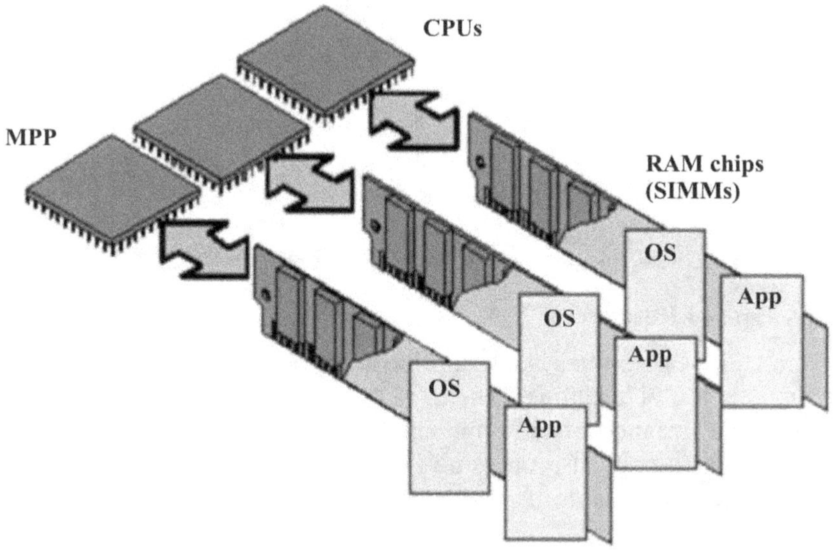

Figure 1.7 Massively parallel processing

In an MPP system, each CPU contains its own memory and copy of the operating system and application. Each subsystem communicates with the others via a high-speed interconnect. In order to use MPP effectively, an information processing problem must be breakable into pieces that can all be solved simultaneously. In the field of artificial intelligence, a chess application must analyze the outcomes of many possible alternatives and formulate the best course of action to take. In scientific environments, certain simulations (such as molecular modeling) and mathematical problems can be split apart and each part processed at the same time. In the business world, a parallel data query

(PDQ) divides a large database into pieces. For example, 26 CPUs could be used to perform a sequential search, each one searching one letter of the alphabet.

To take advantage of more CPUs in an MPP system means that the specific problem has to be broken down further into more parallel groups. However, adding CPUs in an SMP system increases performance in a more general manner. Applications that support parallel operations (multithreading) immediately take advantage of SMP, but performance gains are available to all applications, simply because there are more processors. For example, four CPUs can be running four different applications. MPP machines are not easy to program, but for certain applications, such as data mining, they are the best solution.

1.5   CLUSTER COMPUTING

A cluster is a type of parallel or distributed processing system, which consists of a collection of interconnected stand-alone/complete computers cooperatively working together as a single, integrated computing resource. A node the cluster can be a single or multiprocessor system, such as PC, workstation, or SMP. Each node will have its own memory, I/O devices and operating system. A cluster can be in a single cabinet or physically separated and connected via a LAN. Typically a cluster will appear as a single system to users and applications. Figure 1.8 shows a typical cluster architecture.

In such cluster architecture, the network interface hardware is responsible for transmitting and receiving packets of data between nodes. The communication software should offer a fast and reliable means of data communication between nodes and potentially outside the cluster. For example, clusters with a special network like Myrinet use communication protocol such as Active Messages for fast communication among its nodes. This hardware interface bypasses the operating system and provides direct user-level access to the network interface, thus remove the critical communication overheads.

Cluster middleware is responsible for offering the illusion of a unified system image (single system image) and availability out of a collection of independent but interconnected computers.

Programming environments can offer portable, efficient, and easy-to-use tools for developing applications. Such environments include tools and utilities such as compilers, message passing libraries, debuggers, and profilers. A cluster can execute both sequential and parallel applications.

The cluster components are commonly connected to each other through fast local area networks. Cluster computing can be used for high availability as well as low balancing.

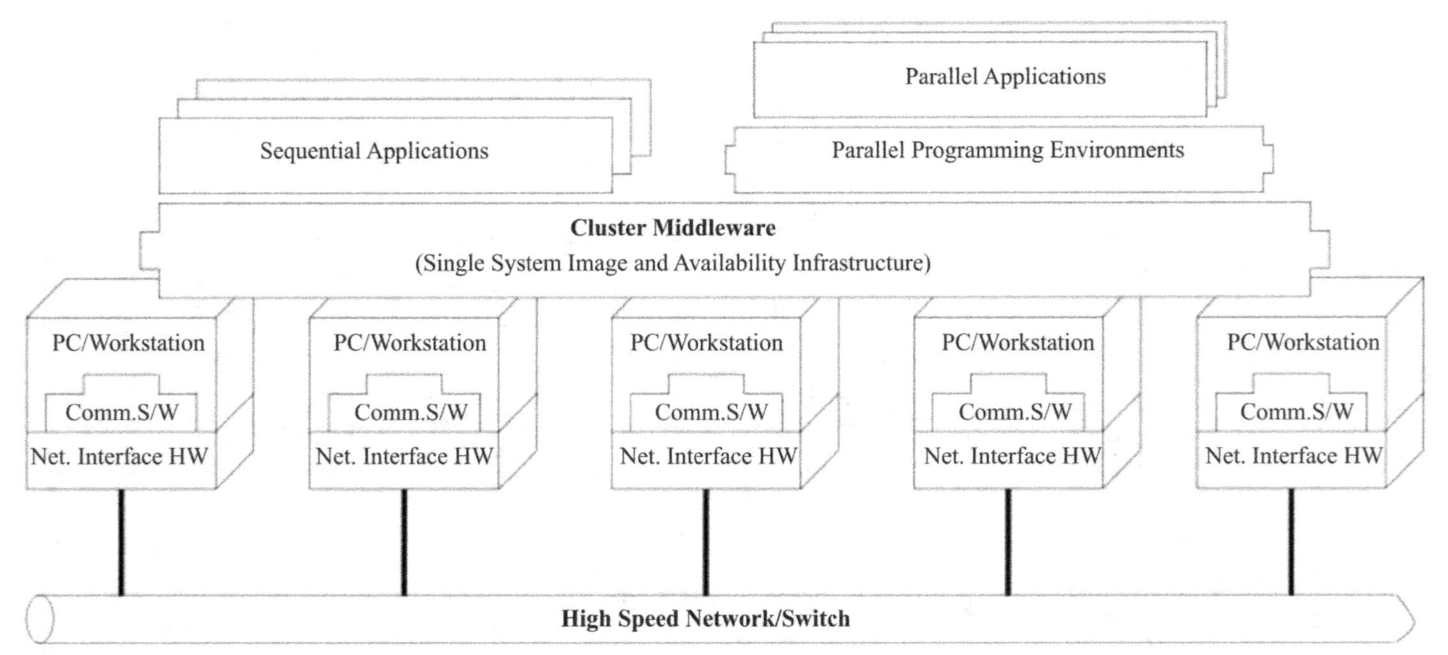

Figure 1.8 Cluster computing architecture

1.5.1 Advantages of Cluster Computing

There are a number of reasons why people use cluster computers for computing tasks. It has many advantages to makes people to use it which are as follows:

Easy to deploy

The cluster computing system is very easy to deploy. In this system software is installed as well as configured automatically. Using web interface, the cluster nodes can be easily added and managed and hence, reduces efforts and saves time.

Complete

The cluster computing system is a rich set of softwares which include common HPC (High Performance Computing) tools. It is a web-based management containing cluster monitoring, reporting and alerting automatically.

Open

As there are no proprietary "lock-in", it is an open system. It is very cost effective to acquire and manage and has various sources of support and supply. The system also supports multiple standard provisioning methods.

Easy to manage

The system is very easy to manage as there is no need to edit shell scripts or XML templates. It changes node group definitions and maintain several software versions with ease. It takes the risk out of software and hardware upgrades as it supports them without upgrading the installer node.

Flexible

As the cluster computing is an open system, it is very flexible. It supports real-world topologies and synchronizes the cluster files without re-installation. The system easily utilizes the power of advanced GPUs (Graphic Processing Units) for general HPC calculations. It can change software configurations at any time.

Optimized

Optimization is an important advantage of cluster computing system. The system is optimized for performance as well as simplicity. As it maintains the libraries that are pre-compiled and tuned for latest hardware, it saves the time of searching the net for latest drivers and math libraries.

Expandable

It is very easy to add new, future hardware models and cluster node at any time. It is easily upgrade to Platform LSF which has proven scalability to 10,000+ CPUs. The commercial add-on-solution makes the cluster growth possible in size and sophistication.

Supported

The system is very supportive as it includes software updates. There is a single point of contact for a fully integrated software and hardware solution. You can enjoy peace of mind with a fully supported computing system.

1.5.2 Different kinds of Clusters

(a) ***High Availability (HA) Clusters:*** High-availability clusters are groups of computers that support server applications that can be reliably utilized. The clusters are designed to maintain redundant nodes that can act as backup systems in the event of failure. The minimum number of nodes in a HA cluster is two - one active and one redundant-though most HA clusters will use considerably more nodes

(b) ***Load Balancing Clusters:*** Load balancing is a computer networking methodology to distribute workload across multiple computers or a computer clusters. Load-balancing clusters operate by routing all work through one or more load-balancing front-end nodes, which then distribute the workload efficiently between the remaining active nodes. Load-balancing clusters are extremely useful for those working with limited IT budgets. Devoting a few nodes to managing the workflow of a cluster ensures that limited processing power can be optimized.

(c) ***High Performance (HP) Clusters:*** High-performance computing uses supercomputers and computer clusters to solve advanced computation problems. HP clusters are designed to exploit the parallel processing power of multiple nodes. They are most commonly used to perform functions that require nodes to communicate as they perform their tasks – for instance, when calculation results from one node will affect future results from another.

1.6   GRID COMPUTING

Grid computing is a form of distributed computing whereby a "super and virtual computer" is composed of a cluster of networked, loosely coupled computers, acting in concert to perform very large tasks. Grid computing is a growing technology that facilitates the executions of large-scale resource intensive applications on geographically distributed computing resources. It facilitates flexible, secure, coordinated large scale resource sharing among dynamic collections of individuals, institutions, and resource.

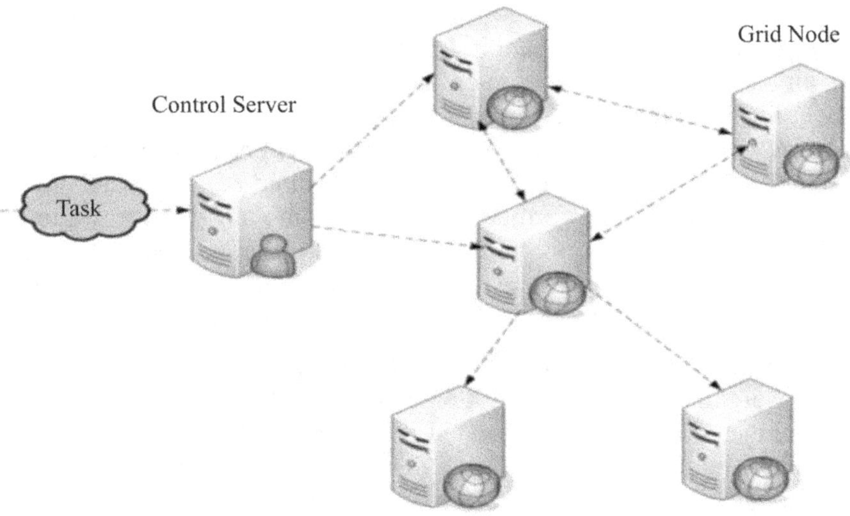

Figure 1.9 Grid Computing

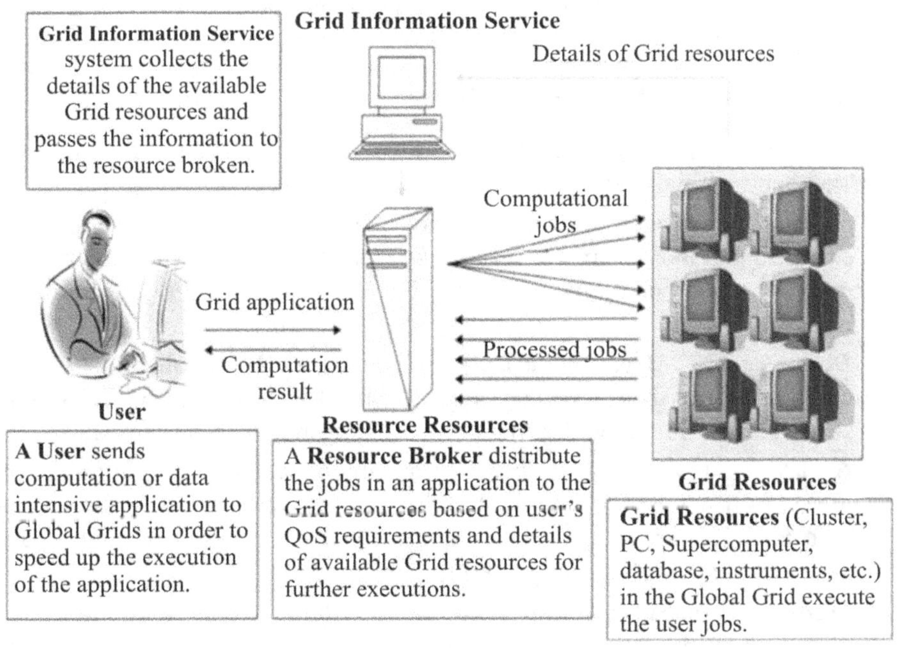

Figure 1.10 A typical view of Grid environment

1.7   VIRTUALIZATION

Virtualization is a method of running multiple independent virtual operating systems on a single physical computer. This approach maximizes the return on investment for the computer. The term was coined in the 1960s in reference to a virtual machine (sometimes called a pseudo-machine). The creation and management of virtual machines has often been called *platform virtualization*. Platform virtualization is performed on a given computer (hardware platform) by software called a control program. The control program creates a simulated environment, a virtual computer, which enables the device to use hosted software specific to the virtual environment, sometimes called guest software.

The guest software, which is often itself a complete operating system, runs just as if it were installed on a stand-alone computer. Frequently, more than one virtual machine is able to be simulated on a single physical computer, their number being limited only by the host device's physical hardware resources. Because the guest software often requires access to specific peripheral devices in order to function, the virtualized platform must support guest interfaces to those devices. Examples of such devices are the hard disk drive, CD-ROM, DVD, and network interface card. Virtualization technology is a way of reducing the majority of hardware acquisition and maintenance costs, which can result in significant savings for any company.

1.7.1 Key Benefits of Virtualization

Virtualization delivers significant benefits throughout the desktop infrastructure. A few key benefits include:

- *Reduced application conflicts:* By handling software and hardware exceptions outside of the standard image, virtualization enables the delivery of applications without time and cost-managing compatibility issues.
- *Lower cost for deployment and maintenance:* By enabling the delivery of applications from a central server, virtualization helps to dramatically streamline software deployment and ongoing patching and updates.
- *Greater computing flexibility:* By virtualizing multiple computing layers, including the desktop, the application, and the profile, organizations are able to deliver personalized computing environments to their end-users anywhere and anytime they need it.
- *Disaster recovery:* As the applications and data are centralized in a secure data center, the backup and recovery could be done more easily and effectively.

- ***Improved security:*** IT managers are easily able to isolate the breached or virus infected systems of clients very quickly and remove the affected systems.

- ***Cost savings:*** It helps in lower acquisition and saves maintenance costs, which also reduces Total Cost of Ownership (TCO) and increases Return of Investment (ROI).

Bit Questions

1. A ---------------- is a collection of independent computers, interconnected via a network, capable of collaborating on a task.

2. -------------- is computing performed in a distributed system.

3. World Wide Web is an example of a --------------------.

4. --------------- is the simultaneous use of multiple compute resources to solve a computational problem.

5. ------------------- occurs when several processes request access to the same resource.

6. ---------------------- is two or more processors share a common workload.

7. Linear arrays of numbers called --------------.

8. ---------------------- is a term used in computer architecture to refer to a computer system with many independent arithmetic units or entire microprocessors that run in parallel.

9. --------------- a collection of interconnected stand-alone/complete computers cooperatively working together as a single, integrated computing resource.

10. A ------------ can execute both sequential and parallel applications.

11. ---------------- computing uses supercomputers and computer clusters to solve advanced computation problems.

12. ---------------- is a method of running multiple independent virtual operating systems on a single physical computer.

13. The creation and management of virtual machines has often been called -----------------.

14. Why did virtualization boost the emergence of Cloud computing?　[　]

   (a) A virtual machine is more secure than a physical machine.

   (b) Virtualization made it easier and cheaper to share resources between users.

   (c) Virtual machines have greater performance than their physical counterparts.

   (d) Virtualization leads to better network utilization.

Exercises

1. Discuss the evolution of cloud computing.

2. Define distributed system?

3. Define Distributed Computing?

4. What are the Strengths and Weaknesses of Distributed Computing?

5. Discuss in detail about Parallel Computing architectures.

6. What is a grid? What are the differences between grid computing and cluster computing?

7. What is a Cluster Computing? Explain the Cluster computing architecture.

8. What is virtualization? Explain the Key Benefits of virtualization.

   (a) Enlist and explain some of the common pitfalls that come with virtualization.

CHAPTER **2**

INTRODUCTION TO CLOUD COMPUTING

2.1 CHAPTER OVERVIEW

In this chapter we will explain what is cloud computing is, cloud collaboration, application architectures, scaling a cloud infrastructure and its models, capacity planning and cloud scale. Let's take a look at how this happened, so we can begin to understand more about the cloud computing.

2.2 CLOUD COMPUTING: WHAT IT IS – AND WHAT IT ISN'T

With traditional desktop computing, you run copies of software programs on each computer you own. The documents you create are stored on the computer on which they were created. Although documents can be accessed from other computers on the network, they can't be accessed by computers outside the network.

The whole scene is PC-centric. With cloud computing, the software programs you use aren't run from your personal computer, but are rather stored on servers accessed via the Internet. If your computer crashes, the software is still available for others to use. Same goes for the documents you create; they are stored on a collection of servers accessed via the Internet. Anyone with permission can not only access the documents, but can also edit and collaborate on those documents in real time. Unlike traditional computing, this cloud computing model isn't PC-centric, it's document-centric. Which PC you use to access a document simply is not important.

But that is a simplification. Let's look in more detail at what cloud computing is—and, just as important, what it isn't.

What Cloud Computing Isn't

First, cloud computing isn't network computing. With network computing, applications or documents are hosted on a single company's server and accessed over the company's network. Cloud computing is a lot bigger than that. It encompasses multiple companies, multiple servers, and multiple networks. Plus, unlike network computing, cloud services and storage are accessible from anywhere in the world over an Internet connection; with network computing, access is over the company's network only.

Cloud computing also is not traditional outsourcing, where a company farms out (subcontracts) its computing services to an outside firm. While an outsourcing firm might host a company's data or applications, those documents and programs are only accessible to the company's employees via the company's network, not to the entire world via the Internet. So, despite superficial similarities, networking computing and outsourcing are not cloud computing.

What Cloud Computing Is

Key to the definition of cloud computing is the "cloud" itself. For our purposes, the cloud is a large group of interconnected computers. These computers can be personal computers or network servers; they can be public or private. For example, Google hosts a cloud that consists of both smallish PCs and larger servers. Google's cloud is a private one (that is, Google owns it) that is publicly accessible (by Google's users).

This cloud of computers extends beyond a single company or enterprise. The applications and data served by the cloud are available to broad group of users, cross-enterprise and cross-platform. Access is via the Internet. Any authorized user can access these docs and apps from any computer over any Internet connection. And, to the user, the technology and infrastructure behind the cloud is invisible. It isn't apparent (and, in most cases doesn't matter) whether cloud services are based on HTTP, HTML, XML, JavaScript, or other specific technologies.

It might help to examine how one of the pioneers of cloud computing, Google, perceives the topic. From Google's perspective, there are six key properties of cloud computing:

- Cloud computing is user-centric: Once you as a user are connected to the cloud, whatever is stored there – documents, messages, images, applications, whatever – becomes yours. In addition, not only is the data yours, but you can also share it with others. In effect, any device that accesses your data in the cloud also becomes yours.

- Cloud computing is task-centric: Instead of focusing on the application and what it can do, the focus is on what you need done and how the application can do it for you., Traditional applications – word processing, spreadsheets, email, and so on – are becoming less important than the documents they create.

- Cloud computing is powerful: Connecting hundreds or thousands of computers together in a cloud creates a wealth of computing power impossible with a single desktop PC.

- Cloud computing is accessible: Because data is stored in the cloud, users can instantly retrieve more information from multiple repositories. You're not limited to a single source of data, as you are with a desktop PC.

- Cloud computing is intelligent: With all the various data stored on the computers in a cloud, data mining and analysis are necessary to access that information in an intelligent manner.

- Cloud computing is programmable: Many of the tasks necessary with cloud computing must be automated. For example, to protect the integrity of the data, information stored on a single computer in the cloud must be replicated on other computers in the cloud. If that one computer goes offline, the cloud's programming automatically redistributes that computer's data to a new computer in the cloud.

2.3   FROM COLLABORATION TO THE CLOUD: A SHORT HISTORY OF CLOUD COMPUTING

Cloud computing has as its antecedents both client/server computing and peer-to-peer distributed computing. It's all a matter of how centralized storage facilitates collaboration and how multiple computers work together to increase computing power.

Client/Server Computing: Centralized Applications and Storage

The term "client/server computing" refers to the process by which data processing chores are shared between the client computer and the more powerful server computer. Figure 2.1 shows a simple client/server network with one server, three clients (computers), and a printer.

The client/server approach can benefit any organization in which many people need continual access to large amounts of data.

The client/server network is the most efficient way to provide:

- Database access and management for applications such as spreadsheets, accounting, communications, and document management.

- Network management.

- Centralized file storage.

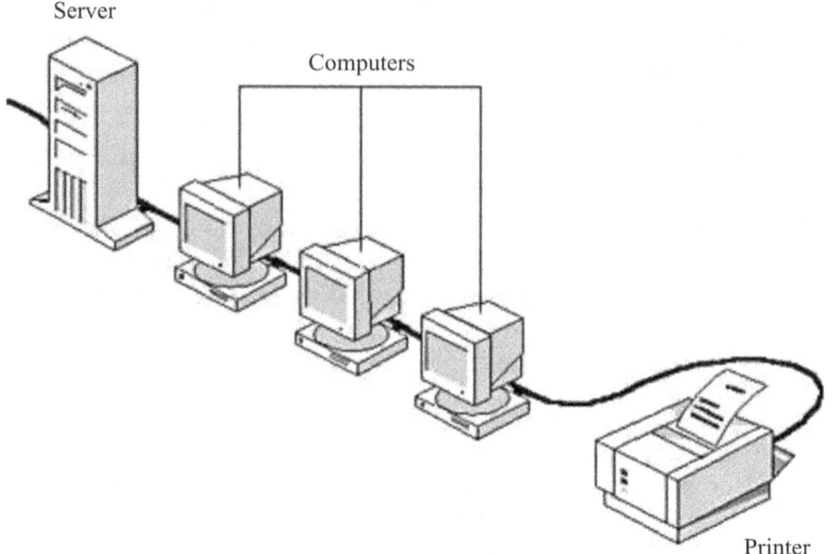

Figure 2.1 A simple client/server network

Most networks operate in the client/server model, also referred to as "server-based networking." A client workstation makes a request for data that is stored on a server. The client workstation processes the data using its own CPU. Data-processing results can then be stored on the server for future use. The data can also be stored on the client workstation and accessed by other client workstations on the network.

Advantages

- Data management is much easier because the files are in one location. This allows fast backups and efficient error management. There are multiple levels of permissions, which can prevent users from doing damage to files.

- The server hardware is designed to serve requests from clients quickly. All the data are processed on the server, and only the results are returned to the client. This reduces the amount of network traffic between the server and the client machine, improving network performance.

- Thin client architectures allow a quick replacement of defect clients, because all data and applications are on the server.

Disadvantages

- Client-Server-Systems are very expensive and need a lot of maintenance.

- The server constitutes a single point of failure. If failures on the server occur, it is possible that the system suffers heavy delay or completely breaks down, which can potentially block hundreds of clients from working with their data or their applications. Within companies high costs could accumulate due to server downtime.

Peer-to-Peer Computing: Sharing Resources

Peer-to-peer (P2P) computing defines a network architecture in which each computer has equivalent capabilities and responsibilities. As opposed to the Client-Server model, where one node provides services and other nodes use the services.

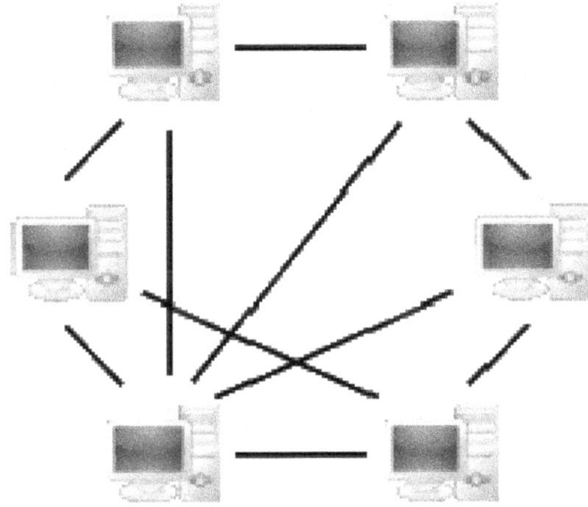

Figure 2.2 Peer-to-Peer network

P2P was an equalizing concept. In the P2P environment, every computer is a client *and* a server; there are no masters and slaves. By recognizing all computers on the network as peers, P2P enables direct exchange of resources and services. There is no need for a central server, because any computer can function in that capacity when called on to do so.

P2P was also a decentralizing concept. Control is decentralized, with all computers functioning as equals. Content is also dispersed among the various peer computers. No centralized server is assigned to host the available resources and services.

Perhaps the most notable implementation of P2P computing is the Internet. Many of today's users forget (or never knew) that the Internet was initially conceived, under its original ARPAnet guise, as a peer-to-peer system that would share computing resources across the United States. The various ARPAnet sites – and there weren't many of them – were connected together not as clients and servers, but as equals.

The P2P nature of the early Internet was best exemplified by the Usenet network. Usenet, which was created back in 1979, was a network of computers (accessed via the Internet), each of which hosted the entire contents of the network. Messages were propagated between the peer computers; users connecting to any single Usenet server had access to all (or substantially all) the messages posted to each individual server. Although the users' connection to the Usenet server was of the traditional client/server nature, the relationship between the Usenet servers was definitely P2P – and presaged the cloud computing of today.

That said, not every part of the Internet is P2P in nature. With the development of the World Wide Web came a shift away from P2P back to the client/server model. On the web, each website is served up by a group of computers, and sites' visitors use client software (web browsers) to access it. Almost all content is centralized, all control is centralized, and the clients have no autonomy or control in the process.

Advantages

- It is easy to install and so is the configuration of computers on this network,
- All the resources and contents are shared by all the peers, unlike server-client architecture where Server shares all the contents and resources.
- P2P is more reliable as central dependency is eliminated. Failure of one peer doesn't affect the functioning of other peers.
- There is no need for full-time System Administrator. Every user is the administrator of his machine. User can control their shared resources.
- The over-all cost of building and maintaining this type of network is comparatively very less.

Disadvantages

- In this network, the whole system is decentralized thus it is difficult to administer. That is one person cannot determine the whole accessibility setting of whole network.
- Data recovery or backup is very difficult. Each computer should have its own back-up system.

Distributed Computing: Providing More Computing Power

One of the most important subsets of the P2P model is that of *distributed computing*, where idle PCs across a network or across the Internet are tapped to provide computing power for large, processor-intensive projects. It's a simple concept, all about *cycle sharing* between multiple computers.

A personal computer, running full-out 24 hours a day, 7 days a week, is capable of tremendous computing power. Most people don't use their computers 24/7, however, so a good portion of a computer's resources go unused. Distributed computing uses those resources.

When a computer is enlisted for a distributed computing project, software is installed on the machine to run various processing activities during those periods when the PC is typically unused. The results of that spare-time processing are periodically uploaded to the distributed computing network, and combined with similar results from other PCs in the project. The result, if enough computers are involved, simulates the processing power of much larger mainframes and supercomputers – which is necessary for some very large and complex computing projects.

For example, genetic research requires vast amounts of computing power. Left to traditional means, it might take years to solve essential mathematical problems. By connecting together thousands (or millions) of individual PCs, more power is applied to the problem, and the results are obtained that much sooner.

Distributed computing dates back to 1973, when multiple computers were networked together at the Xerox PARC labs and worm software was developed to cruise through the network looking for idle resources. A more practical application of distributed computing appeared in 1988, when researchers at the DEC (Digital Equipment Corporation) System Research Center developed software that distributed the work to factor large numbers among workstations within their laboratory. By 1990, a group of about 100 users, utilizing this software, had factored a 100-digit number. By 1995, this same effort had been expanded to the web to factor a 130-digit number.

It wasn't long before distributed computing hit the Internet. The first major Internet-based distributed computing project was distributed.net, launched in 1997, which employed thousands of personal computers to crack encryption codes. Even bigger was SETI@home, launched in May 1999, which linked together millions of individual computers to search for intelligent life in outer space.

Many distributed computing projects are conducted within large enterprises, using traditional network connections to form the distributed computing network. Other, larger, projects utilize the computers of everyday Internet users, with the computing typically taking place offline, and then uploaded once a day via traditional consumer Internet connections.

Collaborative Computing: Working as a Group

From the early days of client/server computing through the evolution of P2P, there has been a desire for multiple users to work simultaneously on the same computer-based project. This type of collaborative computing is the driving force behind cloud computing, but has been around for more than a decade.

Early group collaboration was enabled by the combination of several different P2P technologies. The goal was (and is) to enable multiple users to collaborate on group projects online, in real time.

To collaborate on any project, users must first be able to talk to one another. In today's environment, this means instant messaging for text-based communication, with optional audio/telephony and video capabilities for voice and picture communication. Most collaboration systems offer the complete range of audio/video options, for full-featured multiple-user video conferencing.

In addition, users must be able to share files and have multiple users work on the same document simultaneously. Real-time white boarding is also common, especially in corporate and education environments.

Early group collaboration systems ranged from the relatively simple (Lotus Notes and Microsoft NetMeeting) to the extremely complex (the building-block architecture of the Groove Networks system). Most were targeted at large corporations, and limited to operation over the companies' private networks.

Cloud Computing: The Next Step in Collaboration

With the growth of the Internet, there was no need to limit group collaboration to a single enterprise's network environment. Users from multiple locations within a corporation, and from multiple organizations, desired to collaborate on projects that crossed company and geographic boundaries. To do this, projects had to be housed in the "cloud" of the Internet, and accessed from any Internet-enabled location.

The concept of cloud-based documents and services took wing with the development of large server farms, such as those run by Google and other search companies. Google already had a collection of servers that it used to power its massive search engine; why not use that same computing power to drive a collection of web-based applications – and, in the process, provide a new level of Internet-based group collaboration?

That's exactly what happened, although Google wasn't the only company offering cloud computing solutions. On the infrastructure side, IBM, Sun Systems, and other big iron providers are offering the hardware necessary to build cloud networks. On the software side, dozens of companies are developing cloud-based applications and storage services.

Today, people are using cloud services and storage to create, share, find, and organize information of all different types. Tomorrow, this functionality will be available not only to computer users, but to users of any device that connects to the Internet – mobile phones, portable music players, even automobiles and home television sets.

2.4   CLOUD APPLICATION ARCHITECTURES

Cloud application architectures are grid computing and transactional computing.

Grid Computing

Grid computing is the easiest application architecture to migrate into the cloud. A grid computing application is processor-intensive software that breaks up its processing into small chunks that can then be processed in isolation.

If you have used SETI@home, you have participated in grid computing. SETI (the Search for Extra-Terrestrial Intelligence) has radio telescopes that are constantly listening to activity in space. They collect volumes of data that subsequently need to be processed to search for a non-natural signal that might represent attempts at communication by another civilization. It would take so long for one computer to process all of that data that we might as well wait until we can travel to the stars. But many computers using only their spare CPU cycles can tackle the problem extraordinarily quickly.

These computers running SETI@home – perhaps including your desktop – form the grid. When they have extra cycles, they query the SETI servers for data sets. They process the data sets and submit the results back to SETI. Your results are double-checked against processing by other participants, and interesting results are further checked.

Back in 1999, SETI elected to use the spare cycles of regular consumers desktop computers for its data processing. Commercial and government systems used to network a number of supercomputers together to perform the same calculations. More recently, server farms were created for grid computing tasks such as video rendering. Both supercomputers and server farms are very expensive, capital-intensive approaches to the problem of grid computing.

The cloud makes it cheap and easy to build a grid computing application. When you have data that needs to be processed, you simply bring up a server to process that data. Afterward, that server can either shut down or pull another data set to process.

Figure 2.3 illustrates the process flow of a grid computing application. First, a server or server cluster receives data that requires processing. It then submits that job to a message queue (1). Other servers—often called workers (or, in the case of SETI@home, other desktops)—watch the message queue (2) and wait for new data sets to appear. When a data set appears, the first computer to see it processes it and then sends the results back into the message queue (3). The two components can operate independently of each other, and one can even be running when no computer is running the other.

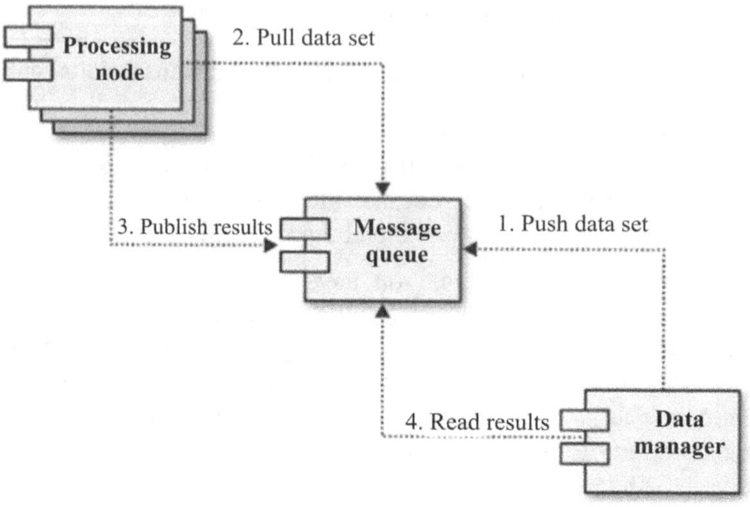

Figure 2.3 The grid application architecture separates the core application from its data processing nodes

Cloud computing comes to the rescue here because you do not need to own any servers when you have no data to process. You can then scale the number of servers to support the number of data sets that are coming into your application. In other words, instead of having idle computers process data as it comes in, you have servers turn themselves on as the rate of incoming data increases, and turn themselves off as the data rate decreases.

Transactional Computing

Transactional computing makes up the bulk of business software. A transaction system is one in which one or more pieces of incoming data are processed together as a single transaction and establish relationships with other data already in the system. The core of a transactional system is generally a relational database that manages the relations among all of the data that make up the system.

Figure 2.4 shows the logical layout of a high-availability transactional system. Under this kind of architecture, an application server typically models the data stored in the database and presents it through a web-based user interface that enables a person to interact with the data. Most of the websites and web applications that you use every day are some form of transactional system. For high availability, all of these components may form a cluster, and the presentation/business logic tier can hide behind a load balancer.

Deploying a transactional system in the cloud is a little more complex and less obvious than deploying a grid system. Whereas nodes in a grid system are designed to be short-lived, nodes in a transactional system must be long-lived.

A key challenge for any system requiring long-lived nodes in a cloud infrastructure is the basic fact that the mean time between failures (MTBF) of a virtual server is necessarily less than that for the underlying hardware. An admittedly gross oversimplification of the problem shows that if you have two physical servers with a three-year MTBF, you will be less likely to experience an outage across the entire system than you would be with a single physical server running two virtual nodes. The number of physical nodes basically governs the MTBF, and since there are fewer physical nodes, there is a higher MTBF for any given node in your cloud-based transactional system.

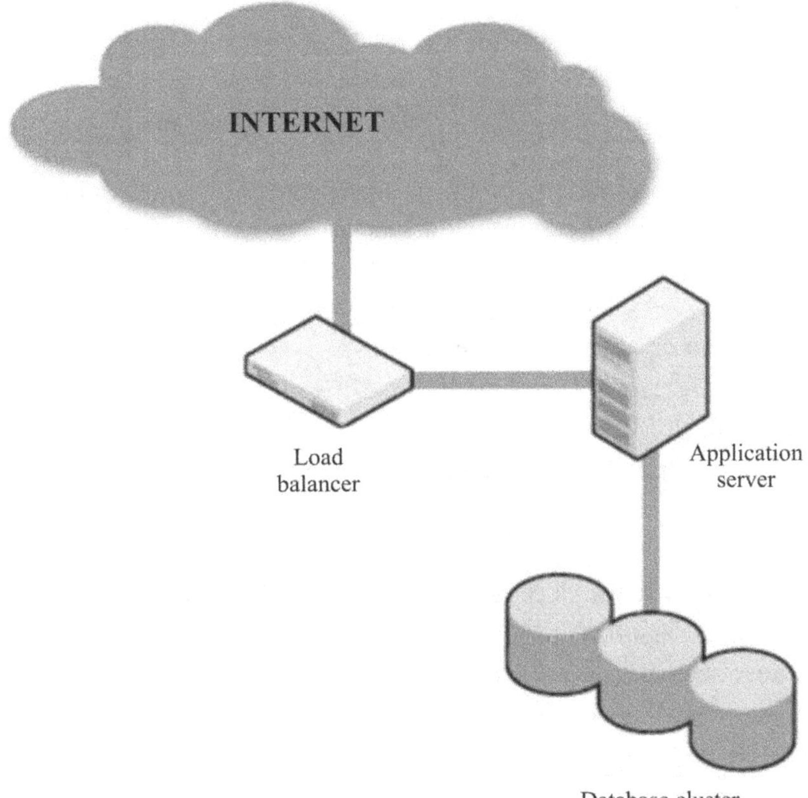

Figure 2.4 A transactional application separates an application into presentation, business logic, and data storage

2.5   THE VALUE OF CLOUD COMPUTING

If you can deploy all of your custom-built software systems on cloud hardware and leverage SaaS systems for your packaged software, you might be able to achieve an all-cloud IT infrastructure. Table 2.1 lists the components of the typical small- or medium-sized business.

Table 2.1 The old IT infrastructure versus the cloud

Traditional	Cloud
File server	Google Docs
Ms Outlook, Apple Maill	Gmail, Yahoo!, MSN
SAP CRM/Oracle CRM/Siebel	SalesForce.com
Quicken/Oracle Financials	Intacct/NetSuit
Microsoft Office/Lotus Notes	Google Apps
Stellent	Valtira
Off-site backup	Amazon S3
Serves, racks, and firewall	Amazon EC2, Go Grid Mosso

The potential impact of the cloud is significant. For some organizations – particularly small- to medium-sized businesses – it makes it possible to never again purchase a server or own any software licenses. In other words, all of these worries diminish greatly or disappear altogether:

- Am I current on all my software licenses?

  SaaS systems and software with cloud-friendly licensing simply charge your credit card for what you use.

- When do I schedule my next software upgrade?

  SaaS vendors perform the upgrades for you; you rarely even know what version you are using.

- What do I do when a piece of hardware fails at 3 a.m.?

  Cloud infrastructure management tools are capable of automating even the most traumatic disaster recovery policies.

- How do I manage my technology assets?

  When you are in the cloud, you have fewer technology assets (computers, printers, etc.) to manage and track.

- What do I do with my old hardware?

  You don't own the hardware, so you don't have to dispose of it.

- How do I manage the depreciation of my IT assets?

  Your costs are based on usage and thus don't involve depreciable expenses.

- When can I afford to add capacity to my infrastructure?

  In the cloud, you can add capacity discretely as the business needs it.

SaaS vendors can run all their services in a hardware cloud provided by another vendor, and therefore offer a robust cloud infrastructure to their customers without owning their own hardware.

Options for an IT Infrastructure

The cloud competes against two approaches to IT:

- Internal IT infrastructure and support

- Outsourcing to managed services

If you own the boxes, you have an internally managed IT infrastructure, even if they are sitting in a rack in someone else's data center. For you, the key potential benefit of cloud computing (certainly financially) is the lack of capital investment required to leverage it.

Internal IT infrastructure and support is one in which you own the boxes and pay people – whether staff or contract employees—to maintain those boxes. When a box fails, you incur that cost, and you have no replacement absent a cold spare that you own.

Managed services outsourcing has similar benefits to the cloud in that you pay a fixed fee for someone else to own your servers and make sure they stay up. If a server goes down, it is the managed services company who has to worry about replacing it immediately (or within whatever terms have been defined in your service-level agreement). They provide the expertise to make sure the servers are fixed with the proper operating system patches and manage the network infrastructure in which the servers operate.

Table 2.2 Provides a comparison between internal IT, managed services, and cloud-based IT with respect to various facets of IT infrastructure development

	Internal IT	**Managed services**	**The Cloud**
	Significant	**Moderate**	**Negligible**
Capital investment	How much cash do you have to cough up in order to set up your infrastructure or make change to it? With internal IT, you have to pay for your hardware before you need it (financing is not important in this equation). Under managed serves, you are typically required to pay a moderate setup fee. In the cloud, you generally have no up-front costs and no commitment.		

Table 2.2 *Contd...*

	Moderate	Significant	Based on usage
Ongoing costs	Your ongoing costs for internal IT are based on the cost of staff and/or contractors to manage the infrastructures, as well as space at your hosting provider and/or real estate and utilities costs. You can see significant variances in the ongoing costs – especially with contract resources – as emergencies occur and other issues arise. Although managed services are often quite pricey, you generally know exactly what you are going to pay each month and it rarely varies. The cloud, on the other hand, can be either pricey or cheap, depending on your needs. Its key advantage is that you pat for exactly what you use and nothing more. Your staff costs are greater than with a managed services provider, but less than with internal IT.		
	Significant	**Moderate**	**None**
Provisioning time	How long does it take to ass a new component into your infrastructure? Under both the internal IT and managed services models, you need to plan ahead of time, place an order, wait for the component to arrive, and then set it up in the data center. The wait is typically significantly shorter with a managed services provider, since they make purchases ahead to time in bulk. Under the cloud however, you can have a new "server" operational within minutes of deciding you want it.		
	Limited	**Moderate**	**Flexible**
Flexibility	How easily can your infrastructure adapt to unexpected peaks in resource demands? For example, do you have a limit on disk space? What happens if you suddenly approach that limit? Internal IT has a very fixed capacity and can meet increased resource demands only through further capital investment. A managed services provider , on the other hand, usually can offer temporary capacity relief by uncapping your bandwidth, giving you short-term access to alternative storage options, and so on. The cloud, however, can be set up to automatically add capacity into your infrastructure as needed, and to let go of that capacity when it is no longer required.		
	Significant	**Limited**	**Moderate**
Staff experience requirements	How much expertise do you need in-house to support your environments? With internal IT, you obviously need staff or contractors who know that ins and outs of your infrastructure, from opening the boxes up and fiddling with the hardware to making sure the operating systems are up-to-date with the latest patches. The advantage here goes to the managed services infrastructure, which enables you to be largely ignorant of all things IT. Finally, the cloud may require a lot of skill or very little skill, depending on how you are using it. You can often find a cloud infrastructure manager (enstratus or RightScale, for example) to manage the environment, but you still must have the skills to set up your machine images.		

Table 2.2 Contd...

	Varies	High	Moderate to high
Reliability	How certain are you that your services will stay up 24/7? The ability to create a high-availability infrastructure with an internal IT staff is a function of the skill level of your staff and the amount of cash you invest in the infrastructure. A managed services provider is the safest, most proven alternative, but this option can lack the locational redundancy of the cloud. A cloud infrastructure, finally, has significant locational redundancies but lacks a proven track record of stability		

The Economics

Perhaps the biggest benefit of cloud computing over building out your own IT infrastructure has nothing to do with technology – it's financial. The "pay for what you use" model of cloud computing is significantly cheaper for a company than the "pay for everything up front" model of internal IT.

Capital costs

The primary financial problem with an internally based IT infrastructure is the capital cost. A capital cost is cash you pay for assets prior to their entering into operations. If you buy a server, that purchase is a capital cost because you pay for it all up front, and then you realize its benefits (in other words, you use it) over the course of 2–3 years.

Let's look at the example of a $5,000 computer that costs $2,000 to set up. The $5,000 is a capital cost and the $2,000 is a one-time expense. From an accounting perspective, the $5,000 cost is just a "funny money" transaction, in that $5,000 is moved from one asset account (your bank account) into another asset account (your fixed assets account). The $2,000, on the other hand, is a real expense that offsets your profits.

The server is what is called a depreciable asset. As it is used, the server is depreciated in accordance with how much it has been used. In other words, the server's value to the company is reduced each month it is in use until it is worth nothing and removed from service. Each reduction in value is considered an expense that offsets the company's profits.

Finance managers hate capital costs for a variety of reasons. In fact, they hate any expenses that are not tied directly to the current operation of the company. The core rationale for this dislike is that you are losing cash today for a benefit that you will receive slowly over time (technically, over the course of the depreciation of the server). Any business owner or executive wants to focus the organization's cash on things that benefit them today. This concern is most acute with the small- and medium-sized business that may not have an easy time walking into the bank and asking for a loan.

The key problem with this delayed realization of value is that money costs money. A company will often fund their operational costs through revenues and pay for capital expenses through loans. If you can grow the company faster than the cost of money, you win. If you cannot grow that rapidly or—worse—you cannot get access to credit, the capital expenses become a significant drain on the organization.

Cost comparison

Managed services infrastructures and the cloud are so attractive to companies because they largely eliminate capital investment and other up-front costs. The cloud has the added advantage of tying your costs to exactly what you are using, meaning that you can often connect IT costs to revenue instead of treating them as overhead.

Table 2.3 compares the costs of setting up an infrastructure to support a single "moderately high availability" transactional web application with a load balancer, two application servers, and two database servers. I took typical costs at the time of writing, October 2008.

Table 2.3 Comparing the cost of different IT infrastructure

	Internal IT	**Managed services**	**The cloud**
Capital investment	$40,000	$0	$0
Setup	$10,000	$5,000	$1,000
Monthly service fees	$0	$4,000	$2,400
Monthly staff costs	$3,200	$0	$1,000
Net cost over three years	$149,000	$129,000	$106,000

Table 2.3 makes the following assumptions:

- The use of fairly standard server systems, such as a Dell 2950 and the high-end Amazon instances.
- The use of a hardware load balancer in the internal IT and managed services configuration and a software load balancer in the cloud.
- No significant data storage or bandwidth needs (different bandwidth or storage needs can have a significant impact on this calculation).
- The low end of the cost spectrum for each of the options (in particular, some managed services providers will charge up to three times the costs listed in the table for the same infrastructure).
- Net costs denominated in today's dollars (in other words, don't worry about inflation).

- A cost of capital of 10% (cost of capital is what you could have done with all of the upfront cash instead of sinking it into a server and setup fees—basically the money's interest rate plus opportunity costs).

- The use of third-party cloud management tools such as enStratus or RightScale, incorporated into the cloud costs.

- Staff costs representing a fraction of an individual (this isolated infrastructure does not demand a full-time employee under any model).

- Perhaps the most controversial element of this analysis is what might appear to be an "apples versus oranges" comparison on the load balancer costs. The reality is that this architecture doesn't really require a hardware load balancer except for extremely high-volume websites. So you likely could get away with a software load balancer in all three options.

- A software load balancer, however, is very problematic in both the internal IT and managed services infrastructures for a couple of reasons:

  A normal server is much more likely to fail than a hardware load balancer. Because it is much harder to replace a server in the internal IT and managed services scenarios, the loss of that software load balancer is simply unacceptable in those two scenarios, whereas it would go unnoticed in the cloud scenario.

  If you are investing in actual hardware, you may want a load balancer that will grow with your IT needs. A hardware load balancer is much more capable of doing that than a software load balancer. In the cloud, however, you can cheaply add dedicated software load balancers, so it becomes a nonissue.

In addition, some cloud providers (GoGrid, for example) include free hardware load balancing, which makes the entire software versus hardware discussion moot. Furthermore, Amazon is scheduled to offer its own load-balancing solution at some point in 2009. Nevertheless, if you don't buy into my rationale for comparing the hardware load balancers against the software load balancers, here is the comparison using all software load balancers: $134K for internal IT, $92K for managed services, and $106K for a cloud environment.

The bottom line

If we exclude sunk costs, the right managed services option and cloud computing are always financially more attractive than managing your own IT. Across all financial metrics – capital requirements, total cost of ownership, complexity of costs – internal IT is always the odd man out.

As your infrastructure becomes more complex, determining whether a managed services infrastructure, a mixed infrastructure, or a cloud infrastructure makes more economic sense becomes significantly more complex.

If you have an application that you know has to be available 24/7/365, and even 1 minute of downtime in a year is entirely unacceptable, you almost certainly want to opt for a managed services environment and not concern yourself too much with the cost differences (they may even favor the managed services provider in that scenario).

On the other hand, if you want to get high-availability on the cheap, and 99.995% is good enough, you can't beat the cloud.

2.6   CLOUD INFRASTRUCTURE MODELS

Cloud infrastructure models represent a continuum from managed services through something people call Infrastructure as a Service (IaaS) to Platform as a Service (PaaS).

Platform as a Service Vendor

PaaS environments provide you with an infrastructure as well as complete operational and development environments for the deployment of your applications. You program using the vendor's specific application development platform and let the vendor worry about all deployment details.

The most commonly used example of pure PaaS is Google App Engine. To leverage Google App Engine, you write your applications in Python against Google's development frameworks with tools for using the Google file system and data repositories. This approach works well for applications that must be deployed rapidly and don't have significant integration requirements.

The downside to the PaaS approach is vendor lock-in. With Google, for example, you must write your applications in the Python programming language to Google-specific APIs.

Python is a wonderful programming language – in fact, my favorite – but it isn't a core competency of most development teams. Even if you have the Python skills on staff, you still must contend with the fact that your Google App Engine application may only ever work well inside Google's infrastructure.

Infrastructure as a Service

The focus of this book is the idea of IaaS. I spend a lot of time in this book using examples from the major player in this environment, Amazon Web Services. A number of significant AWS competitors exist who have different takes on the IaaS problem. These different approaches have key value propositions for different kinds of cloud customers.

AWS is based on pure virtualization. Amazon owns all the hardware and controls the network infrastructure, and you own everything from the guest operating system up. You request virtual instances on-demand and let them go when you are done. Amazon sees one of its key benefits is a commitment to not overcommitting resources to virtualization.

AppNexus represents a different approach to this problem. As with AWS, AppNexus enables you to gain access to servers on demand. AppNexus, however, provides dedicated servers with virtualization on top. You have the confidence in knowing that your applications are not fighting with anyone else for resources and that you can meet any requirements that demand full control over all physical server resources.

Hybrid computing takes advantage of both worlds, offering virtualization where appropriate and dedicated hardware where appropriate. In addition, most hybrid vendors such as Rackspace and GoGrid base their model on the idea that people still want a traditional data center – they just want it in the cloud.

There are a number of reasons why a purely virtualized solution might not work for you:

- Regulatory requirements that demand certain functions operate on dedicated hardware
- Performance requirements – particularly in the area of I/O – that will not support portions of your application
- Integration points with legacy systems that may lack any kind of web integration strategy

Private Clouds

In a private cloud, an organization sets up a virtualization environment on its own servers, either in its own data centers or in those of a managed services provider. This structure is useful for companies that either have significant existing IT investments or feel they absolutely must have total control over every aspect of their infrastructure.

The key advantage of private clouds is control. You retain full control over your infrastructure, but you also gain all of the advantages of virtualization. The reason I am not a fan of the term "private cloud" is simply that, based on the criteria I defined earlier in this chapter, I don't see a private cloud as a true cloud service. In particular, it lacks the freedom from capital investment and the virtually unlimited flexibility of cloud computing. As James Urquhart noted in his "Urquhart on Barriers to Exit" on page 16, I also believe that private clouds may become an excuse for not moving into the cloud, and could thus put the long-term competitiveness of an organization at risk.

2.7   SCALING A CLOUD INFRASTRUCTURE

One of the most useful features of cloud infrastructures is the ability to automatically scale an infrastructure vertically and horizontally with little or no impact to the applications running in that infrastructure. In truth, useful is an understatement. This feature fundamentally alters IT managers' relationships to their infrastructures and changes the way finance managers look at IT funding. But the feature is a double-edged sword.

The obvious benefit of cloud scaling is that you pay only for the resources you use. The non-cloud approach is to buy infrastructure for peak capacity, waste resources, and pray your capacity planning was spot on. The downside of cloud scaling, however, is that it can become a crutch that lazy system architects use to avoid capacity planning. In addition, over-reliance on cloud scaling can lead an organization to respond to demand and thus add cloud instances,when the demand in question simply has no business benefit.

2.8   CAPACITY PLANNING

Capacity planning is basically developing a strategy that guarantees your infrastructure can support the resource demands placed on it.

The core concerns for scaling in the cloud:

- Knowing your expected usage patterns as they vary during the day, over the course of a week, during holidays, and across the seasonal variance of your business

- Knowing how your application responds to load so that you can identify when and what kind of additional capacity you will need

- Knowing the value of your systems to the business so you can know when adding capacity provides value—and when it doesn't.

Expected Demand

You absolutely need to know what demands you expect to be placed on your application. I am not suggesting you need to be a seer and accurately predict the number of page views on your website every day. You simply need to have a well-quantified expectation that will enable you to:

- Plan out an infrastructure to support expected loads

- Recognize when actual load is diverging in a meaningful way from expected load

- Understand the impact of changing application requirements on your infrastructure

The most obvious value of demand estimation is that—combined with understanding how your system responds to load—it tells you how many servers you need, what kind of servers you need, and what resources those servers require. If you have no idea how many people will use your website or web application, you literally have no idea whether the infrastructure you have put together will work right. It could fail within an hour of deployment, or you could waste countless amounts of money on unnecessary infrastructure.

You cannot possibly be expected to predict the future. The point of capacity planning is not to eliminate unexpected peaks in demand; you will always have unexpected peaks in demand. The point of capacity planning is to help you plan for the expected, recognize the unexpected, and react appropriately to the deviation.

Consider, for example, the scenario in which you have an infrastructure that supports 10 million transactions/second and you have a growth from your average load of 1 million transactions/second to 5 million transactions/second. If you had properly estimated the load, you would recognize whether the sudden surge was expected (and thus nothing to be concerned about) or unexpected and thus something to watch for potential capacity problems. Without proper load estimation, you would not know what to do about the variation (In Fig. 2.5 and Fig.2.6, X and Y represents transactions and load).

Determining your expected demand

Figures 2.5 and 2.6 provide charts illustrating the expected traffic for an e-commerce site over the course of a typical day as well as projected peak volumes over the next 12 months.

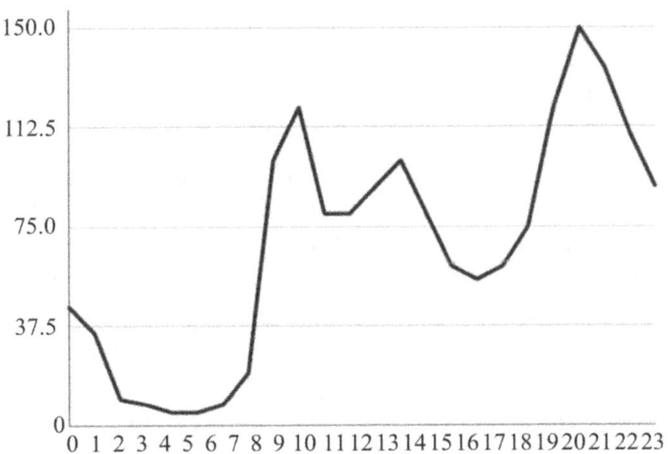

Figure 2.5 The projected daily load on an e-commerce site

The daily chart shows peaks in the morning, at lunch, and in the early evening. A major lull-almost nonexistent traffic—balances out these peaks in the early morning hours.

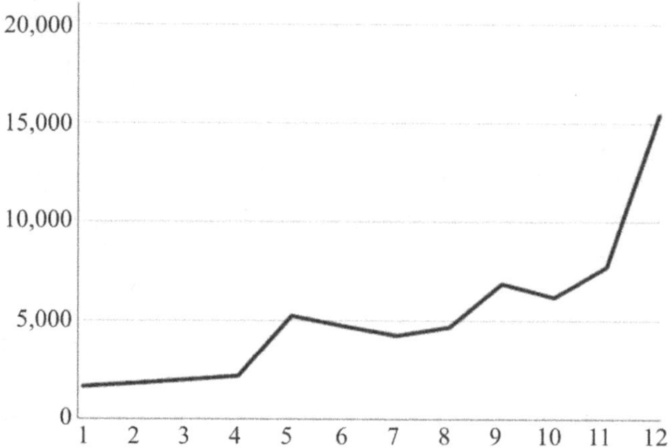

Figure 2.6 The expected load on the e-commerce site over the next 12 months

As a growing company, we expect gradually increasing volumes over the course of the year, punctuated by two product launches in May and September. Finally, we also have a seasonal increase in purchasing at the end of the year.

How do we get these numbers? As with many things, it depends on the application. In the case of the daily chart, historical patterns should form the basis of your expectations. If you have a steady business, the historical patterns are your expectations. A growing business, however, will see behavior alter with the changing market.

A more challenging situation is one in which you have no historical data. If you understand your market, a best guess is good enough until you develop historical data.

At the annual level, however, much of your projections are based on projections coming from other parts of the business. If you are selling goods to consumers, chances are that you expect seasonal variation, especially at the end of the year. Beyond general seasonal availability, however, you are at the mercy of what the business is doing to drive traffic to your website.

You should therefore become good friends with sales, marketing, and anyone else who is driving traffic into the site. As we saw in Figure 2.5, you need to know about the intended product launch in May and the demand the company is projecting for the product in order to take that into account in your projections.

Analyzing the unexpected

You will see unexpected traffic. Sometimes the company launches a product that exceeds expectations; sometimes you receive unplanned media coverage; sometimes you are simply going to be wrong. Any time significant unexpected traffic hits your web systems, it's important to understand why traffic is varying from the unexpected. (As we will discuss later in this section, that) unexpected traffic could be either good news or bad news. It may require a change in all your projections, or it may simply be a wayward blip on the radar screen.

The Impact of Load

The ability to scale a web application or website is tied directly to understanding where the resource constraints lie and what impact the addition of various resources has on the application. Unfortunately, architects more often than not assume that simply adding another server into the mix can fix any performance problem. In reality, adding an application server into an infrastructure with a disk I/O bound database server will only make your problem worse. System architects must therefore understand the expected usage patterns of the applications they manage and execute tests to see how different scenarios create stress points in the infrastructure.

Assuming a perfectly efficient web application and database engine, the typical web application deployed into the cloud has all of these potential capacity constraints:

- The bandwidth into the load balancer
- The CPU and RAM of the load balancer
- The ability of the load balancer to properly spread load across the application servers
- The bandwidth between the load balancer and the application servers
- The CPU and RAM of the application server
- The disk I/O for read operations on the application server
- The write I/O for disk operations on the application server, a secondary disk constraint if the application is caching on the disk
- The bandwidth between the application server and any network storage devices (such as Amazon elastic block storage devices)
- The bandwidth between the application server and the database server
- The disk I/O for read operations on the read database
- The disk I/O for write operations on the write database
- The amount of space on the disk to support data storage needs

Application architecture and database architecture revisited

Guidelines:

- Use the fastest storage devices available to you for database access
- Avoid keeping transactional data at the application server layer
- Enable multiple copies of your application server to run against the same database without any communication between the application servers
- Properly index your database
- If possible, use a master/slave setup with read operations directed to slaves
- With Amazon EC2, design your redundancies to minimize traffic across availability zones

Points of scale

Depending on your application, the most likely initial stress points will be one of the following three components:

- The CPU on your application server
- The RAM on your application server
- The disk I/O on your database server

Every application has stress points. If it didn't, it could run on a single Intel 386 under indefinite load. For the Valtira application (a Java-based web application I architected for the company by the same name), our first bottleneck is always CPU on the application server. As it scales horizontally, CPU ceases to be a significant factor, but (depending on the content inside the Valtira deployment) we encounter a new bottleneck on either bandwidth into the network or database disk I/O. In the cloud, it's the disk I/O.

So our next point of scale is to split out read operations across multiple database slaves and use the master only for write operations. The next choke point tends to become the disk I/O for write operations on the database master. At that point, we need to segment the database or look at a more expensive database solution.

In other words, we have a firm grasp over how our application operates, where we run into capacity constraints, and what we can do about those capacity constraints. Without that knowledge, I might be deluded into believing the solution is always to add application servers.

Of course, you could do a very expensive analysis to try to determine the exact number of users at which you need to take each scaling action. That's not really necessary, however. Just launch your environment at the expected level of scale, begin running realistic load tests, and make notes on the impact of load and additional scale. It should take very little time and cost very little money, and the information you use should be good enough, except for situations in which hiring expert capacity planners is absolutely necessary.

The Value of Your Capacity

In a web application, you don't simply add more capacity to the system just because your CPUs have hit 90% utilization. It's important to be able to answer the question, "What does supporting this additional load get me?" Knowing the value of the demand on your system will help answer that question.

In a grid computing system, it's often easy to understand the value of additional load. For example, a video-rendering farm scales specifically to render more video. If that's your business, you should be able to determine what rendering each video is worth to you and do an appropriate cost/benefit analysis. Understanding whether you are launching more capacity to support one video – as opposed to waiting for existing capacity to become available – will help you be more efficient in your spending. For the most part, however, the decision to add capacity in many non-web systems is generally straightforward.

Web applications aren't that cut-and-dried. A website or web application typically supports dozens or hundreds of different use cases, each with its own value to the business. The value on an e-commerce site of the shopping experience is much different from the value of the CMO's blog. A 100% spike in activity related to a successful product promotion is thus more important than a 100% spike in activity due to a Twitter reference to the CMO's latest blog entry.

A simple thought experiment

(Let's look at a simple example of what I am talking about). We have a simple web application with basic corporate content that serves as our main sales generation tool. We use SalesForce.com's Web2Lead to take leads from the website and get them into SalesForce.com.

An intranet component behind the website enables the marketing team to set up campaigns and landing pages and do basic reporting.

The website begins seeing a sudden, unexpected spike in activity. As load approaches capacity, do we add more capacity or do we let it ride the storm?

To make the call, we need to know how much it is going to cost to add capacity and the value of that capacity to the business. The critical questions we need to answer are:

- How is the lack of capacity impacting site visitors?

- Do we think this spike represents appropriate uses of the system? Is there a bigger issue we need to be concerned with?

- Do we expect the demand to increase further? Do we think we are near the peak?

- Does it cost us anything to let things ride? If so, is that cost greater than the cost of adding capacity into the system?

For the purposes of this thought experiment, we will assume all scaling is done manually. Now we can do some research. Imagine we find the following answers to our questions:

How is the lack of capacity impacting site visitors?

As we approach capacity, the website begins to slow down and the system stops processing logins. If the system gets too bogged down, the speed of the site will eventually become unusable.

Do we think the spike is legitimate?

An analysis of site traffic shows that the CMO said something controversial in her blog and a number of social media sites picked up on it. The blog is being hammered pretty heavily, but the rest of site traffic is pretty much normal.

Do we expect things to get worse?

It does not look like it, as the traffic has begun to level out. But is this a new usage plateau?

Does it cost us anything to let things ride?

The cost of letting this play out is largely insignificant, as regular site visitors are still getting through. The only people significantly impacted are internal marketing users who can put up with a few hours of limited or no access. On the other hand, because we are in the cloud and we have done load testing, we know that adding a single additional application server will return system operation to normal. In other words, it will cost us a few dollars.

The answer

We add the capacity. It does not buy us much, but it also does not cost us much.

How might the outcome have been different?

The most important lesson of this experiment is how different the results and our decision would have been if we were not in a cloud. The cost of adding more capacity would have been huge and, by the time we got it, the unexpected demand would have subsided.

Another outcome worth considering, however, is if there was something peculiar about the traffic—for instance, if it appeared to be some kind of out-of-control botnet looking for site vulnerabilities. The issues become much more difficult in that scenario because it is unclear whether adding capacity is going to help you. In fact, you might end up in a situation in which as you add capacity, the botnet increases its probes and forces you to add more capacity. In short, you would be in a spiral in which you increasingly become a victim to the botnet. The net impact of additional capacity on normal traffic is negligible. As a result, you could be incurring greater cost and greater exposure to an external threat without incurring any business benefit.

The key point here is that additional demand does not automatically mean that you must add more capacity.

2.9   CLOUD SCALE

The cloud empowers you to alter your computing resources to meet your load requirements. You can alter your capacity both manually (by executing a command on a command line or through a web interface) and programmatically (through predefined changes in capacity or through software that automatically adjusts capacity to meet actual demand).

The ability to manually adjust capacity is a huge advantage over traditional computing. But the real power of scaling in the cloud lies in dynamic scaling.

Dynamic scaling

This term – which I sometimes also refer to as cloud scaling—enables software to adjust the resources in your infrastructure without your interactive involvement. Dynamic scaling can take the form of proactive scaling or reactive scaling.

Proactive scaling

This involves a schedule for altering your infrastructure based on projected demand. If you would configure our cloud management tools to run with a minimal infrastructure that supports our availability requirements during the early morning hours, add capacity in the late morning, drop back to the baseline until lunch, and so on. This strategy does not wait for demand to increase, but instead increases capacity based on a plan.

Reactive scaling

In this strategy, your infrastructure reacts to changes in demand by adding and removing capacity on its own accord. In the capacity valuation thought experiment, an environment engaging in reactive scaling might have automatically added capacity when it detected the unexpected spike in activity on the CMO blog.

Tools and Monitoring Systems

Cloud infrastructure management tools and monitoring systems as being critical to the management of a cloud infrastructure. I run one such company, enStratus, but there are a number of other good systems out there, including RightScale and Morph. Which one is right for you depend on your budget, the kinds of applications you manage, and what parts of infrastructure management matter most to you.

Whatever tool you pick, it should minimally have the following capabilities:

- To schedule changes in capacity for your application deployments
- To monitor the deployments for excess (and less than normal) demand
- To adjust capacity automatically based on unexpected spikes or falloffs in demand

Monitoring involves a lot more than watching for capacity caps and switching servers off and on. You can also roll your own monitoring system if you don't want to pay for someone else's software. A monitoring system has the architecture described in Figure 2.7.

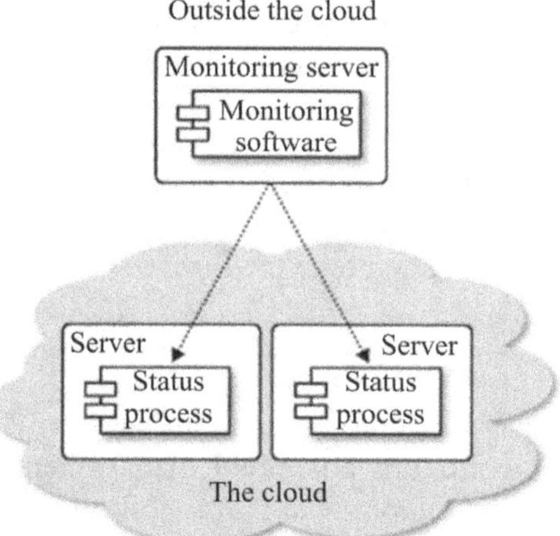

Figure 2.7 General architecture for a system monitoring your cloud health

Compared to disaster recovery, it's not as critical for capacity planning purposes that your monitoring server is outside the cloud. Nevertheless, it's a very good idea, and a critical choice if bandwidth management is part of your monitoring profile.

The monitoring checks on each individual server to get a picture of its current resource constraints. Each cloud instance has a process capable of taking the vitals of that instance and reporting back to the monitoring server. Most modern operating systems have the ability to operate as the status process for core system data, such as CPU, RAM, and other SNMP-related data. In addition, Java application servers support the JMX interfaces that enable you to query the performance of your Java virtual machines.

For security purposes, I prefer having the monitoring server poll the cloud instances rather than making the cloud instances regularly report into the monitoring server. By polling, you can put your monitoring server behind a firewall and allow no incoming traffic into the server.

It's also important to keep in mind that you need the ability to scale the monitoring server as the number of nodes it must monitor grows.

The process that checks instance vitals must vary for each instance based on its function. A load balancer can be fairly dumb, and so all the monitor needs to worry about is the server's RAM and CPU utilization. A database server needs to be slightly more intelligent: the vitals process must review disk I/O performance for any signs of trouble. The most difficult monitoring process supports your application servers. It should be capable of reporting not simply how much the instance's resources are being utilized, but what the activity on the instance looks like.

The monitoring server then uses analytics to process all of that data. It knows when it is time to proactively add and remove scale, how to recognize unexpected activity, and how to trigger rules in response to unexpected activity.

The procurement process in the cloud

Whether you scale dynamically or through a human pulling the levers, the way you think about spending money in the cloud is very different from a traditional infrastructure. When you add new resources into your internal data center or with a managed services provider, you typically need to get a purchase order approved through your company procurement processes. Finance approves the purchase order against your department's budget, and the order goes off to the vendor. You don't spend $3,000 on a server unless that spend is cleared through Finance.

Nothing in the AWS infrastructure prevents you from executing ec2-run-instances just one time on an EC2 extra-large instance and spending $7,000 over the course of a year. Anyone who has access to launch new instances or alter the scaling criteria of your cloud management tools has full procurement rights in the cloud. There's no justification that an IT manager needs to make to

Finance; it's just a configuration parameter in a program that Finance may never touch.

Finance should therefore be involved in approving the monthly budget for the team managing the cloud infrastructure. Furthermore, controls should be in place to make sure any alterations in the resources you have deployed into the cloud are aligned with the approved budget. If you don't put this human process in place, you may find Finance turning from the biggest supporter of your move into the cloud to your biggest critic.

Managing proactive scaling

A well-designed proactive scaling system enables you to schedule capacity changes that match your expected changes in application demand. When using proactive scaling, you should understand your expected standard deviation. You don't need to get out the statistics textbooks…or worse, throw out this book because I mentioned a term from statistics. I simply mean you should roughly understand how much normal traffic deviates from your expectations. If you expect site activity of 1,000 page views/hour around noon and you are seeing 1,100, is that really unexpected? Probably not.

Your capacity for any point in time should therefore be able to handle the high end of your expected capacity with some room to spare. The most efficient use of your resources is just shy of their capacity, but scheduling things that way can create problems when your expectations are wrong—even when combined with reactive scaling. Understanding what constitutes that "room to spare" is probably the hardest part of capacity planning.

Managing reactive scaling

Reactive scaling is a powerful rope you can easily hang yourself with. It enables you to react quickly to unexpected demand. If you fail to do any capacity planning and instead rely solely on reactive scaling to manage a web application, however, you probably will end up hanging yourself with this rope.

The crudest form of reactive scaling is utilization-based. In other words, when your CPU or RAM or other resource reaches a certain level of utilization, you add more of that resource into your environment. It makes for very simple logic for the monitoring system, but realistically, it's what you need only a fraction of the time. We've already seen some examples of where this will fail:

- Hiked-up application server processing that suffers from an I/O bound database server. The result is increased loads on the database server that further aggravate the situation.

- An attack that will use up whatever resources you throw at it. The result is a spiraling series of attempts to launch new resources while your costs go through the roof.

- An unexpected spike in web activity that begins taxing your infrastructure but only mildly impacts the end user experience. You know the activity will subside, but your monitor launches new instances simply because it perceives load.

A good monitoring system will provide tools that mitigate these potential problems with reactive scaling. I have never seen a system, however, that is perfectly capable of dealing with the last scenario. It calls for an understanding of the problem domain and the pattern of activity that determines you should not launch new instances—and I don't know of an algorithmic substitute for human intuition for these decisions.

However your monitoring system defines its rules for reactive scaling, you should always have a governor in place. A governor places limits on how many resources the monitoring system can automatically launch, and thus how much money your monitoring system can spend on your behalf. In the case of the attack on your infrastructure, your systems would eventually end up grinding to a halt as you hit your governor limit, but you would not end up spending money adding an insane number of instances into your cloud environment.

A final issue of concern that affects both proactive and reactive scaling – but more so for reactive scaling – is the fallibility of Amazon S3 and the AWS APIs. If you are counting on reactive scaling to make sure you have enough resources, Amazon S3 issues will weaken your plans. Your system will then fail you.

A recommended approach

I am not terribly fond of reactive scaling, but it does have its uses. I prefer to rely heavily on proactive scaling to manage my infrastructure based on expected demand, including excess capacity roughly one to two times the difference between expected demand and the highest expected demand (about three to five standard deviations from the expected demand). With this setup, reactive scaling should almost never kick in.

Unexpected demand does occur. Instead of using reactive scaling to manage unexpected load, I instead use it to give people time to react and assess the situation. My governors are thus generally set to 150% to 200% of the baseline configuration. In other words, if my baseline configuration has two application servers and my application will scale to 200% of the baseline capacity by adding two more application servers, I direct the governor to limit scaling at two application servers and notify me well in advance of the need to add even one.

As a result of using reactive scaling in this way, my infrastructure should scale in a controlled manner automatically in reaction to the unexpected demand up to a certain point. I should also have the time to examine the unexpected activity to determine whether I want to bump up the governors, change my baseline configuration, or ignore the event altogether. Because I am not running near capacity and I am not relying on reactive scaling to keep things running, Amazon S3 failures are unlikely to impact me.

Although the absolute numbers I have mentioned may not make sense for your web application, the general policy should serve you well. Whatever numbers make sense for your application, you should have an approved budget to operate at the peak capacity for at least long enough a time period to approve increasing the budget. If your budget is approved for expected capacity and you find yourself operating at the limits of your governors, your finance department will not be pleased with you.

Scaling Vertically

So far, I have been entirely focused on horizontal scaling, which is scaling through the addition of new servers. Vertical scalability, on the other hand, is scaling by replacing an existing server with a beefier one or a more specialized one. All virtualized environments – and cloud environments in particular – are very good at horizontal scaling. When it comes to vertical scaling, however, the cloud has some important strengths and some very important weaknesses.

The strength of the cloud with respect to vertical scaling is the ease with which you can try out smaller or less-specialized configurations and the ability to make the system prove the need for more configurations. Clouds (and the Amazon cloud more so than its competitors) do a poor job of providing specialized system configurations.

Amazon currently provides you with five different system choices. If a component of your application requires more RAM than one of the Amazon instances supports, you are out of luck. GoGrid, in contrast, provides a greater degree of customization, including the ability to design high I/O configurations. In the end, none of these options will match your ability to configure a very specialized system through Dell's configurator.

Though I have spent a lot of time in this book talking about horizontal scaling, I always scale vertically first.

Vertical scalability in the Amazon cloud is most effective when you need more RAM. The Valtira application I mentioned earlier in this chapter is an excellent example of such an application. I left out that the first point of scale for Valtira is actually RAM. Most systems deployed on the Valtira platform don't need a lot of RAM – 1 to 2 GB is generally sufficient. Some applications that leverage certain components of the Valtira platform, however, require a lot more RAM. Because Valtira will essentially duplicate its memory footprint across all servers in a cluster, adding more servers into the equation does not help at all. Moving to a server with more RAM, however, makes all the difference in the world.

Vertical scalability can help with other capacity constraints as well. Table 2.4 describes how a theoretical application responds to different kinds of scaling.

Table 2.4 Example of Amazon server CPU options

Configuration	Capacity	Cost
Eight Amazon medium	8,000 page views/minute	$0.80/hour
Two Amazon large	10,000 page views/minute	$0.80/hour
One Amazon extra-large	10,000 page views/minute	$0.80/hour

If you assume linear scalability horizontally, you want to switch the infrastructure from eight medium instances to two large instances rather than adding a ninth medium instance.

Admittedly, this example is absurdly simplistic. The point, however, is that sometimes it simply makes financial sense to scale vertically.

Vertical dynamic scaling is trickier than horizontal. More to the point, scaling vertically is a special case of horizontal scaling. It requires the following rules:

- Add an instance into the cloud of the beefier system, as if you were scaling horizontally. The only difference is that you are using one of the larger machine instances instead of a duplicate of the existing infrastructure instances.
- Wait for the new instance to begin responding to requests.
- Remove one or more of the old, smaller instances from the system.

When you put horizontal scaling together with vertical scaling, you end up with an infrastructure that makes the most efficient use of computing resources.

Bit Questions

1. P2P is a ------------ concept.

2. Properties of cloud computing are ----------------.

3. Client-Server is a ------------ concept.

4. A -------------- application is processor-intensive software that breaks up its processing into small chunks that can then be processed in isolation.

5. The term----------------------- has been used historically as a metaphor for the Internet.

6. ----------------------- can be defined as the provision of computational and storage resources as a metered service.

7. "Cloud" in cloud computing represents what?   [   ]

    (a) Wireless   (b) Hard drives   (c) People   (d) Internet

8. Which one of these is not a cloud computing pricing model?   [   ]

    (a) Free   (b) Pay Per Use   (c) Subscription   (d) Ladder

9. Which of the following is an example of a cloud computing application?

                                                                         [   ]

    (a) Facebook Apps.   (b) Twitter or RSS.

    (c) Salesforce.com   (d) Skype.

10. What is grid computing ?   [   ]

    (a) It's a network of computers that share resources -- the network can be local or distributed across the Internet. Hardware as a Service

    (b) It's a physical arrangement of computer terminals that optimizes computing power -- the computers in the center are the most powerful.

    (c) It's a temporary cloud computer network that only exists as long as a single project is active.

    (d) All the above

11. What is an important benefit of Cloud?   [   ]

    (a) highly protected data

    (b) independency from the Internet

    (c) reduced cost

    (d) small bandwidth

12. What is not a valid reason for the customer asking a Cloud provider where their servers are located?   [   ]

    (a) Geographical location may tell something about network latency.

    (b) The geographical location may tell something about legislation.

    (c) The number of sites tells you something about disaster recovery possibilities.

    (d) When a server breaks down, the customer wants to send a technician to fix the   problem as soon as possible.

13. Which cloud deployment model is operated solely for a single organization and its authorized users?

    (a) Community cloud   (b) Hybrid cloud

    (c) Public cloud   (d) Private cloud

14. Which cloud deployment model is managed by a cloud provider, has an infrastructure that is offsite, and is accessible to the general public?

    (a) Community cloud   (b) Hybrid cloud

    (c) Public cloud   (d) Private cloud

15. Interoperability is enabled by --------------.

    (a) a cloud operating system   (b) middleware

    (c) a community cloud   (d) a composite cloud

16. What is/are the key characteristic/s of cloud computing?   [   ]

    (a) Service offering   (b) Reliability

    (c) Scalability   (d) All

17. Which one is delivering software services to end users and running code?   [   ]

    (a) SOA   (b) Grid

    (c) Cloud   (d) None

Exercises

1. Define Cloud Computing, enlist and explain essential characteristics of cloud computing.

2. Is the cloud model reliable? Explain its benefits and limitations.

3. Discuss about the Pros and Cons of Cloud Computing.

4. Explain collaboration to cloud.

5. Explain about Cloud application architectures.

6. Explain in detail about the Cloud Infrastructure models.

7. Explain in brief, how cloud helps reducing capital expenditure?

8. Write short notes on the following:

   (a)   Capacity planning   (b) Cloud Scale

CHAPTER 3

SERVICES DELIVERED FROM THE CLOUD

3.1 CHAPTER OVERVIEW

In this chapter we will examine some of the web services delivered from the cloud. We will take a look at Communication-as-a-Service (CaaS) and explain some of the advantages of using CaaS. Infrastructure is also a service in cloud land, and there are many variants on how infrastructure is managed in cloud environments. When vendors outsource Infrastructure-as-a-Service (IaaS), it relies heavily on modern on-demand computing technology and high-speed networking. We will look at some vendors who provide Software-as-a-Service (SaaS), such as Amazon.com with their elastic cloud platform, and foray into the implementation issues, the characteristics, benefits, and architectural maturity level of the service. Outsourced hardware environments (called platforms) are available as Platforms-as-a-Service (PaaS), and we will look at Mosso (Rackspace) and examine key characteristics of their PaaS implementation. Now, let's examine some of the more common web service offerings.

3.2 COMMUNICATION-AS-A-SERVICE (CAAS)

CaaS is an Outsourced enterprise communications solution. Providers of this type of cloud-based solution (known as CaaS vendors) are responsible for the management of hardware and software required for delivering Voice over IP (VoIP) services, Instant Messaging (IM), and video conferencing capabilities to their customers. This model began its evolutionary process from within the telecommunications (Telco) industry, not unlike how the SaaS model arose from the software delivery services sector. CaaS vendors are responsible for all of the hardware and software management consumed by their user base. CaaS vendors typically offer guaranteed quality of service (QoS) under a service-level agreement (SLA).

A CaaS model allows a CaaS provider's business customers to selectively deploy communications features and services throughout their company on a pay-as-you-go basis for service(s) used. CaaS is designed on a utility-like pricing model that provides users with comprehensive, flexible, and (usually) simple-to-understand service plans.

A CaaS solution includes redundant switching, network, POP and circuit diversity, customer premises equipment redundancy, and WAN fail-over that specifically addresses the needs of their customers. All VoIP transport components are located in geographically diverse, secure data centers for high availability and survivability.

CaaS offers flexibility and scalability that small and medium-sized business might not otherwise be able to afford. CaaS service providers are usually prepared to handle peak loads for their customers by providing services capable of allowing more capacity, devices, modes or area coverage as their customer demand necessitates. Network capacity and feature sets can be changed dynamically, so functionality keeps pace with consumer demand and provider-owned resources are not wasted. From the service provider customer's perspective, there is very little to virtually no risk of the service becoming obsolete, since the provider's responsibility is to perform periodic upgrades or replacements of hardware and software to keep the platform technologically current.

CaaS requires little to no management oversight from customers. It eliminates the business customers need for any capital investment in infrastructure, and it eliminates expense for ongoing maintenance and operations overhead for infrastructure. With a CaaS solution, customers are able to leverage enterprise-class communication services without having to build a premises-based solution of their own. This allows those customers to reallocate budget and personnel resources to where their business can best use them.

3.2.1 Advantages of CaaS

From the handset found on each employee's desk to the PC-based software client on employee laptops, to the VoIP private backbone, and all modes in between, every component in a CaaS solution is managed 24/7 by the CaaS vendor. As we said previously, the expense of managing a carrier-grade data center is shared across the vendor's customer base, making it more economical for businesses to implement CaaS than to build their own VoIP network.

Some of the advantages of a hosted approach for CaaS.

Hosted and Managed Solutions

Remote management of infrastructure services provided by third parties once seemed an unacceptable situation to most companies. However, over the past decade, with enhanced technology, networking, and software, the attitude has changed, due to cost savings achieved in using those services. However, unlike the "one-off" services offered by specialist providers, CaaS delivers a complete communications solution that is entirely managed by a single vendor. Along with features such as VoIP and unified communications, the integration of core PBX features with advanced functionality is managed by one vendor, who is responsible for all of the integration and delivery of services to users.

3.2.2   Fully Integrated, Enterprise-Class Unified Communications

With CaaS, the vendor provides voice and data access and manages LAN/WAN, security, routers, email, voice mail, and data storage. By managing the LAN/WAN, the vendor can guarantee consistent quality of service from a user's desktop across the network and back. Advanced unified communications features that are most often a part of a standard CaaS deployment include:

- Chat
- Multimedia conferencing
- Microsoft Outlook integration
- Real-time presence
- "Soft" phones (software-based telephones)
- Video calling
- Unified messaging and mobility

No Capital Expenses Needed

When business outsource their unified communications needs to a CaaS service provider, the provider supplies a complete solution that fits the company's exact needs. Customers pay a fee (usually billed monthly) for what they use. Customers are not required to purchase equipment, so there is no capital outlay. Bundled in these types of services are ongoing maintenance and upgrade costs, which are incurred by the service provider. The use of CaaS services allows companies the ability to collaborate across any workspace. Advanced collaboration tools are now used to create high-quality, secure, adaptive work spaces throughout any organization. This allows a company's workers, partners, vendors, and customers to communicate and collaborate more effectively. Better communication allows organizations to adapt quickly to market changes and to build competitive advantage. CaaS can also accelerate decision making within an organization. Innovative unified communications capabilities (such as presence, instant messaging, and rich media services) help ensure that information quickly reaches whoever needs it.

Flexible Capacity and Feature Set

When customers outsource communications services to a CaaS provider, they pay for the features they need when they need them. The service provider can distribute the cost services and delivery across a large customer base. This makes the use of shared feature functionality more economical for customers to implement. Economies of scale allow service providers enough flexibility that they are not tied to a single vendor investment. They are able to leverage best-of-breed providers such as Avaya, Cisco, Juniper, Microsoft, Nortel and ShoreTel more economically than any independent enterprise.

No Risk of Obsolescence

Rapid technology advances, predicted long ago and known as Moore's law, have brought about product obsolescence in increasingly shorter periods of time. Moore's law describes a trend he recognized that has held true since the beginning of the use of integrated circuits (ICs) in computing hardware. Since the invention of the integrated circuit in 1958, the number of transistors that can be placed inexpensively on an integrated circuit has increased exponentially, doubling approximately every two years.

Unlike IC components, the average life cycles for PBXs and key communications equipment and systems range anywhere from five to 10 years. With the constant introduction of newer models for all sorts of technology(PCs, cell phones, video software and hardware, etc.), these types of products now face much shorter life cycles, sometimes as short as a single year. CaaS vendors must absorb this burden for the user by continuously upgrading the equipment in their offerings to meet changing demands in the marketplace.

No Facilities and Engineering Costs Incurred

CaaS providers host all of the equipment needed to provide their services to their customers, virtually eliminating the need for customers to maintain data center space and facilities. There is no extra expense for the constant power consumption that such a facility would demand. Customers receive the benefit of multiple carrier-grade data centers with full redundancy and it's all included in the monthly payment.

Guaranteed Business Continuity

If a catastrophic event occurred at your business's physical location, would your company disaster recovery plan allow your business to continue operating without a break? If your business experienced a serious or extended communications outage, how long could your company survive? For most businesses, the answer is "not long." Distributing risk by using geographically dispersed data centers has become the norm today. It mitigates risk and allows companies in a location hit by a catastrophic event to recover as soon as possible.   This process is implemented by CaaS providers because most companies don't even contemplate voice continuity if catastrophe strikes.Unlike data continuity, eliminating single points of failure for a voice network is usually cost-prohibitive because of the large scale and management complexity of the project. With a CaaS solution, multiple levels of redundancy are built into the system, with no single point of failure.

3.3   INFRASTRUCTURE-AS-A-SERVICE (IaaS)

According to the online reference Wikipedia, IaaS is the delivery of computer infrastructure (typically a platform virtualization environment) as a service. IaaS leverages significant technology, services, and data center investments to deliver IT as a service to customers. Unlike traditional outsourcing, which requires extensive due diligence, negotiations ad infinitum, and complex, lengthy contract vehicles, IaaS is centered around a model of service delivery that provisions a predefined, standardized infrastructure specifically optimized for the customer's applications. Simplified statements of work and à la carte service-level choices make it easy to tailor a solution to a customer's specific application requirements. IaaS providers manage the transition and hosting of selected applications on their infrastructure. Customers maintain ownership and management of their application(s) while off-loading hosting operations and infrastructure management to the IaaS provider. Provider-owned implementations typically include the following layered components:

- Computer hardware (typically set up as a grid for massive horizontal scalability)
- Computer network (including routers, firewalls, load balancing, etc.)
- Internet connectivity (often on OC 192 backbones)
- Platform virtualization environment for running client-specified virtual machines
- Service-level agreements
- Utility computing billing

The chief benefits of using this type of outsourced service include:

- Ready access to a preconfigured environment that is generally ITIL-based (The Information Technology Infrastructure Library is a customized framework of best practices designed to promote quality computing services in the IT sector.)

- Use of the latest technology for infrastructure equipment

- Secured, "sand-boxed" (protected and insulated) computing platforms that are usually security monitored for breaches

- Reduced risk by having off-site resources maintained by third parties

- Ability to manage service-demand peaks and valleys

- Lower costs that allow expensing service costs instead of making capital investments

- Reduced time, cost, and complexity in adding new features or capabilities

3.3.1 Modern On-Demand Computing

On-demand computing is an increasingly popular enterprise model in which computing resources are made available to the user as needed. Computing resources that are maintained on a user's site are becoming fewer and fewer, while those made available by a service provider are on the rise. The on-demand model evolved to overcome the challenge of being able to meet fluctuating resource demands efficiently. Because demand for computing resources can vary drastically from one time to another, maintaining sufficient resources to meet peak requirements can be costly.

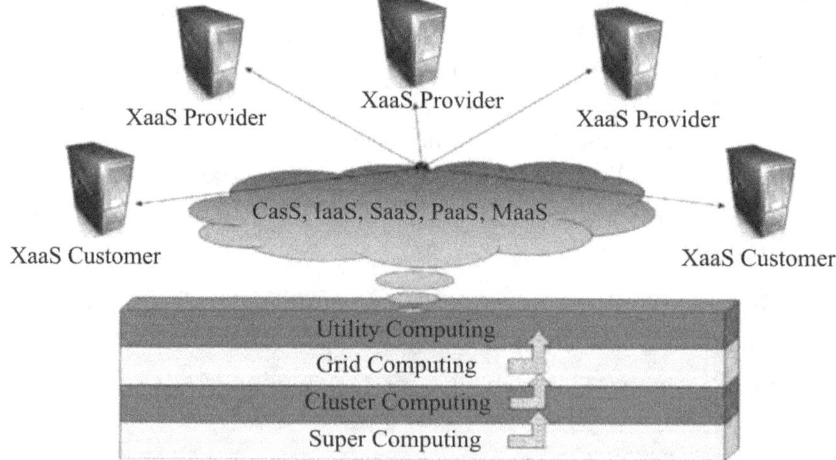

Figure 3.1 Building blocks to the cloud

Over engineering a solution can be just as adverse as a situation where the enterprise cuts costs by maintaining only minimal computing resources, resulting in insufficient resources to meet peak load requirements. Concepts such as clustered computing, grid computing, utility computing, etc., may all seem very similar to the concept of on-demand computing, but they can be better understood if one thinks of them as building blocks that evolved over time and with techno-evolution to achieve the modern cloud computing model we think of and use today (see Figure 3.1).

One example we will examine is Amazon's Elastic Compute Cloud (Amazon EC2). This is a web service that provides resizable computing capacity in the cloud. It is designed to make web-scale computing easier for developers and offers many advantages to customers:

- It's web service interface allows customers to obtain and configure capacity with minimal effort.

- It provides users with complete control of their (leased) computing resources and lets them run on a proven computing environment.

- It reduces the time required to obtain and boot new server instances to minutes, allowing customers to quickly scale capacity as their computing demands dictate.

- It changes the economics of computing by allowing clients to pay only for capacity they actually use.

- It provides developers the tools needed to build failure-resilient applications and isolate themselves from common failure scenarios.

3.3.2 Amazon's Elastic Cloud

Amazon EC2 presents a true virtual computing environment, allowing clients to use a web-based interface to obtain and manage services needed to launch one or more instances of a variety of operating systems (OSs). Clients can load the OS environments with their customized applications. They can manage their network's access permissions and run as many or as few systems as needed. In order to use Amazon EC2, clients first need to create an Amazon Machine Image (AMI). This image contains the applications, libraries, data, and associated configuration settings used in the virtual computing environment.

Amazon EC2 offers the use of preconfigured images built with templates to get up and running immediately. Once users have defined and configured their AMI, they use the Amazon EC2 tools provided for storing the AMI by uploading the AMI into Amazon S3. Amazon S3 is a repository that provides safe, reliable, and fast access to a client AMI. Before clients can use the AMI, they must use the Amazon EC2 web service to configure security and network access. (see Fig. 3.2)

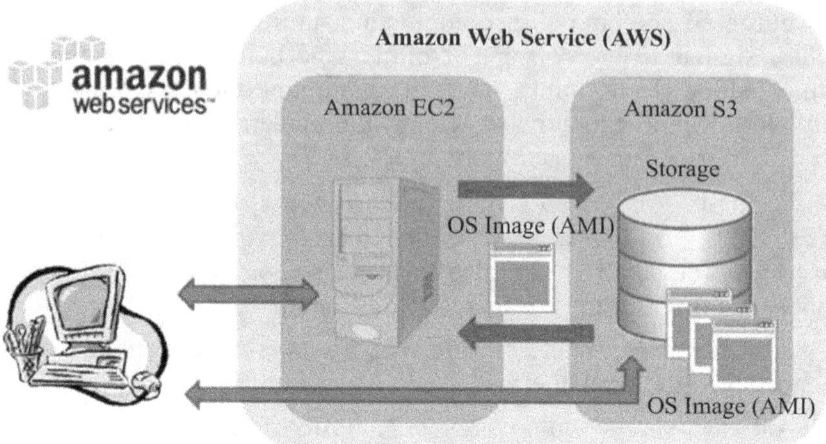

Figure 3.2 Amazon EC2 & S3

Using Amazon EC2 to Run Instances

During configuration, users choose which instance type(s) and operating system they want to use. Available instance types come in two distinct categories, Standard or High-CPU instances. Most applications are best suited for Standard instances, which come in small, large, and extra-large instance platforms. High-CPU instances have proportionally more CPU resources than RAM and are well suited for compute-intensive applications. With the High-CPU instances, there are medium and extra large platforms to choose from. After determining which instance to use, clients can start, terminate, and monitor as many instances of their AMI as needed by using web service Application Programming Interfaces(APIs) or a wide variety of other management tools that are provided with the service. Users are able to choose whether they want to run in multiple locations, use static IP endpoints, or attach persistent block storage to any of their instances, and they pay only for resources actually consumed. They can also choose from a library of globally available AMIs that provides useful instances. For example, if all that is needed is a basic Linux server, clients can choose one of the standard Linux distribution AMIs.

3.3.3 Amazon EC2 Service Characteristics

Amazon EC2 provides financial benefits. Because of Amazon's massive scale and large customer base, it is an inexpensive alternative to many other possible solutions. The costs incurred to set up and run an operation are shared over many customers, making the overall cost to any single customer much lower than almost any other alternative. Customers pay a very low rate for the compute capacity they actually consume. Security is also provided through Amazon EC2 web service interfaces. These allow users to configure firewall settings that control network access to and between groups of instances. Amazon EC2 offers a highly reliable environment where replacement instances can be rapidly provisioned.

When one compares this solution to the significant up-front expenditures traditionally required to purchase and maintain hardware, either in-house or hosted, the decision to outsource is not hard to make. Outsourced solutions like EC2 free customers from many of the complexities of capacity planning and allow clients to move from large capital investments and fixed costs to smaller, variable, expensed costs. This approach removes the need to overbuy and overbuild capacity to handle periodic traffic spikes. The EC2 service runs within Amazon's proven, secure, and reliable network infrastructure and data center locations.

Amazon EC2 Service Characteristics

- Dynamic Scalability
- Full Control of Instances
- Configuration Flexibility
- Integration with Other Amazon Web Services
    - Amazon S3
    - Amazon SimpleDB
    - Amazon Simple Queue Service (Amazon SQS)
    - Amazon CloudFront
    - Reliable and Resilient Performance
    - Amazon Elastic Block Store (EBS)
    - Support for Use in Geographically Disparate Locations
    - Elastic IP Addressing

Dynamic Scalability

Amazon EC2 enables users to increase or decrease capacity in a few minutes. Users can invoke a single instance, hundreds of instances, or even thousands of instances simultaneously. Because this is all controlled with web service APIs, an application can automatically scale itself up or down depending on its needs. This type of dynamic scalability is very attractive to enterprise customers because it allows them to meet their customers' demands without having to overbuild their infrastructure.

Full Control of Instances

Users have complete control of their instances. They have root access to each instance and can interact with them as one would with any machine. Instances can be rebooted remotely using web service APIs. Users also have access to console output of their instances. Once users have set up their account and uploaded their AMI to the Amazon S3 service, they just need to boot that instance. Possible to start an AMI on any number of instances (or any type) by calling the *RunInstances* API that is provided by Amazon.

Configuration Flexibility

Configuration settings can vary widely among users. They have the choice of multiple instance types, operating systems, and software packages. Amazon EC2 allows them to select a configuration of memory, CPU, and instance storage that is optimal for their choice of operating system and application. For example, a user's choice of operating systems may also include numerous Linux distributions, Microsoft Windows Server, and even an OpenSolaris environment, all running on virtual servers.

Integration with Other Amazon Web Services

Amazon EC2 works in conjunction with a variety of other Amazon web services.

Examples:

- Amazon Simple Storage Service (Amazon S3)
- Amazon SimpleDB
- Amazon Simple Queue Service (Amazon SQS) and
- Amazon CloudFront is all integrated to provide a complete solution for computing, query processing, and storage across a wide range of applications.

Amazon S3

Amazon S3 provides a web services interface that allows users to store and retrieve any amount of data from the Internet at anytime, anywhere. It gives developers direct access to the same highly scalable, reliable, fast, inexpensive data storage infrastructure Amazon uses to run its own global network of web sites. The S3 service aims to maximize benefits of scale and to pass those benefits on to developers.

Amazon SimpleDB

Amazon SimpleDB is another web-based service, designed for running queries on structured data stored with the Amazon Simple Storage Service (Amazon S3) in real time. This service works in conjunction with the Amazon EC2 to provide users the capability to store, process, and query data sets within the cloud environment. These services are designed to make web-scale computing easier and more cost effective for developers. Traditionally, this type of functionality was provided using a clustered relational database that requires a sizable investment. Implementations of this nature brought on more complexity and often required the services of a database administer to maintain it.

By comparison to traditional approaches, Amazon SimpleDB is easy to use and provides the core functionality of a database (e.g., real-time lookup and simple querying of structured data) without inheriting the operational complexity involved in traditional implementations. Amazon SimpleDB requires no schema, automatically indexes data, and provides a simple API for data storage and access. This eliminates the need for customers to perform tasks such as data modeling, index maintenance, and performance tuning.

Amazon Simple Queue Service (Amazon SQS)

It is a reliable, scalable, hosted queue for storing messages as they pass between computers. Using Amazon SQS, developers can move data between distributed components of applications that perform different tasks without losing messages or requiring 100% availability for each component. Amazon SQS works by exposing Amazon's web-scale messaging infrastructure as a service. Any computer connected to the Internet can add or read messages without the need for having any installed software or special firewall configurations. Components of applications using Amazon SQS can run independently and do not need to be on the same network, developed with the same technologies, or running at the same time.

Amazon CloudFront

Amazon CloudFront is a web service for content delivery. It integrates with other Amazon web services to distribute content to end users with low latency and high data transfer speeds. Amazon CloudFront delivers content using a global network of edge locations. Requests for objects are automatically routed to the nearest edge server, so content is delivered with the best possible performance. An edge server receives a request from the user's computer and makes a connection to another computer called the origin server, where the application resides. When the origin server fulfills the request, it sends the application's data back to the edge server, which, in turn, forwards the data to the client computer that made the request.

Reliable and Resilient Performance

Amazon Elastic Block Store (EBS) is yet another Amazon EC2 feature that provides users powerful features to build failure-resilient applications. Amazon EBS offers persistent storage for Amazon EC2 instances. Amazon EBS volumes provide "off-instance" storage that persists independently from the life of any instance. Amazon EBS volumes are highly available, highly reliable data shares that can be attached to a running Amazon EC2 instance and are exposed to the instance as standard block devices. Amazon EBS volumes are automatically replicated on the back end. The service provides users with the ability to create point-in-time snapshots of their data volumes, which are stored using the Amazon S3 service. These snapshots can be used as a starting point for new Amazon EBS volumes and can protect data indefinitely.

Support for Use in Geographically Disparate Locations

Amazon EC2 provides users with the ability to place one or more instances in multiple locations. Amazon EC2 locations are composed of Regions (such as North America and Europe) and Availability Zones. Regions consist of one or more Availability Zones, are geographically dispersed, and are in separate geographic areas or countries. Availability Zones are distinct locations that are engineered to be insulated from failures in other Availability Zones and provide inexpensive, low-latency network connectivity to other Availability Zones in the same Region. For example, the North America Region may be split into the following Availability Zones: Northeast, East, SouthEast, NorthCentral, Central, SouthCentral, NorthWest, West, SouthWest, etc. By launching instances in any one or more of the separate Availability Zones, you can insulate your applications from a single point of failure. Amazon EC2 has a service-level agreement that commits to 99.95% uptime availability for each Amazon EC2 Region. Amazon EC2 is currently available in two regions, the United States and Europe.

Elastic IP Addressing

Elastic IP (EIP) addresses are static IP addresses designed for dynamic cloud computing. An Elastic IP address is associated with your account and not with a particular instance, and you control that address until you choose explicitly to release it. Unlike traditional static IP addresses, however, EIP addresses allow you to mask instance or Availability Zone failures by programmatically remapping your public IP addresses to any instance in your account. Rather than waiting on a technician to reconfigure or replace your host, or waiting for DNS to propagate to all of your customers, Amazon EC2 enables you to work around problems that occur with client instances or client software by quickly remapping their EIP address to another running instance. A significant feature of Elastic IP addressing is that each IP address can be reassigned to a different instance when needed.

Now, let's Review how the Elastic IPs work with Amazon EC2 services:

First of all, Amazon allows users to allocate up to five Elastic IP addresses per account (which is the default). Each EIP can be assigned to a single instance. When this reassignment occurs, it replaces the normal dynamic IP address used by that instance. By default, each instance starts with a dynamic IP address that is allocated upon startup. Since each instance can have only one external IP address, the instance starts out using the default dynamic IP address. If the EIP in use is assigned to a different instance, a new dynamic IP address is allocated to the vacated address of that instance. Assigning or reassigning an IP to an instance requires only a few minutes. The limitation of designating a single IP at a time is due to the way Network Address Translation (NAT) works. Each instance is mapped to an internal IP address and is also assigned an external (public) address. The public address is mapped to the internal address using Network Address Translation tables (hence, NAT). If two external IP addresses happen to be translated to the same internal IP address, all inbound traffic (in the form of data packets) would arrive without any issues. However, assigning outgoing packets to an external IP address would be very difficult because a determination of which external IP address to use could not be made. This is why implementers have built in the limitation of having only a single external IP address per instance at any one time.

3.3.4 Mosso (Rackspace)

Mosso, a direct competitor of Amazon's EC2 service is a web application hosting service and cloud platform provider that bills on a utility computing basis. Mosso was launched in February 2008 and is owned and operated by Rackspace, a web hosting provider that has been around for some time. Most new hosting platforms require custom code and architecture to make an application work. What makes Mosso different is that it has been designed to run an application with very little or no modifications. The Mosso platform is built on existing web standards and powered by proven technologies. Customers reap the benefits of a scalable platform for free. They spend no time coding custom APIs or building data schemas. Mosso has also branched out into cloud storage and cloud infrastructure.

Mosso Cloud Servers and Files

Mosso Cloud Servers (MCS) came into being from the acquisition of a company called Slicehost by Rackspace. Slicehost was designed to enable deployment of multiple cloud servers instantly. In essence, it touts capability for the creation of advanced, high-availability architectures. In order to create a full-service offering, Rackspace also acquired another company, JungleDisk. JungleDisk was an online backup service. By integrating JungleDisk's backup features with virtual servers that Slicehost provides, Mosso, in effect, created a new service to compete with Amazon's EC2. Mosso claims that these "cloud sites" are the fastest way for customers to put their site in the cloud. Cloud sites are capable of running Windows or Linux applications across banks of servers numbering in the hundreds.

Mosso's Cloud Files provide unlimited storage for content by using a partnership formed with Limelight Networks. This partnership allows Mosso to offer its customers a content delivery network (CDN). With CDN services, servers are placed around the world and, depending on where you are located, you get served via the closest or most appropriate server. CDNs cut down on the hops back and forth to handle a request. The chief benefit of using CDN is a scalable, dynamic storage platform that offers a metered service by which customers pay only for what they use. Customers can manage files through a web-based control panel or programmatically through an API.

Integrated backups with the CDN offering implemented in the Mosso services platform began in earnest with Jungle Disk version 2.5 in early 2009. Jungle Disk 2.5 is a major upgrade, adding a number of highly requested features to its portfolio. Highlights of the new version include running as a background service. The background service will keep running even if the Jungle Disk Monitor is logged out or closed. Users do not have to be logged into the service for automatic backups to be performed. There is native file system support on both 32-bit and 64-bit versions of Windows (Windows 2000, XP, Vista, 2003 and 2008), and Linux. A new download resume capability has been added for moving large files and performing restore operations. A time-slice restore interface was also added, allowing restoration of files from any given point-in-time where a snapshot was taken. Finally, it supports automatic updates on Windows (built-in) and Macintosh (using Sparkle).

3.4   MONITORING-AS-A-SERVICE (MaaS)

MaaS is the outsourced provisioning of security, primarily on business platforms that leverage the Internet to conduct business. MaaS has become increasingly popular over the last decade. Since the advent of cloud computing, its popularity has, grown even more. Security monitoring involves protecting an enterprise or government client from cyber threats. A security team plays a crucial role in securing and maintaining the confidentiality, integrity, and availability of IT assets. However, time and resource constraints limit security operations and their effectiveness for most companies. This requires constant vigilance over the security infrastructure and critical information assets.

Many industry regulations require organizations to monitor their security environment, server logs, and other information assets to ensure the integrity of these systems. However, conducting effective security monitoring can be a daunting task because it requires advanced technology, skilled security experts, and scalable processes – none of which come cheap. MaaS security monitoring services offer real-time, 24/7 monitoring and nearly immediate incident response across a security infrastructure – they help to protect critical information assets of their customers. Prior to the advent of electronic security systems, security monitoring and response were heavily dependent on human resources and human capabilities, which also limited the accuracy and effectiveness of monitoring efforts. Over the past two decades, the adoption of information technology into facility security systems, and their ability to be connected to security operations centers (SOCs) via corporate networks, has significantly changed that picture.

This means two important things:

1. The total cost of ownership (TCO) for traditional SOCs is much higher than for a modern-technology SOC; and

2. Achieving lower security operations costs and higher security effectiveness means that modern SOC architecture must use security and IT technology to address security risks.

3.4.1 Protection Against Internal and External Threats

SOC-based security monitoring services can improve the effectiveness of a customer security infrastructure by actively analyzing logs and alerts from infrastructure devices around the clock and in real time. Monitoring teams correlate information from various security devices to provide security analysts with the data they need to eliminate false positives and respond to true threats against the enterprise. Having consistent access to the skills needed to maintain the level of service an organization requires for enterprise-level monitoring is a huge issue. The information security team can assess system performance on a periodically recurring basis and provide recommendations for improvements as needed.

Typical services provided by many MaaS vendors are:

- Early Detection
- Platform, Control, and Services Monitoring
- Intelligent Log Centralization and Analysis
- Vulnerabilities Detection and Management
- Continuous System Patching/Upgrade and Fortification
- Intervention, Forensics, and Help Desk Services

Early Detection

An early detection service detects and reports new security vulnerabilities shortly after they appear. Generally, the threats are correlated with third-party sources, and an alert or report is issued to customers. This report is usually sent by email to the person designated by the company. Security vulnerability reports, aside from containing a detailed description of the vulnerability and the platforms affected, also include information on the impact the exploitation of this vulnerability would have on the systems or applications previously selected by the company receiving the report. Most often, the report also indicates specific actions to be taken to minimize the effect of the vulnerability, if that is known.

Platform, Control, and Services Monitoring

Platform, control, and services monitoring is often implemented as a dashboard interface and makes it possible to know the operational status of the platform being monitored at any time. It is accessible from a web interface, making remote access possible. Each operational element that is monitored usually provides an operational status indicator, always taking into account the critical impact of each element. This service aids in determining which elements may be operating at or near capacity or beyond the limits of established parameters. By detecting and identifying such problems, preventive measures can be taken to prevent loss of service.

Intelligent Log Centralization and Analysis

Intelligent log centralization and analysis is a monitoring solution based mainly on the correlation and matching of log entries. Such analysis helps to establish a baseline of operational performance and provides an index of security threat. Alarms can be raised in the event an incident moves the established baseline parameters beyond a stipulated threshold. These types of sophisticated tools are used by a team of security experts who are responsible for incident response once such a threshold has been crossed and the threat has generated an alarm or warning picked up by security analysts monitoring the systems.

Vulnerabilities Detection and Management

Vulnerabilities detection and management enables automated verification and management of the security level of information systems. The service periodically performs a series of automated tests for the purpose of identifying system weaknesses that may be exposed over the Internet, including the possibility of unauthorized access to administrative services, the existence of services that have not been updated, the detection of vulnerabilities such as phishing, etc. The service performs periodic follow-up of tasks performed by security professionals managing information systems security and provides reports that can be used to implement a plan for continuous improvement of the system's security level.

Continuous System Patching/Upgrade and Fortification

Security posture is enhanced with continuous system patching and upgrading of systems and application software. New patches, updates, and service packs for the equipment's operating system are necessary to maintain adequate security levels and support new versions of installed products. Keeping abreast of all the changes to all the software and hardware requires a committed effort to stay informed and to communicate gaps in security that can appear in installed systems and applications.

Intervention, Forensics, and Help Desk Services

Quick intervention when a threat is detected is crucial to mitigating the effects of a threat. This requires security engineers with ample knowledge in the various technologies and with the ability to support applications as well as infrastructures on a 24/7 basis. MaaS platforms routinely provide this service to their customers. When a detected threat is analyzed, it often requires forensic analysis to determine what it is, how much effort it will take to fix the problem, and what effects are likely to be seen. When problems are encountered, the first thing customers tend to do is pick up the phone. Help desk services provide assistance on questions or issues about the operation of running systems. This service includes assistance in writing failure reports, managing operating problems, etc.

3.4.2 Delivering Business Value

Some consider balancing the overall economic impact of any build-versus-buy decision as a more significant measure than simply calculating a return on investment (ROI).

The key cost categories that are most often associated with MaaS are:

1. Service fees for security event monitoring for all firewalls and intrusion detection devices, servers, and routers;

2. Internal account maintenance and administration costs; and

3. Preplanning and development costs.

Based on the total cost of ownership, whenever a customer evaluates the option of an in-house security information monitoring team and infrastructure compared to outsourcing to a service provider, it does not take long to realize that establishing and maintaining an in-house capability is not as attractive as outsourcing the service to a provider with an existing infrastructure. Having an in-house security operations center forces a company to deal with issues such as staff attrition, scheduling, around the clock operations, etc.

Losses incurred from external and internal incidents are extremely significant, as evidenced by a regular stream of high-profile cases in the news. The generally accepted method of valuing the risk of losses from external and internal incidents is to look at the amount of a potential loss, assume a frequency of loss, and estimate a probability for incurring the loss. Although this method is not perfect, it provides a means for tracking information security metrics. Risk is used as a filter to capture uncertainty about varying cost and benefit estimates. If a risk-adjusted ROI demonstrates a compelling business case, it raises confidence that the investment is likely to succeed, because the risks that threaten the project have been considered and quantified. Flexibility represents an investment in additional capacity or agility today that can be turned into future business benefits at some additional cost. This provides an organization with the ability to engage in future initiatives, but not the obligation to do so. The value of flexibility is unique to each organization, and willingness to measure its value varies from company to company.

3.4.3   Real-Time Log Monitoring Enables Compliance

Security monitoring services can also help customers comply with industry regulations by automating the collection and reporting of specific events of interest, such as log-in failures. Regulations and industry guidelines often require log monitoring of critical servers to ensure the integrity of confidential data. MaaS providers' security monitoring services automate this time consuming process.

3.5   PLATFORM-AS-A-SERVICE (PAAS)

Cloud computing has evolved to include platforms for building and running custom web-based applications, a concept known as Platform-as-a-Service. Paas is an outgrowth of the SaaS application delivery model. The PaaS model makes all of the facilities required to support the complete life cycle of building and delivering web applications and services entirely available from the Internet, all with no software downloads or installation for developers, IT managers, or end users. Unlike the IaaS model, where developers may create a specific operating system instance with homegrown applications running, PaaS developers are concerned only with web based development and generally do not care what operating system is used. PaaS services allow users to focus on innovation rather than complex infrastructure. Organizations can redirect a significant portion of their budgets to creating applications that provide real business value instead of worrying about all the infrastructure issues in a roll-your-own delivery model. The PaaS model is thus driving a new era of mass innovation. Now, developers around the world can access unlimited computing power. Anyone with an Internet connection can build powerful applications and easily deploy them to users globally.

3.5.1 The Traditional On-Premises Model

The traditional approach of building and running on-premises applications has always been complex, expensive, and risky. Building your own solution has never offered any guarantee of success. Each application was designed to meet specific business requirements. Each solution required a specific set of hardware, an operating system, a database, often a middleware package, email and web servers, etc. Once the hardware and software environment was created, a team of developers had to navigate complex programming development platforms to build their applications. Additionally, a team of network, database, and system management experts was needed to keep everything up and running. Inevitably, a business requirement would force the developers to make a change to the application. The changed application then required new test cycles before being distributed. Large companies often needed specialized facilities to house their data centers. Enormous amounts of electricity also were needed to power the servers as well as to keep the systems cool. Finally, all of this required use of fail-over sites to mirror the data center so that information could be replicated in case of a disaster. Old days, old ways – now, let's fly into the silver lining of today's cloud.

3.5.2 The New Cloud Model

PaaS offers a faster, more cost-effective model for application development and delivery. PaaS provides the entire infrastructure needed to run applications over the Internet. Such is the case with companies such as Amazon.com, eBay, Google, iTunes, and YouTube. The new cloud model has made it possible to deliver such new capabilities to new markets via the web browsers. PaaS is based on a metering or subscription model, so users pay only for what they use. PaaS offerings include workflow facilities for application design, application development, testing, deployment, and hosting, as well as application services such as virtual offices, team collaboration, database integration, security, scalability, storage, persistence, state management, dashboard instrumentation, etc.

3.5.3 Key Characteristics of PaaS

The Services to develop, test, deploy, host, and manage applications to support the application development life cycle. Web-based user interface creation tools typically provide some level of support to simplify the creation of user interfaces, based either on common standards such as HTML and JavaScript or on other, proprietary technologies. Supporting a multitenant architecture helps to remove developer concerns regarding the use of the application by many concurrent users. PaaS providers often include services for concurrency management, scalability, fail-over and security. Another characteristic is the integration with web services and databases. Support for Simple Object Access Protocol (SOAP) and other interfaces allows PaaS offerings to create combinations of web services (called mashups) as well as having the ability to access databases and reuse services maintained inside private networks. The ability to form and share code with ad-hoc, predefined, or distributed teams greatly enhance the productivity of PaaS offerings. Integrated PaaS offerings provide an opportunity for developers to have much greater insight into the inner workings of their applications and the behavior of their users by implementing dashboard-like tools to view the inner workings based on measurements such as performance, number of concurrent accesses, etc. Some PaaS offerings leverage this instrumentation to enable pay-per-use billing models.

3.6   SOFTWARE-AS-A-SERVICE (SaaS)

The traditional model of software distribution, in which software is purchased for and installed on personal computers, is sometimes referred to as Software-as-a-Product. Software-as-a-Service is a software distribution model in which applications are hosted by a vendor or service provider and made available to customers over a network, typically the Internet. SaaS is becoming an increasingly prevalent delivery model as underlying technologies that support web services and service-oriented architecture (SOA) mature and new developmental approaches become popular. SaaS is also often associated with a pay-as-you-go subscription licensing model. Meanwhile, broadband service has become increasingly available to support user access from more areas around the world. The huge strides made by Internet Service Providers (ISPs) to increase bandwidth, and the constant introduction of ever more powerful microprocessors coupled with inexpensive data storage devices, is providing a huge platform for designing, deploying, and using software across all areas of business and personal computing. SaaS applications also must be able to interact with other data and other applications in an equally wide variety of environments and platforms. SaaS is closely related to other service delivery models we have described. IDC identifies two slightly different delivery models for SaaS. The hosted application management model is similar to an Application Service Provider (ASP) model. Here, an ASP hosts commercially available software for customers and delivers it over the Internet. The other model is a software on demand model where the provider gives customers network-based access to a single copy of an application created specifically for SaaS distribution. IDC predicted that SaaS would make up 30% of the software market by 2007 and would be worth $10.7 billion by the end of 2009.

SaaS is most often implemented to provide business software functionality to enterprise customers at a low cost while allowing those customers to obtain the same benefits of commercially licensed, internally operated software without the associated complexity of installation, management, support, licensing, and high initial cost. Most customers have little interest in the how or why of software implementation, deployment, etc., but all have a need to use software in their work. Many types of software are well suited to the SaaS model (e.g., accounting, customer relationship management, email software, human resources, IT security, IT service management, video conferencing, web analytics, and web content management). The distinction between SaaS and earlier applications delivered over the Internet is that SaaS solutions were developed specifically to work within a web browser. The architecture of SaaS-based applications is specifically designed to support many concurrent users (multitenancy) at once.

3.6.1 SaaS Implementation Issues

Many types of software components and applications frameworks may be employed in the development of SaaS applications. Using new technology found in these modern components and application frameworks can drastically reduce the time to market and cost of converting a traditional on-premises product into a SaaS solution. According to Microsoft, SaaS architectures can be classified into one of four maturity levels whose key attributes are ease of configuration, multitenant efficiency, and scalability. Each level is distinguished from the previous one by the addition of one of these three attributes.

The levels described by Microsoft are as follows:

- SaaS Architectural Maturity Level 1—Ad-Hoc/Custom
- SaaS Architectural Maturity Level 2—Configurability
- SaaS Architectural Maturity Level 3—Multitenant Efficiency
- SaaS Architectural Maturity Level 4—Scalable

SaaS Architectural Maturity Level 1—Ad-Hoc/Custom

The first level of maturity is actually no maturity at all. Each customer has a unique, customized version of the hosted application. The application runs its own instance on the host's servers. Migrating a traditional non-networked or client-server application to this level of SaaS maturity typically requires the least development effort and reduces operating costs by consolidating server hardware and administration.

SaaS Architectural Maturity Level 2—Configurability

The second level of SaaS maturity provides greater program flexibility through configuration metadata. At this level, many customers can use separate instances of the same application. This allows a vendor to meet the varying needs of each customer by using detailed configuration options. It also allows the vendor to ease the maintenance burden by being able to update a common code base.

SaaS Architectural Maturity Level 3—Multitenant Efficiency

The third maturity level adds multitenancy to the second level. This results in a single program instance that has the capability to serve all of the vendor's customers. This approach enables more efficient use of server resources without any apparent difference to the end user, but ultimately this level is limited in its ability to scale massively.

SaaS Architectural Maturity Level 4—Scalable

At the fourth SaaS maturity level, scalability is added by using a multitiered architecture. This architecture is capable of supporting a load-balanced farm of identical application instances running on a variable number of servers, sometimes in the hundreds or even thousands. System capacity can be dynamically increased or decreased to match load demand by adding or removing servers, with no need for further alteration of application software architecture.

3.6.2 Key Characteristics of SaaS

Deploying applications in a service-oriented architecture is a more complex problem than is usually encountered in traditional models of software deployment. As a result, SaaS applications are generally priced based on the number of users that can have access to the service. There are often additional fees for the use of help desk services, extra bandwidth, and storage. SaaS revenue streams to the vendor are usually lower initially than traditional software license fees. However, the trade-off for lower license fees is a monthly recurring revenue stream, which is viewed by most corporate CFOs as a more predictable gauge of how the business is faring quarter to quarter. These monthly recurring charges are viewed much like maintenance fees for licensed software.

The key characteristics of SaaS software are the following:

- Network-based management and access to commercially available software from central locations rather than at each customer's site, enabling customers to access applications remotely via the Internet.

- Application delivery from a one-to-many model (single-instance, multitenant architecture), as opposed to a traditional one-to-one model.

- Centralized enhancement and patch updating that obviates any need for downloading and installing by a user. SaaS is often used in conjunction with a larger network of communications and collaboration software, sometimes as a plug-in to PaaS architecture.

3.6.3 Benefits of the SaaS Model

- Streamlined administration
- Automated update and patch management services
- Data compatibility across the enterprise (all users have the same version of software)
- Facilitated, enterprise-wide collaboration
- Global accessibility

Bit Questions

1. CaaS stands for ----------------

2. ---------------- is an Outsourced enterprise communications solution.

3. IaaS stands for ----------------

4. SaaS stands for ----------------

5. PaaS stands for ----------------

6. AWS stands for ----------------

7. With a ---------------- solution, customers are able to leverage enterprise class communication services without having to build a premises-based solution of their own.

8. ---------------- is the delivery of computer infrastructure (typically a platform virtualization environment) as a service.

9. ---------------- is a web service that provides resizable computing capacity in the cloud.

10. AWS is based on -----------------------.

11. --------------------is the ability to automatically scale an infrastructure vertically and horizontally with little or no impact to the applications running in that infrastructure.

12. Which of these is not a major type of cloud computing usage?   [   ]

    (a) Hardware as a Service   (b) Platform as a Service

    (c) Software as a Service   (d) Infrastructure as a Service

13. Which is considered the most widely used cloud computing service?   [   ]

    (a)   Infrastructure-as-a-Service (IaaS)

    (b)   Platform-as-a-Service (PaaS)

    (c)   Communication-as-a-Service (CaaS)

    (d)   Software-as-a-Service (SaaS)

14. Which service model allows the customer to choose more layers in the computing architecture?   [   ]

    (a)   Infrastructure as a Service (IaaS)

    (b)   Platform as a Service (PaaS)

    (c)   Software as a Service (SaaS)

    (d)   There is no difference between the service models.

15. In which category of SaaS services does customer relationship management (CRM) software fall?

    (a) Consumer services   (b) Communication services

    (c) Infrastructure services   (d) Business services

Exercises

1. Explain in detail about the following :

    (a) CaaS   (b) IaaS   (c) Maa

    (d) PaaS   (e) SaaS

2. Explain in detail about Amazon EC2.

3. Write short notes on the following:

    (a) Amazon S3

    (b) Amazon SimpleDB

    (c) Amazon SQS

    (d) Amazon CloudFront

    (e) Amazon Elastic Block Store

BUILDING CLOUD NETWORKS

4.1 CHAPTER OVERVIEW

In this chapter, we will describe what it takes to build a cloud network and data center to cloud. You will learn how and why companies build these highly automated private cloud networks providing resources that can be managed from a single point. We will discuss the significant reliance of cloud computing architectures on server and storage virtualization as a layer between applications and distributed computing resources and learn the basics of how flexible cloud computing networks such as those modeled after public providers such as Google and Amazon are built, and how they interconnect with corporate IT private clouds designed as service-oriented architectures (SOAs). We provide an overview of how SOA is used as an intermediary step for cloud computing and the basic approach to SOA as it applies to data center design. We then describe the role and use of open source software in data centers.

4.2 THE EVOLUTION FROM THE MSP (MANAGED SERVICE PROVIDERS) MODEL TO CLOUD COMPUTING AND SOFTWARE-AS-A-SERVICE

Organizations with frame relay were essentially singular clouds that were interconnected to other frame relay-connected organizations using a carrier/provider to transport data communications between the two entities. Everyone within the frame network sharing a common Private Virtual Connection (PVC) could share their data with everyone else on the same PVC. To go outside their cloud and connect to another cloud, users had to rely on the I-1.0 infrastructure's routers and switches along the way to connect the dots between the clouds. The endpoint for this route between the clouds and the I-1.0 pathway was a demarcation point between the cloud and the provider's customer. Where the dots ended between the clouds (i.e., the endpoints) was where access was controlled by I-1.0 devices such as gateways, proxies, and firewalls on the customer's premises.

From customers' perspective, this endpoint was known as the main point of entry (MPOE) and marked their authorized pathway into their internal networking infrastructure. By having applications use specific protocols to transport data (e.g., Simple Mail Transfer Protocol [SMTP] for sending mail or File Transfer Protocol [FTP] for moving files from one location to another), applications behind the MPOE could accept or reject traffic passing over the network and allow email and file transfer to occur with little to no impedance from the network infrastructure or their administrators. Specialized applications often required a client/server implementation using specific portals created through the firewall to allow their traffic protocols to proceed unhindered and often required special administrative setup before they could work properly. While some of this may still hold, that was, for the most part, how it was done "old school." Things have changed considerably since that model was considered state of the art. However state of the art it was, it was difficult to manage and expensive. Because organizations did not want to deal with the complexities of managing I-1.0 infrastructure, a cottage industry was born to do just that.

4.2.1 From Single-Purpose Architectures to Multipurpose Architectures

In the early days of MSPs, the providers would actually go onto customer sites and perform their services on customer-owned premises. Over time, these MSPs specialized in implementation of infrastructure and quickly figured out ways to build out data centers and sell those capabilities off in small chunks commonly known as monthly recurring services, in addition to the basic fees charged for ping, power, and pipe (PPP).

- ping, power, and pipe (PPP)
- *Ping* refers to the ability to have a live Internet connection
- *Power* is obvious enough(understood), and
- *Pipe* refers to the amount of data throughput that a customer is willing to pay for. Generally, the PPP part of the charge was built into the provider's monthly service fee in addition to their service offerings.

Common services provided by MSPs

- Remote network, desktop and security monitoring, incident response, patch management, and remote data backup, as well as technical support.

Advantage: for customers using an MSP is that by purchasing a defined set of services, MSPs bill a flat or near-fixed monthly fee, which benefits customers by having a predictable IT cost to budget for over time. *Disadvantage*: time-consuming and expensive.

4.2.2 Data Center Virtualization

By allowing the infrastructure to be virtualized and shared across many customers, the providers have changed their business model to provide remotely managed services at lower costs, making it attractive to their customers. X-as-a-Service models (XaaS) are continually growing and evolving, as we are currently standing at the forefront of a new era of computing service driven by a huge surge in demand by both enterprises and individuals. SaaS as a subset or segment of the cloud computing market that is growing all the time. Typically, cloud computing has been viewed as a broad array of Internet Protocol (IP) services (Web browser as the main interface) in order to allow users to obtain a specific set of functional capabilities on a "pay for use" basis. Previously, obtaining such services required tremendous hardware/software investments and professional skills that were required in hosting environments such as Exodus Communications, Cable & Wireless, SAVVIS, and Digital Island. SaaS over the traditional hosting environment are expensive out-sourced data centers. SaaS is a "pay as you go" model that evolved as an alternative to using classical (more expensive) software licensing solutions. The cloud evolved from the roots of managed service provider environments and data centers and is a critical element of next-generation data centers when compared to the MSPs they evolved from. Today, customers no longer care where the data is physically stored or where servers are physically located, as they will only use and pay for them when they need them. What drives customer decision making today is lower cost, higher performance and productivity, and currency of solutions.

4.3 SOA AS A STEP TOWARD CLOUD COMPUTING

An SOA (**Service-Oriented Architectures**) involves policies, principles, and a framework that illustrate how network services can be leveraged by enterprise applications to achieve desired business outcomes. These outcomes include enabling the business capabilities to be provided and consumed as a set of services. SOA is thus an architectural style that encourages the creation of coupled business services. The "services" in SOA are business services. For example, updating a customer's service-level agreement is a business service, updating a record in a database is not. A service is a unit of work done by a service provider to achieve desired end results for a service consumer.

An SOA solution consists of a linked set of business services that realize an end-to-end business process. At a high level, SOA can be viewed as enabling improved management control, visibility, and metrics for business processes, allowing business process integration with a holistic view of business processes, creating a new capability to create composite solutions, exposing granular business activities as services, and allowing reuse of existing application assets.

4.3.1 Difference between SOA and Cloud Computing

SOA delivers web services from applications to other programs. Whereas the cloud is about delivering software services to end users and running code. Thus the cloud-versus- SOA debate is like comparing apples and oranges. A couple of areas that SOA has brought to the table have been mostly ignored in the rapid evolution to cloud computing. The first is governance. The second is an end-to-end architectural approach.

Cloud service providers such as Amazon, The Web Service, Force.com, and others have evolved from the typically poorly designed SOA service models and have done a pretty good job in architecting and delivering their services. SOA model is to architect and design services into the cloud so that it can expand and be accessed as needed. Expanding services in an SOA is typically a difficult and expensive process. Virtual resources and computing assets are accessed through the cloud, including not only externally hosted services but also those provided globally by companies. Provides the basis for the next generation of enterprise data centers which, like the Internet, will provide extreme scalability and fast access to networked users. A big advantage over grid computing, which distributes IT only for a specific task.

Placing information, services, and processes outside the enterprise without a clear strategy is not productive. A process, architecture, and methodology using SOA and for leveraging cloud computing is used. As part of the enterprise architecture, SOA provides the framework for using cloud computing resources. In this context, SOA provides the evolutionary step to cloud computing by creating the necessary interfaces from the IT infrastructure to the cloud outside the enterprise. Cloud computing essentially becomes an extension of SOA. Services and processes may be run inside or outside the enterprise, as required by the business. By connecting the enterprise to a web platform or cloud, businesses can take advantage of Internet delivered resources that provide access to prebuilt processes, services, and platforms delivered as a service, when and where needed, to reduce overhead costs. SOA as an enterprise architecture is the intermediate step toward cloud computing.

4.4   BASIC APPROACH TO A DATA CENTER-BASED SOA

SOA is essentially a collection of services. A service is, in essence, a function that is well defined, self-contained, and does not depend on the context or state of other services. Services most often reflect logical business activities. Some means of connecting services to each other is needed, so services communicate with each other, have an interface, and are message-oriented. The communication between services may involve simple data passing or may require two or more services coordinating an activity. The services generally communicate using standard protocols, which allows for broad interoperability. SOA encompasses legacy systems and processes, so the effectiveness of existing investments is preserved. New services can be added or created without affecting existing services.

The first service-oriented architectures are usually considered to be the Distributed Component Object Model (DCOM) or Object Request Brokers (ORBs), which were based on the Common Object Requesting Broker Architecture (CORBA) specification. The introduction of SOA provides a platform for technology and business units to meet business requirements of the modern enterprise. With SOA, your organization can use existing application systems to a greater extent and may respond faster to change requests.

Benefits are attributed to several critical elements of SOA:

1. Free-standing, independent components
2. Combined by loose coupling
3. Message (XML)-based instead of API-based
4. Physical location, etc., not important

4.4.1   Planning for Capacity

It is important to create a capacity plan for an SOA architecture. To accomplish this, it is necessary to set up an initial infrastructure and establish a baseline of capacity. It should be based on known capacity requirements and vendor recommendations for software and hardware. Once the infrastructure is set up, it is necessary to establish a set of processing patterns. These patterns will be used to test capacity and should include a mix of simple, medium, and complex patterns. They need to cover typical SOA designs and should exercise all the components within the SOA infrastructure.

4.4.2   Planning for Availability

Availability planning includes performing a business impact analysis (BIA) and developing and implementing a written availability plan. The goal is to ensure that system administrators adequately understand the criticality of a system and implement appropriate safeguards to protect it. This requires proper planning and analysis at each stage of the systems development life cycle (SDLC).

A BIA is the first step in the availability planning process. A BIA provides the necessary information for a administrator to fully understand and protect systems. This process should fully characterize system requirements, processes, and interdependencies that will determine the availability requirements and priorities.

Once this is done, a written availability plan is created. It should define the overall availability objectives and establish the organizational framework and responsibilities for personnel. Management should be included in the process of developing availability structure, objectives, roles, and responsibilities to support the development of a successful plan.

4.4.3   Planning for SOA Security

The foundations include public key infrastructure (PKI), the common security authentication method Kerberos, XML (Extensible Markup Language) encryption, and XML digital signatures.

The main areas of SOA security are:

- message-level security
- Security-as-a-Service
- declarative and policy-based security

Message-level security provides the ability to ensure that security requirements are met in an SOA environment, where transport-level security is inadequate because transactions are no longer point-to-point in SOA.

Security-as-a-Service provides the ability to implement security requirements for services.

Declarative and policy-based security provides the ability to implement security requirements that are transparent to security administrators and can be used to quickly implement emerging new security requirements for services that implement new business functionalities.

Message-Level Security: The OASIS set of WS-Security standards addresses message-level security concerns. These standards are supported by key vendors including IBM, Microsoft, and Oracle. The standards provide a model describing how to manage and authenticate message exchanges between parties (including security context exchange) as well as establishing and deriving session keys. The standards recommend a Web service endpoint policy describing the capabilities and constraints of the security and other business policies on intermediaries and endpoints including required security tokens, supported encryption algorithms, and privacy rules. The standards include a Web service trust model that describes a framework for trust models that enables Web services to operate securely.

Security-as-a-Service: Accomplished by collecting an inventory of service security requirements throughout the enterprise architecture (EA) and specifying the set of discrete security services that will be needed for the enterprise. The organization must complete the process of designing and implementing these security services as services themselves. Often, a toolkit approach can help specify the set of typical security services that may be used to provide most of the requirements and accelerate the establishment of Security-as-a-Service in an organization.

Declarative and Policy-based Security: Implementation of declarative and policy-based security requires tools and techniques for use at the enterprise management level and at the service level. These tools and techniques should provide transparency for security administrators, policy enforcement, and policy monitoring. When policy violations are detected, alerts should be issued. Traceability of such violations, both for data and users, should be included as a critical element.

Bit Questions

1. SaaS is a ------------- model.

2. Benefits of SOA are ------------------.

3. --------------- provides the ability to implement security requirements for services.

4. PPP stands for-----------------.

5. Services provided by MSPs are --------------------.

6. -------------- can reduce your costs on facilities, power, cooling, and hardware, simplify administration and maintenance, and give you a greener IT profile.

7. The main areas of SOA security are ------------------------

8. Provides the ability to implement security requirements for services.

Exercises

1. Describe Data Center Virtualization

2. What is Service-Oriented Architecture?

3. Compare and contrast SOA and Cloud Computing. What are the Basic approaches to a Data Center-Based SOA?

CHAPTER 5

VIRTUALIZATION IN CLOUD

5.1 INTRODUCTION

The IT industry's focus on virtualization technology has increased considerably in the past few years. However, the concept has been around much longer, as you can read in the brief history below. This chapter also provides a high level view of the virtualization technology and methods that exist today, and highlights a number of reasons why organizations are embracing virtualization more and more.

5.1.1 Brief History of Virtualization

The concept of virtualization is generally believed to have its origins in the mainframe days in the late 1960s and early 1970s, when IBM invested a lot of time and effort in developing robust time-sharing solutions. Time-sharing refers to the shared usage of computer resources among a large group of users, aiming to increase the efficiency of both the users and the expensive computer resources they share. This model represented a major breakthrough in computer technology: the cost of providing computing capability dropped considerably and it became possible for organizations, and even individuals, to use a computer without actually owning one. Similar reasons are driving virtualization for industry standard computing today: the capacity in a single server is so large that it is almost impossible for most workloads to effectively use it. The best way to improve resource utilization, and at the same time simplify data center management, is through virtualization.

Data centers today use virtualization techniques to make abstraction of the physical hardware, create large aggregated pools of logical resources consisting of CPUs, memory, disks, file storage, applications, networking, and offer those resources to users or customers in the form of agile, scalable, consolidated virtual machines. Even though the technology and use cases have evolved, the core meaning of virtualization remains the same: to enable a computing environment to run multiple independent systems at the same time.

5.1.2   Virtual Machines and Virtualization Middleware

A conventional computer has a single OS image. This offers a rigid architecture that tightly couples application software to a specific hardware platform. Some software running well on one machine may not be executable on anther platform with a different instruction set under a fixed OS management. *Virtual machines* (VM) offer novel solutions to underutilized resources, application inflexibility, software manageability, and security concerns in existing physical machines.

Virtual Machines: The concept of virtual machines is illustrated in Figure 5.1. The host machine is equipped with the physical hardware shown at the bottom. For example, a desktop with x-86 architecture running its installed Windows OS as shown in Figure 5.1 (a). The VM can be provisioned to any hardware system. The VM is built with virtual resources managed by a guest OS to run a specific application. Between the VMs and the host platform, we need to deploy a middleware layer called a *virtual machine monitor* (VMM).

Figure 5.1 (b) shows a native VM installed with the use a VMM called a *hypervisor* at the privileged mode. For example, the hardware has a X-86 architecture running the Windows system. The guest OS could be a Linux system and the hypervisor is the XEN system developed at Cambridge University. This hypervisor approach is also called bare-metal VM, because the hypervisor handles the bare hardware (CPU, memory, and I/O) directly.

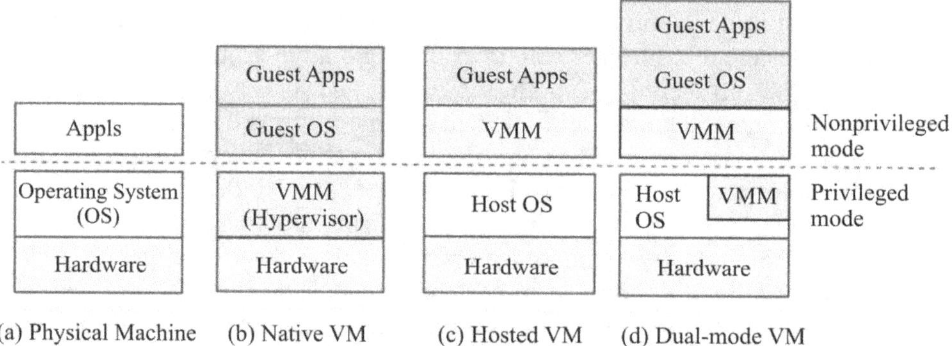

Figure 5.1 Three ways of constructing a virtual machine (VM) embedded in a physical machine. The VM could run on an OS different from that of the host computer

Another architecture is the host VM shown in Figure 5.1 (c). Here the VMM runs with a non-privileged mode. The host OS need not be modified. The VM can be also implemented with a dual mode as shown in Figure 5.1 (d). Part of VMM runs at the user level and another portion runs at the supervisor level. In this case, the host OS may have to be modified to some extent. Multiple VMs can be ported to one given hardware system, to support the virtualization process. The VM approach offers hardware-independence of the OS and applications. The user application and its dedicated OS could be bundled together as a virtual appliance that can be easily ported on various hardware platforms.

Virtualization Operations: The VMM provides the VM abstraction to the guest OS. With full virtualization, the VMM exports a VM abstraction identical to the physical machine; so that a standard OS such as Windows 2000 or Linux can run just as they would on the physical hardware. Low-level VMM operations are indicated by Mendel Rosenblum and illustrated in Figure 5.2.

- First, the VMs can be multiplexed between hardware machines as shown in Figure 5.2(a).

- Second, a VM can be suspended and stored in a stable storage as shown in Figure 5.2 (b).

- Third, a suspended VM can be resumed or provisioned to a new hardware platform in Figure 5.2 (c).

- Finally, a VM can be migrated from one hardware platform to another platform as shown in Figure 5.2 (d).

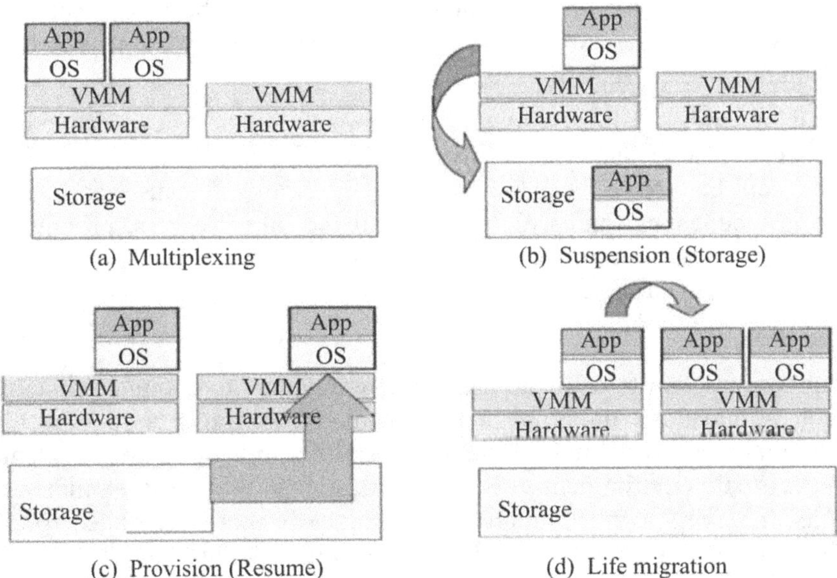

Figure 5.2 Virtual machine multiplexing, suspension, provision, and migration in a distributed computing environment

(Courtesy of M. Rosenblum, Keynote address, *ACM ASPLOS* 2006)

These VM operations enable a virtual machine to be provisioned to any available hardware platform. They make it flexible to port distributed application executions. Furthermore the VM approach will significantly enhance the utilization of server resources. Multiple server functions can be consolidated on the same hardware platform to achieve higher system efficiency. This will eliminate server sprawl via deployment of systems as VMs. These VMs move transparency to the shared hardware. According to a claim by VMWare, the server utilization could be increased from current 5-15% to 60-80%.

5.2   REASONS TO USE VIRTUALIZATION

There are many different good reasons for companies and organizations to invest in virtualization today, but it is probably safe to assume that financial motivation is number one on the list: virtualization can save a lot of money. Below is an overview of the key benefits of virtualization.

Resource optimization

Today's enterprise level computer resources are so powerful that they often have excess capacity. By virtualizing the hardware and allocating parts of it based on the real needs of users and applications, the available computing power, storage space and network bandwidth can be used much more effectively. Computers no longer need to be idle or performing below their capabilities because there are fewer connected users, or because the hosted application happens to be less demanding than the server can handle.

Virtual machines offer software developers isolated, constrained, test environments. Rather than purchasing dedicated physical hardware, virtual machines can be created on the existing hardware. Because each virtual machine is independent and isolated from all the other servers, programmers can run software without having to worry about affecting other applications, or external components affecting the execution of their code.

Consolidation

It is common practice to dedicate individual computers to a single application. If several applications only use a small amount of processing power, the administrator can consolidate several computers into one server running multiple virtual environments. For organizations that own hundreds or thousands of servers, consolidation can dramatically reduce the need for floor space, HVAC, A/C power, and co-location resources. This means the cost of ownership is reduced significantly, since less physical servers and floor and rack space are required, which in turn leads to less heat and power consumption, and ultimately a smaller carbon footprint.

Maximizing Uptime

Agility is all about being able to respond to changing requirements as quickly and flexibly as possible. Virtualization brings new opportunities to data center administration, allowing users to enjoy:

- Guaranteed uptime of servers and applications; speedy disaster recovery if large scale failures do occur.
- Instant deployment of new virtual machines or even aggregated pools of virtual machines via template images.
- Elasticity, that is, resource provisioning when and where required instead of keeping the entire data center in an always-on state.
- Reconfiguration of running computing environments without impacting the users.

Automatically Protect Applications from Server Failure

Server virtualization provides a way to implement redundancy without purchasing additional hardware. Redundancy, in the sense of running the same application on multiple servers, is a safety measure: if for any reason a server fails, another server running the same application takes over, thereby minimizing the interruption in service. This kind of redundancy works in two ways when applied to virtual machines:

- If one virtual system fails, another virtual system takes over.
- By running the redundant virtual machines on separate physical hardware you can also provide better protection against physical hardware failure.

Easily Migrate Workloads as Needs Change

Migration refers to moving a server environment from one place to another. With most virtualization solutions it is possible to move a virtual machine from one physical machine in the environment to another. With physical servers this was originally possible only if both physical machines ran on the same hardware, operating system and processor. In the virtual world, a server can be migrated between physical hosts with entirely different hardware configurations. Migration is typically used to improve reliability and availability: in case of hardware failure the guest system can be moved to a healthy server with limited downtime, if any. It is also useful if a virtual machine needs to scale beyond the physical capabilities of the current host and must be relocated to physical hardware with better performance.

Protect Investment in Existing, Legacy Systems

Server hardware will eventually become obsolete, and switching from one system to another can be difficult. In order to continue offering the services provided by these legacy systems, you can run it as a virtual machine on new, modern hardware, while the legacy system itself still behaves as if it were running on the same legacy hardware. From an application perspective, nothing has changed. In fact, its performance may well benefit from the newer underlying hardware. This gives the organization the time to transition to new processes without worrying about hardware issues, particularly in situations where the manufacturer of the legacy hardware no longer exists or cannot fix broken equipment.

5.3   DIFFERENT TYPES OF VIRTUALIZATION

Today the term virtualization is widely applied to a number of concepts including:

- Server Virtualization
- Client / Desktop / Application Virtualization
- Network Virtualization
- Storage Virtualization
- Service / Application Infrastructure Virtualization

In most of these cases, either virtualizing one physical resource into many virtual resources or turning many physical resources into one virtual resource is occurring.

Server Virtualization

Server virtualization is the most active segment of the virtualization industry featuring established companies such as VMware, Microsoft, and Citrix. With server virtualization one physical machine is divided into many virtual servers. At the core of such virtualization is the concept of a hypervisor (virtual machine monitor). A hypervisor is a thin software layer that intercepts operating system calls to hardware. Hypervisors typically provide a virtualized CPU and memory for the guests running on top of them. The term was first used in conjunction with the IBM CP-370.

Hypervisors are classified as one of two types:

Type 1 : This type of hypervisor is also known as native or bare-metal. They run directly on the hardware with guest operating systems running on top of them. Examples include VMware ESX, Citrix XenServer, and Microsoft's Hyper-V.

Type 2 : This type of hypervisor runs on top of an existing operating system with guests running at a third level above hardware. Examples include VMware Workstation and SWSoft's Parallels Desktop.

Related to type 1 hypervisors is the concept of para virtualization. Para virtualization is a technique in which a software interface that is similar but not identical to the underlying hardware is presented. Operating systems must be ported to run on top of a para virtualized hypervisor. Modified operating systems use the "hypercalls" supported by the para virtualized hypervisor to interface directly with the hardware. The popular Xen project makes use of this type of virtualization. Starting with version 3.0 however Xen is also able to make use of the hardware assisted virtualization technologies of Intel (VT-x) and AMD (AMD-V). These extensions allow Xen to run unmodified operating systems such as Microsoft Windows.

Server virtualization has a large number of benefits for the companies making use of the technology. Among those frequently listed:

- **Increased Hardware Utilization:** This results in hardware saving, reduced administration overhead, and energy savings.

- **Security:** Clean images can be used to restore compromised systems. Virtual machines can also provide sandboxing and isolation to limit attacks.

- **Development:** Debugging and performance monitoring scenarios can be easily setup in a repeatable fashion. Developers also have easy access to operating systems they might not otherwise be able to install on their desktops.

Correspondingly there are a number of potential downsides that must be considered:

- **Security:** There are now more entry points such as the hypervisor and virtual networking layer to monitor. A compromised image can also be propagated easily with virtualization technology.

- **Administration:** While there are less physical machines to maintain there may be more machines in aggregate. Such maintenance may require new skills and familiarity with software that administrators otherwise would not need.

- **Licensing/Cost Accounting:** Many software-licensing schemes do not take virtualization into account. For example running 4 copies of Windows on one box may require 4 separate licenses.

- **Performance:** Virtualization effectively partitions resources such as RAM and CPU on a physical machine. This combined with hypervisor overhead does not result in an environment that focuses on maximizing performance.

Application/Desktop Virtualization

Virtualization is not only a server domain technology. It is being put to a number of uses on the client side at both the desktop and application level. Such virtualization can be broken out into four categories:

- Local Application Virtualization/Streaming
- Hosted Application Virtualization
- Hosted Desktop Virtualization
- Local Desktop Virtualization

Wikipedia <u>defines</u> application virtualization as follows:

Application virtualization is an umbrella term that describes software technologies that improve manageability and compatibility of legacy applications by encapsulating applications from the underlying operating system on which they are executed. A fully virtualized application is not installed in the traditional sense, although it is still executed as if it is. Application virtualization differs from operating system virtualization in that in the latter case, the whole operating system is virtualized rather than only specific applications.

With streamed and local application virtualization an application can be installed on demand as needed. If streaming is enabled then the portions of the application needed for startup are sent first optimizing startup time. Locally virtualized applications also frequently make use of virtual registries and file systems to maintain separation and cleanness from the user's physical machine. Examples of local application virtualization solutions include Citrix Presentation Server and Microsoft Soft Grid. One could also include virtual appliances into this category such as those frequently distributed via VMware's VMware Player.

Hosted application virtualization allows the user to access applications from their local computer that are physically running on a server somewhere else on the network. Technologies such as Microsoft's RemoteApp allow for the user experience to be relatively seamless include the ability for the remote application to be a file handler for local file types.

Benefits of application virtualization include:

- **Security :** Virtual applications often run in user mode isolating them from OS level functions.

- **Management :** Virtual applications can be managed and patched from a central location.

- **Legacy Support:** Through virtualization technologies legacy applications can be run on modern operating systems they were not originally designed for.

- **Access:** Virtual applications can be installed on demand from central locations that provide failover and replication.

Disadvantages include:

- **Packaging:** Applications must first be packaged before they can be used.

- **Resources:** Virtual applications may require more resources in terms of storage and CPU.

- **Compatibility:** Not all applications can be virtualized easily.

Wikipedia defines desktop virtualization as:

Desktop virtualization (or Virtual Desktop Infrastructure) is a server-centric computing model that borrows from the traditional thin-client model but is designed to give administrators and end users the best of both worlds: the ability to host and centrally manage desktop virtual machines in the data center while giving end users a full PC desktop experience.

Hosted desktop virtualization is similar to hosted application virtualization, expanding the user experience to be the entire desktop. Commercial products include Microsoft's Terminal Services, Citrix's Xen Desktop, and VMware's VDI.

Benefits of desktop virtualization include most of those with application virtualization as well as:

- **High Availability:** Downtime can be minimized with replication and fault tolerant hosted configurations.

- **Extended Refresh Cycles:** Larger capacity servers as well as limited demands on the client PCs can extend their lifespan.

- **Multiple Desktops:** Users can access multiple desktops suited for various tasks from the same client PC.

Disadvantages of desktop virtualization are similar to server virtualization. There is also the added disadvantage that clients must have network connectivity to access their virtual desktops. This is problematic for offline work and also increases network demands at the office.

The final segment of client virtualization is local desktop virtualization. It could be said that this is where the recent resurgence of virtualization began with VMware's introduction of VMware Workstation in the late 90's. Today the market includes competitors such as Microsoft Virtual PC and Parallels Desktop. Local desktop virtualization has also played a key part in the increasing success of Apple's move to Intel processors since products like VMware Fusion and Parallels allow easy access to Windows applications. Some the benefits of local desktop virtualization include:

- **Security:** With local virtualization organizations can _lock down_ and encrypt just the valuable contents of the virtual machine/disk. This can be more preferment than encrypting a user's entire disk or operating system.

- **Isolation:** Related to security is isolation. Virtual machines allow corporations to isolate corporate assets from third party machines they do not control. This allows employees to use personal computers for corporate use in some instances.

- **Development/Legacy Support:** Local virtualization allows a users computer to support many configurations and environments it would otherwise not be able to support without different hardware or host operating system. Examples of this include running Windows in a virtualized environment on OS X and legacy testing Windows 98 support on a machine that's primary OS is Vista.

Network Virtualization

Up to this point the types of virtualization covered have centered on applications or entire machines. These are not the only granularity levels that can be virtualized however. Other computing concepts also lend themselves to being software virtualized as well. Network virtualization is one such concept.

Wikipedia _defines_ network virtualization as:

In computing, network virtualization is the process of combining hardware and software network resources and network functionality into a single, software-based administrative entity, a virtual network. Network virtualization involves platform virtualization, often combined with resource virtualization. Network virtualization is categorized as either external, combining many networks, or parts of networks, into a virtual unit, or internal, providing network-like functionality to the software containers on a single system…

Using the internal definition of the term, desktop and server virtualization solutions provide networking access between both the host and guest as well as between many guests. On the server side virtual switches are gaining acceptance as a part of the virtualization stack. The external definition of network virtualization is probably the more used version of the term however. Virtual Private Networks (VPNs) have been a common component of the network administrators' toolbox for years with most companies allowing VPN use.

Virtual LANs (VLANs) are another commonly used network virtualization concept. With network advances such as 10 gigabit Ethernet, networks no long need to be structured purely along geographical lines. Companies with products in the space include Cisco and 3Leaf.

In general, benefits of network virtualization include:

- **Customization of Access:** Administrators can quickly customize access and network options such as bandwidth throttling and quality of service.
- **Consolidation:** Physical networks can be combined into one virtual network for overall simplification of management.

Similar to server virtualization, network virtualization can bring increased complexity, some performance overhead, and the need for administrators to have a larger skill set.

Storage Virtualization

Another computing concept that is frequently virtualized is storage. Unlike the definitions we have seen up to this point that have been complex at times, Wikipedia defines storage virtualization simply as:

Storage virtualization refers to the process of abstracting logical storage from physical storage.

While RAID at the basic level provides this functionality, the term storage virtualization typically includes additional concepts such as data migration and caching. Storage virtualization is hard to define in a fixed manner due to the variety of ways that the functionality can be provided. Typically, it is provided as a feature of:

- Host Based with Special Device Drivers
- Array Controllers
- Network Switchs
- Stand Alone Network Appliances

Each vendor has a different approach in this regard. Another primary way that storage virtualization is classified is whether it is in-band or out-of-band. In-band (often called symmetric) virtualization sits between the host and the storage device allowing caching. Out-of-band (often called asymmetric) virtualization makes use of special host based device drivers that first lookup the meta data (indicating where a file resides) and then allows the host to directly retrieve the file from the storage location. Caching at the virtualization level is not possible with this approach.

General benefits of storage virtualization include:

- **Migration:** Data can be easily migrated between storage locations without interrupting live access to the virtual partition with most technologies.

- **Utilization:** Similar to server virtualization, utilization of storage devices can be balanced to address over and under utilitization.

- **Management:** Many hosts can leverage storage on one physical device that can be centrally managed.

Some of the disadvantages include:

- **Lack of Standards and Interoperability:** Storage virtualization is a concept and not a standard. As a result vendors frequently do not easily interoperate.

- **Metadata:** Since there is a mapping between logical and physical location, the storage metadata and its management becomes key to a working reliable system.

- **Backout:** The mapping between local and physical locations also makes the backout of virtualization technology from a system a less than trivial process.

Service / Application Infrastructure Virtualization

Enterprise application providers have also taken note of the benefits of virtualization and begun offering solutions that allow the virtualization of commonly used applications such as Apache as well as application fabric platforms that allow software to easily be developed with virtualization capabilities from the ground up.

Application infrastructure virtualization (sometimes referred to as application fabrics) unbundle an application from a physical OS and hardware. Application developers can then write to a virtualization layer. The fabric can then handle features such as deployment and scaling. In essence this process is the evolution of grid computing into a fabric form that provides virtualization level features. Companies such as Appistry and DataSynapse provides features including:

- Virtualized Distribution
- Virtualized Processing
- Dynamic Resource Discovery

IBM has also embraced the virtualization concept at the application infrastructure level with the rebranding and continued of enhancement of

Websphere XD as <u>Websphere Virtual Enterprise</u>. The product provides features such as service level management, performance monitoring, and fault tolerance. The software runs on a variety of Windows, Unix, and Linux based operating systems and works with popular application servers such as WebSphere, Apache, BEA, JBoss, and PHP application servers.   This lets administrators deploy and move application servers at a virtualization layer level instead of at the physical machine level.

5.4   VIRTUALIZATION VENDORS

Virtualization Vendors has the following:

VMWare: VMWare has a suite of products in this area. There are two hosted products, called VMWare workstation and VMWare server. Their hypervisor product is called VMWare ESX. They have one version of ESX that comes burned in the bios. It is called VMWare ESXi. They have virtual center as management product to manage complete virtual machine infrastructure in the data center. Their all the products are based on the dynamic binary translation technology. They support various flavors for Windows and Linux.

Xen: It is an open source project. It is based on para-virtualization and hypervisor technologies. Linux is modified to support para-virtualization. Xen now supports Windows with hardware assisted virtualization. There are number of products based on Xen. Citrix, which bought XenSource has couple of Xen based products, Sun has xVM, Oracle has Oracle VM. Redhat and Suse have been shipping Xen as part of their Linux distributions for some time.

Hyper-V: This is Microsoft's entry in this space. It is similar to the Xen architecture. It also requires hardware assistance. It comes bundled with Windows server 2008, and supports running Windows and Linux guest operating systems in the virtual machines.

5.5   DOWNLOADING SUN XVM VIRTUAL BOX

This practicum will provide you with some guided hands-on experience and help you gain confidence in using virtualization technologies. To begin, the first thing to do is to **download the Sun VirtualBox product.**

To do this, you need to open a browser and go to the web site

http://www.virtualbox.org/wiki/Downloads

Where you will see this page:

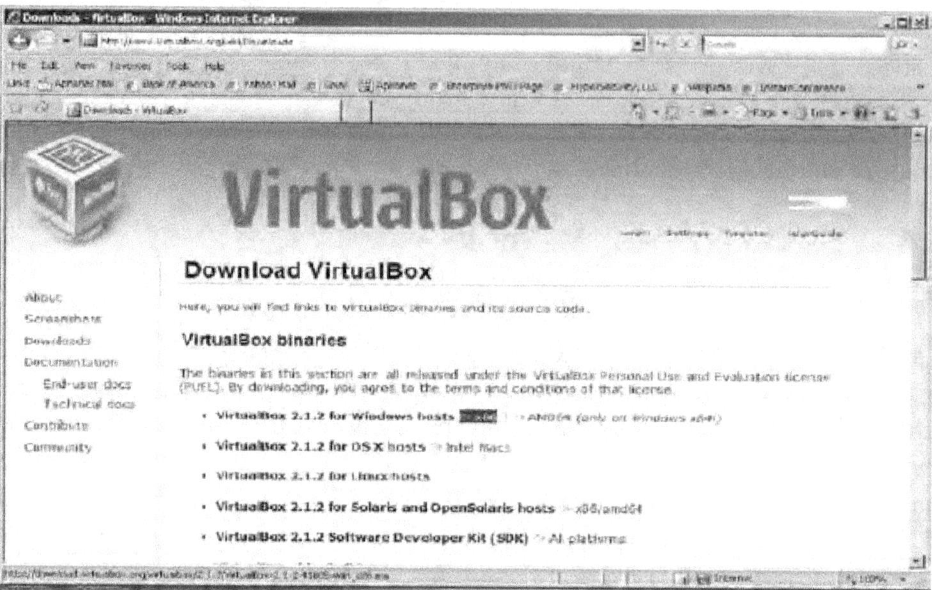

Choose the type of download file that is most suitable to the operating system you are using and download the product. Save the file—in Microsoft Windows, you will be prompted to save the file from the **File Download – Security Warning** dialog:

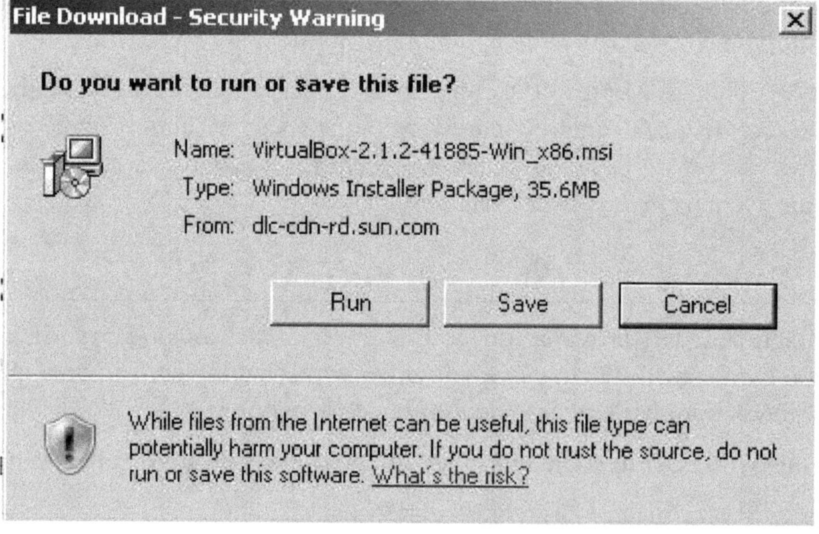

Choose **Save** and you will be shown a **Save As** file selection dialog to choose where you wish to save the downloaded file. The dialog box should look like this:

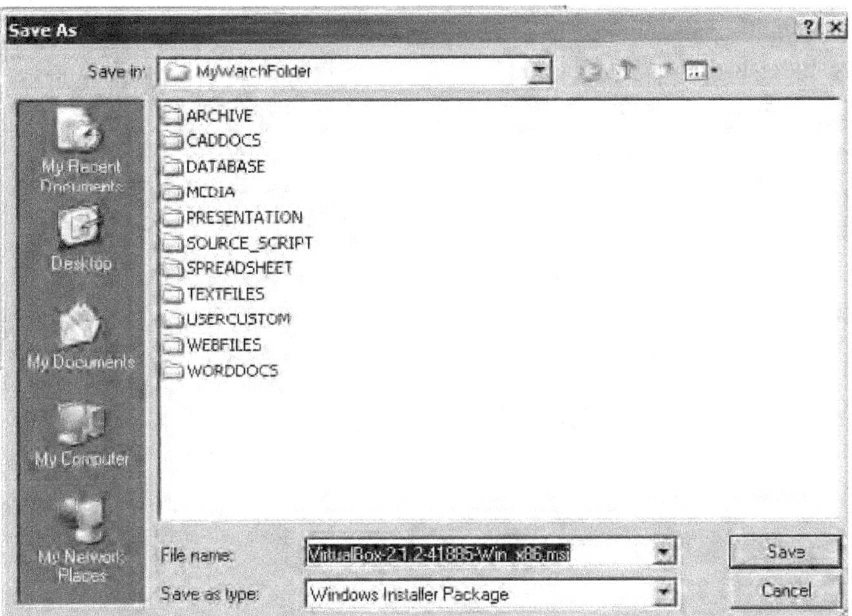

Select a location for the file to be saved to and click the **Save** button to continue. The download status dialog will appear:

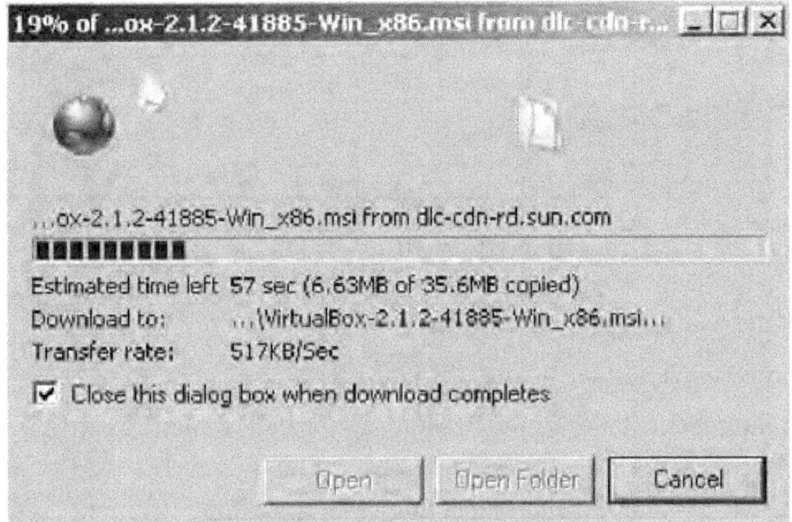

5.6   INSTALLING SUN xVM VIRTUAL BOX

Once the download has completed, you must locate the file wherever you saved it and execute the installer. If you are not using a Microsoft operating system, the procedure for executing the installer will be slightly different than what is shown here. Regardless of which non-Microsoft operating system you may be using, launch the installer according to your specific operating system's instructions. The VirtualBox installation can be started from a Windows environment by double-clicking on its Microsoft Installer archive (MSI file) or by entering this command from the prompt of a commandline interface:

msiexec /i VirtualBox.msi

The figure below shows the highlighted selection of the Sun VirtualBox (Windows version) installer from the root of the D: drive.

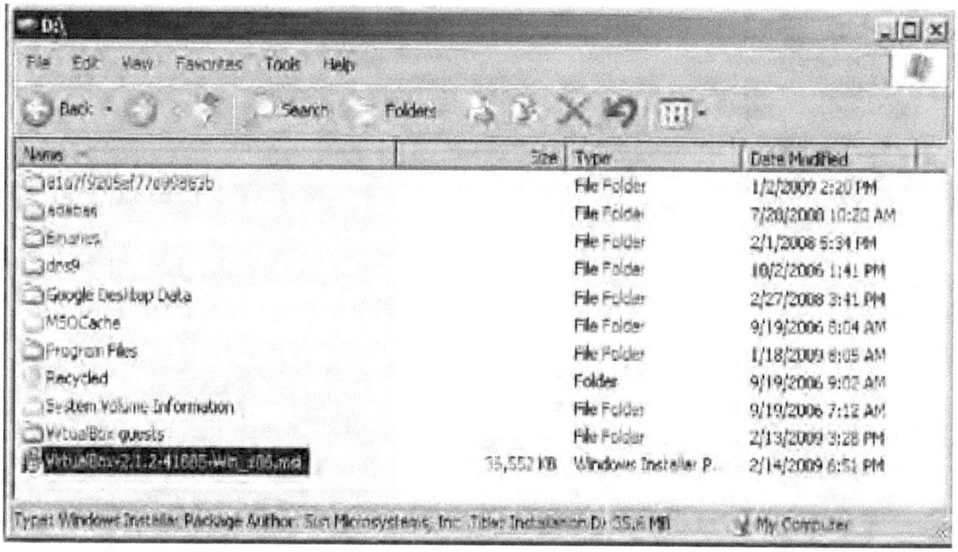

Using just the standard settings, VirtualBox will be installed for all users on the local system. If this is not what you want, it is necessary to invoke the installer from a command-line prompt as follows:

msiexec /i VirtualBox.msi ALLUSERS=2

Executing the installer in this fashion will install VirtualBox for the current user only.

Once the installer begins executing, the first thing you will see is the installation welcome dialog, which looks like this:

Click **Next >**to continue on to the **End-User License Agreement** (EULA), as shown below. In order to proceed, you must accept this agreement to use the product. Click the **Next >** button to continue.

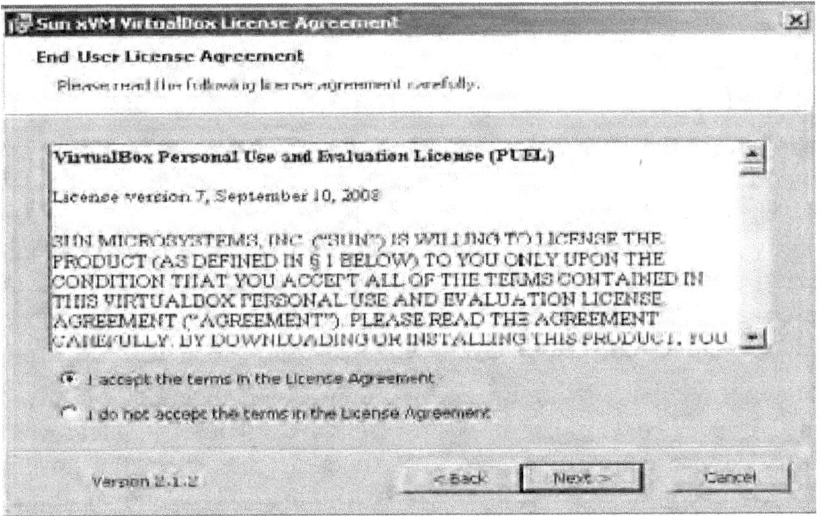

Once the EULA is accepted, the **Custom Setup** screen will appear, as shown below.

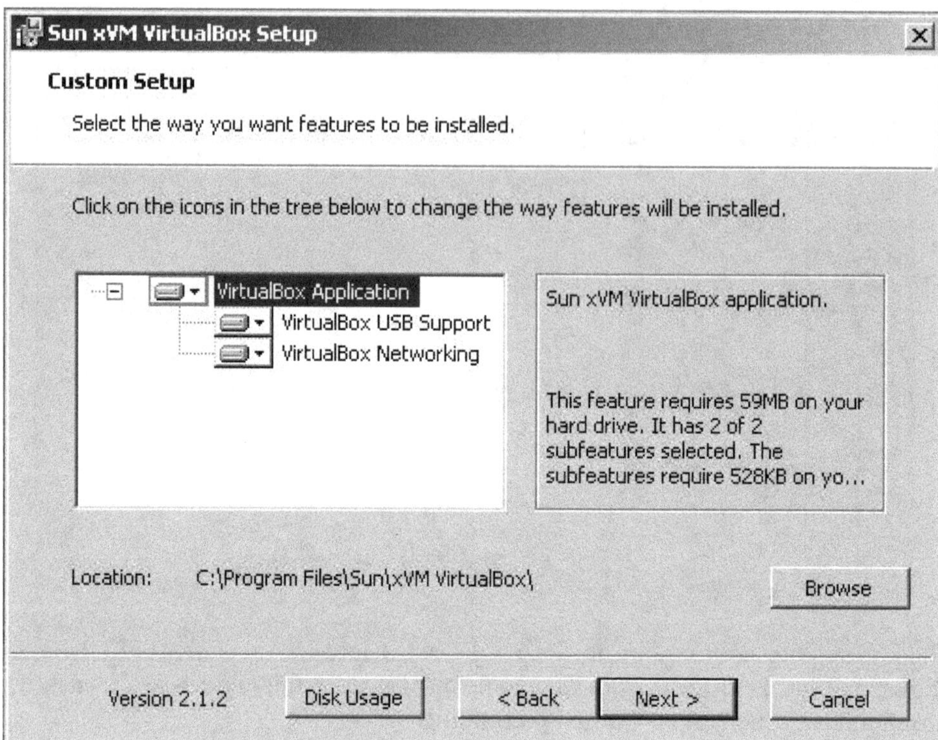

Here you can change the default settings, choosing where and how VirtualBox will be installed. Usually, the defaults are satisfactory for installation. If you choose this option, all features will be installed.

In addition to the VirtualBox application, the components for USB support and networking are available. These packages contains special drivers for your Windows host that VirtualBox requires to fully support networking and USB devices in your virtual machine (VM). The networking package contains extra networking drivers for your Windows host that VirtualBox needs to support Host Interface Networking (to make your VM's virtual network cards accessible from other machines on your physical network).

Depending on your Windows configuration, you may see warnings about "unsigned drivers" or similar messages. Select **Continue** on these warnings, because otherwise VirtualBox may not function correctly after installation. Click **Next >** to continue to the **Ready to Install** dialog box, shown below.

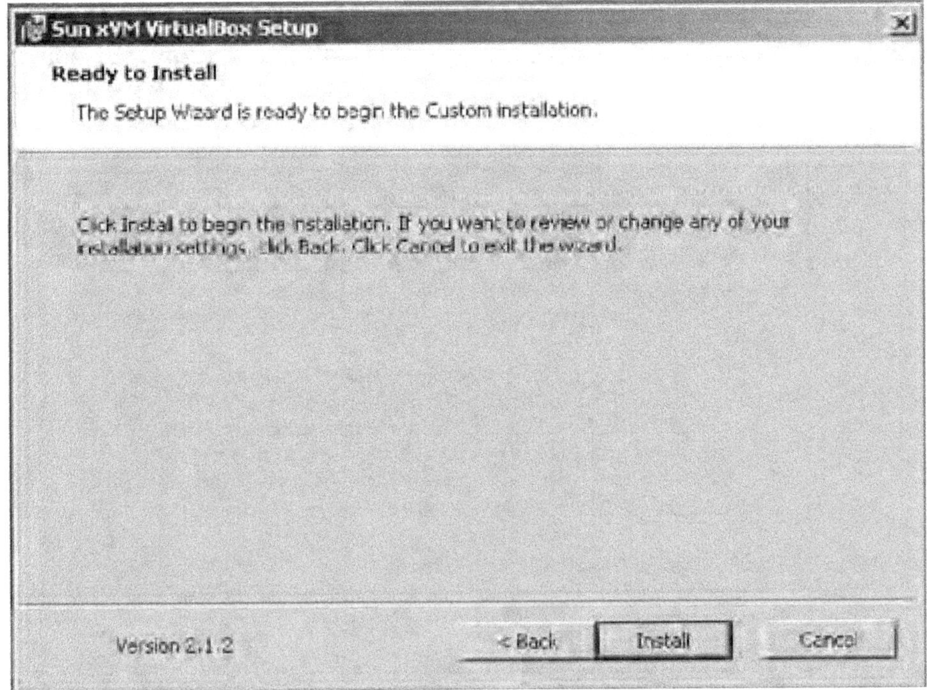

To start the installation process, just click **Install.** It may take a minute or so for the installer to complete, depending on your system's processor and memory resources. You will see an installation progress dialog, similar to this one:

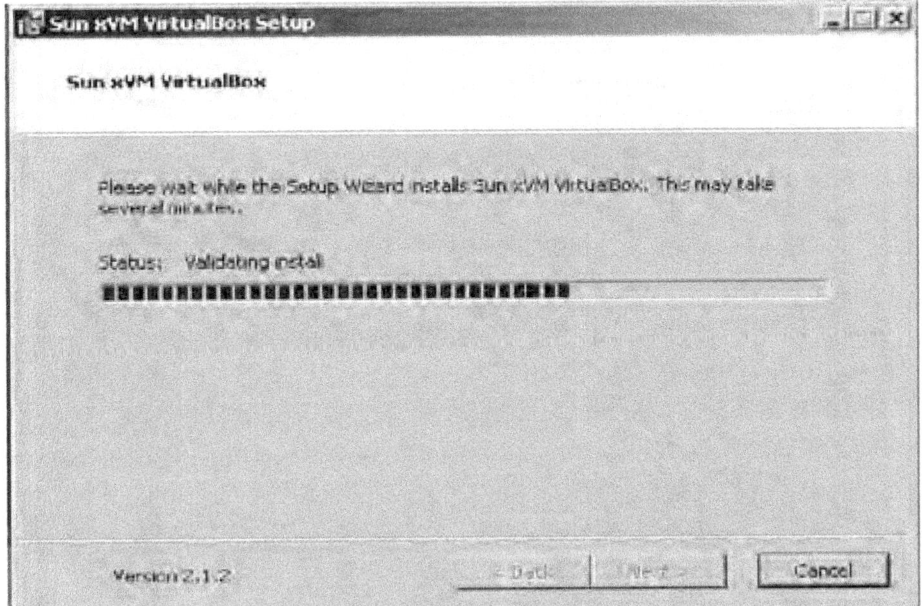

On Microsoft Windows operating systems, you may see the **Software Installation** dialog box shown below, warning you that the product you are installing has not passed Windows Logo testing to verify its compatibility with Windows XP. Click the **Continue Anyway** button to proceed.

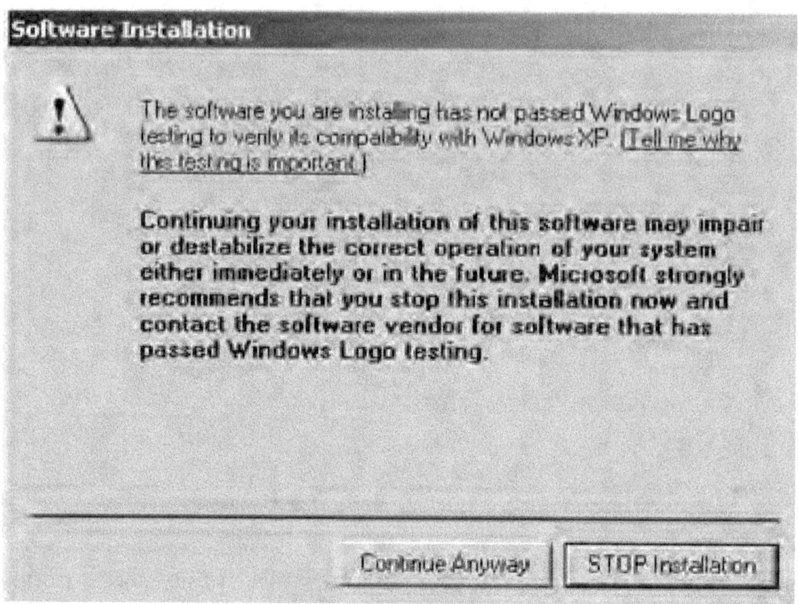

You will be notified when the installation has completed, and given the opportunity to launch the application automatically. Be sure the box in the following dialog is checked:

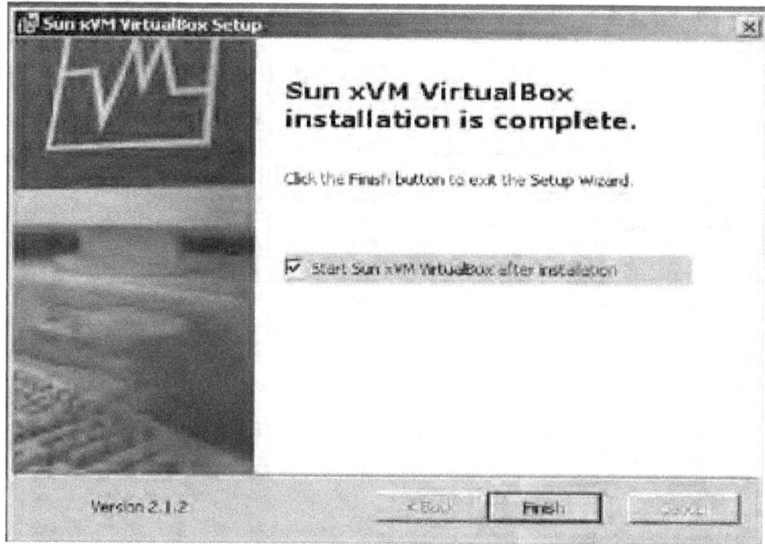

Click **Finish** to complete the installation process and continue. The **VirtualBox Registration Dialog** will appear:

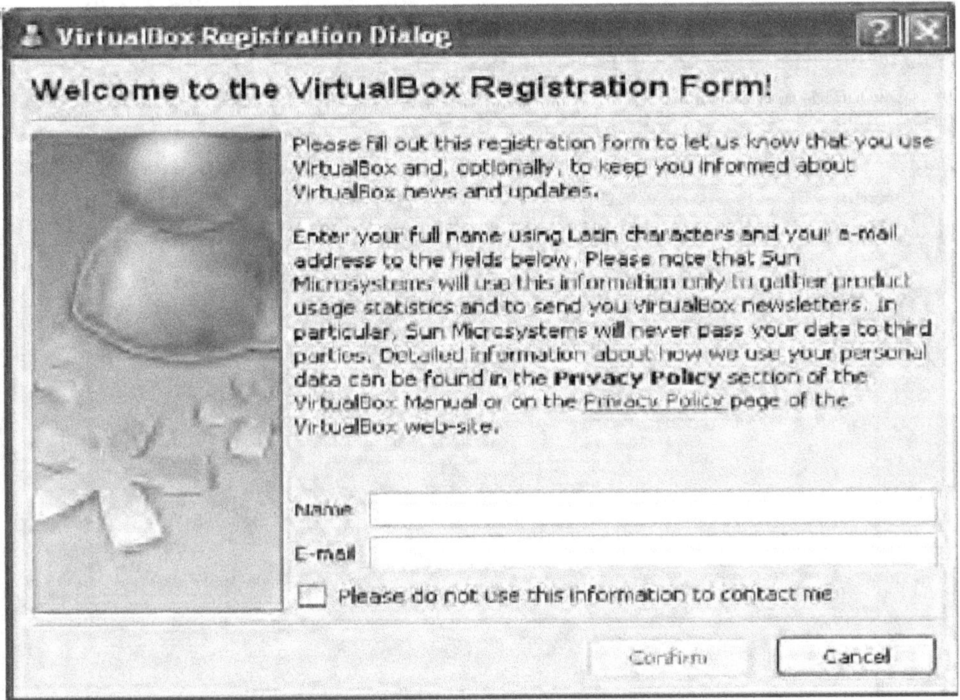

Registration is very simple, and it is recommended that you register your product. Just fill in your name and an email address. Once the registration form has been completed, a **Confirm** button will appear. You can choose to allow Sun to contact you or not by checking or checking the box above the **Confirm** button. Once you have clicked **Confirm,** instant kudos appear:

Click **OK** and you are rewarded with the initial display of the Sun xVM VirtualBox product. For Microsoft Windows-based systems, the installer will create a **VirtualBox** group in the Programs folder of the Start menu, which will allow you to launch the application and access its documentation. If you choose later to uninstall this product, VirtualBox can be safely uninstalled at any time by choosing the program entry in the **Add/Remove Programs** applet in the Windows **Control Panel.** For non-Windows operating systems, you must uninstall according to your system's recommended procedures. However, let's not do that yet! The following picture shows you what the opening screen looks like after you have installed and filled out the product registration form:

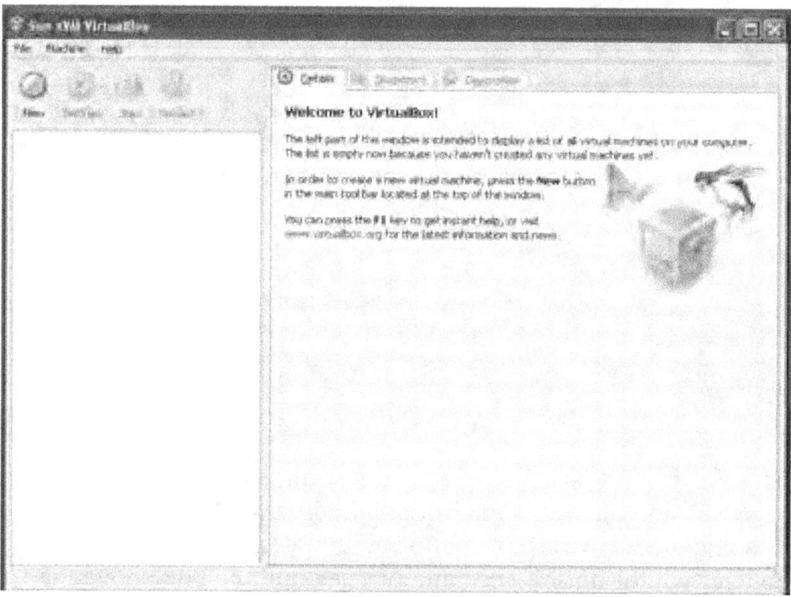

5.7   ADDING A GUEST OPERATING SYSTEM TO VIRTUAL BOX

VirtualBox allows you to run *guest operating systems* using its own virtual computer system, which is why it is called a "virtual machine". The guest system will run in its VM environment just as if it were installed on a real computer. It operates according to the VM settings you have specified (we will talk about settings a bit more later in this chapter). All software that you choose to run on the guest system will operate just as it would on a physical computer.

With the options available, you have quite a bit of latitude in deciding what virtual hardware will be provided to the guest. The virtual hardware you specify can be used to communicate with the host system or even with other guests. For instance, if you provide VirtualBox with the image of a CD-ROM in the form of an ISO file, VirtualBox can make this image available to a guest system just as if it were a physical CD-ROM. You can also give a guest system access to the real network (and network shares) via its virtual network card. It is even possible to give the host system, other guests, or computers on the Internet access to the guest system.

5.8   DOWNLOADING FREEDOS AS A GUEST OS

For our first guest, we will be adding an open source operating system called FreeDOS to the host machine. In order to do this, we must first go to the Internet and download FreeDOS. Minimize the VirtualBox application for now and open a web browser. Go to

http://virtualbox.wordpress.com/images

When your browser has brought up the site, it should look similar to the figure below. You will see a list of virtual operating systems, with the sponsoring web site for each one in parentheses.

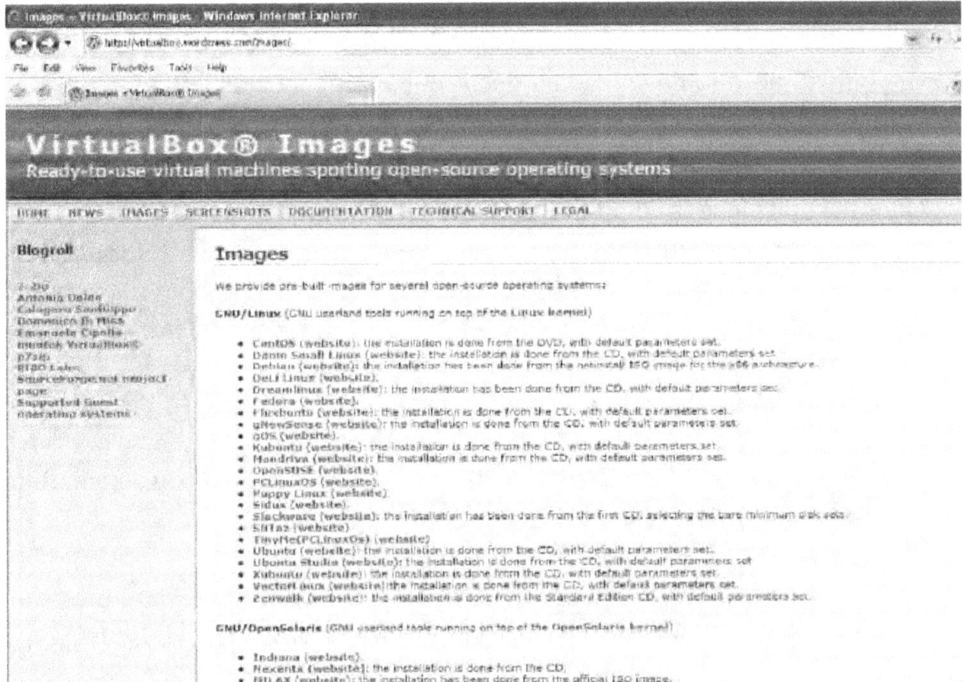

Towards the bottom of the page, you will find the FreeDOS entry. The reader is encouraged to go to the web site of each operating system and check it out before downloading a file. Click on the Free-DOS entry to start the download process. When you click on any of the operating system links, you will be taken to that system's download page. There, you are given the choice of which architecture (i.e., 32-bit or 64-bit) you want to install. What is important for almost every operating system displayed on this page is that you must *write down the passwords for the root user and default user.*

An example similar to what you will see is shown below:

FreeDOS There are several FreeDOS images available.

FreeDOS 1.0

Size (compressed/<u>uncompressed</u>): 82.3 MBytes / <u>394 MBytes</u>

Link: http://downloads.sourceforge.net/virtualboximage/freedos

Of course, FreeDOS is the exception to the rule above, since it does not require a root or user password. Click the link to download the image and save it to a location you will remember—later in this practicum, you will need to unzip this file and extract the images. We recommend that you choose to save the files on a drive with plenty of space available.

5.9   DOWNLOADING THE 7-ZIP ARCHIVE TOOL

Next, you will need to download an open source product called 7-zip (it works on both Linux and Windows platforms), which can be accessed from

> http://www.7-zip.org/download.html

Once the download is complete, perform the following steps *in sequence:*

1. Pick a drive with plenty of spare room on it and create a folder named **VirtualGuests.**

2. Download the **7-zip file** to the VirtualGuests folder and install it using the standard options.

3. Once you have installed 7-zip, find the FreeDOS file you downloaded previously.

4. Highlight the file and right-click on it—choose the **7-zip extraction** option to extract files.

5. Extract the files to your VirtualGuests folder.

6. Your VirtualGuests folder will now contain two folders,**Machines** and **VDI.** The virtualBox image for FreeDOS will be in the VDI folder.

5.10   ADDING A GUEST OS TO SUN xVM VIRTUAL BOX

Now you will add the FreeDOS guest operating system to your virtualBox host. Start by clicking on the **New** button. The **New Virtual Machine Wizard** dialog box will appear:

The wizard is an easy-to-follow guided setup for installation of your guest operating system. Click **Next >** to continue and you will be presented with the **Virtual Machine Name and OS Type** dialog box:

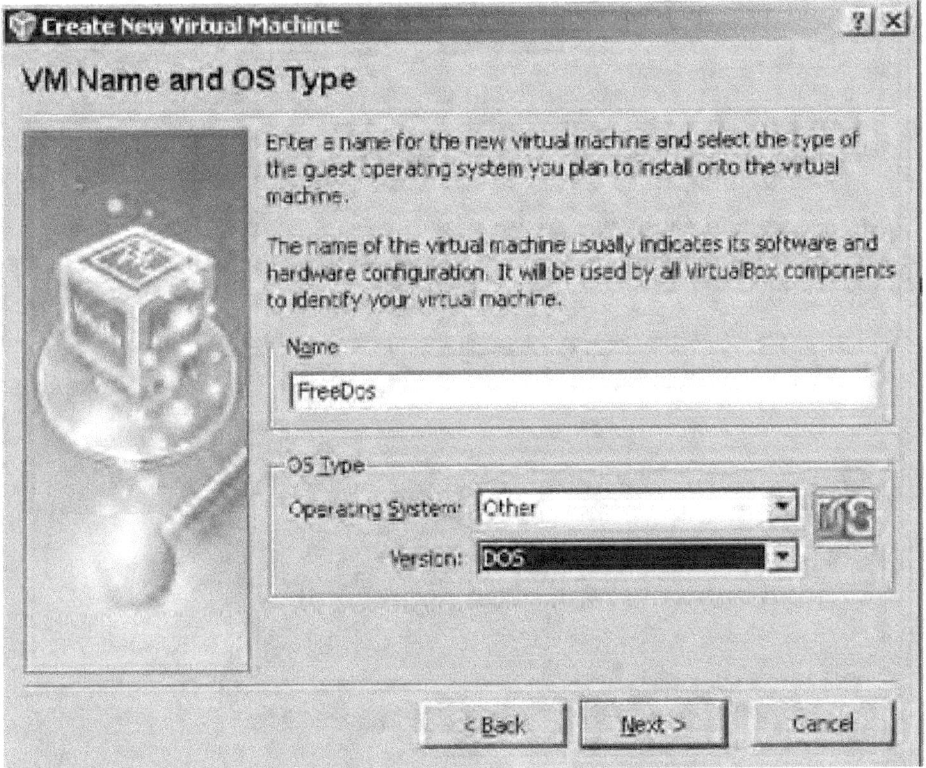

Type **FreeDOS** in the **Name** field. Select **Other** for the **Operating System,** and for the **Version** we will choose **DOS.** Click **Next >** to continue on to the dialog for memory configuration. In this part of the wizard, you have the option of increasing or decreasing the amount of memory that will be used for the guest operating system. For those of us old enough to remember DOS, 32 MB of memory is plenty.

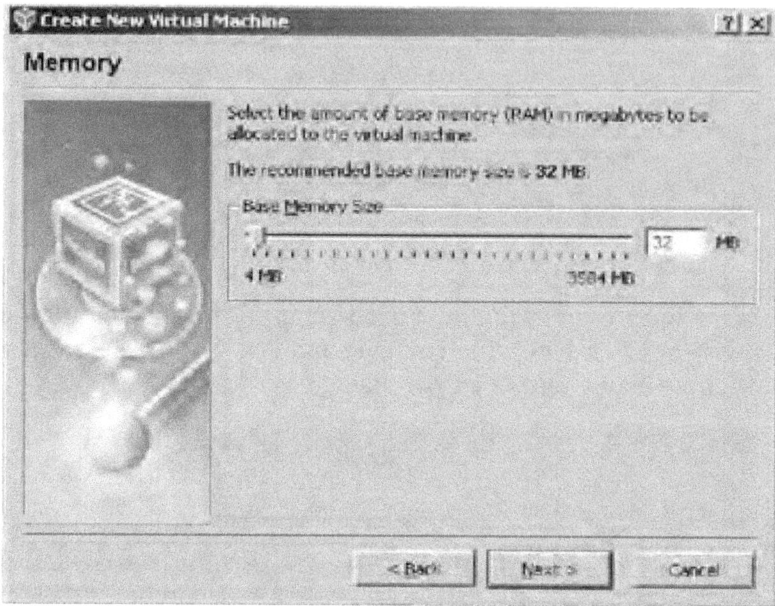

Just accept the default settings for now (you can always change them later) and click **Next >** to proceed to the next section of the wizard, the **Virtual Hard Disk** dialog box:

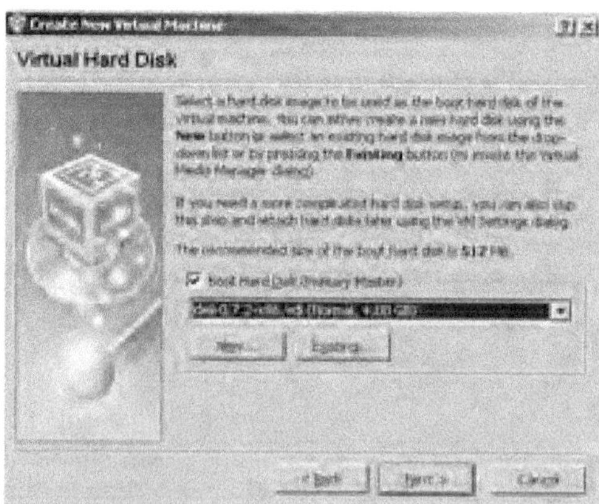

This dialog box allows you to select the virtual device image file (.vdi file) that was previously downloaded and saved to the VirtualGuests folder you created. What you see displayed in the dialog box is the name of the last image added. In this case, it was an image of Damn Small Linux (dsl). If no images have been installed on the host, the default selection will be similar to the one shown below:

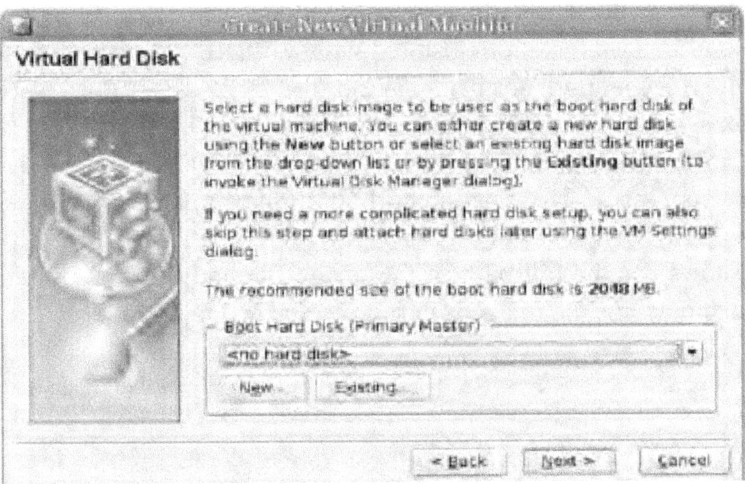

If you had previously created any virtual hard disks which have not been attached to other virtual machines, you could select from among those using the drop-down list in the Wizard window. Since we have downloaded and extracted a new image of FreeDos, it won't be in the list. Click the **Existing...** button to continue on to the **Virtual Media Manager.** In the figure below, FreeDOS is listed as an available selection. If it is not listed, then you need to add it by clicking on the **Add** button at the top of the dialog box.

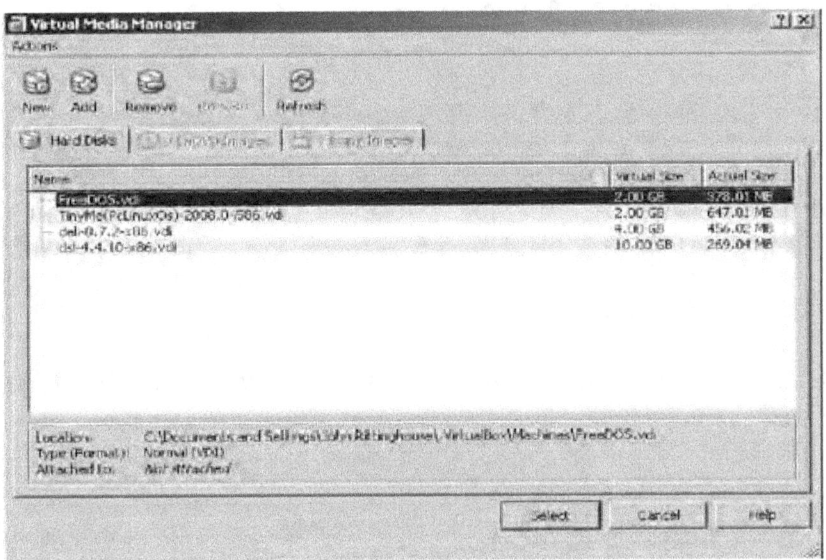

VirtualBox's Virtual Media Manager keeps an internal registry of all available hard disk, CD/DVD-ROM, and floppy disk images. This registry can be viewed and changed in the Virtual Disk Manager, which you can access from the **File** menu in the VirtualBox main window. The **Disk Image Manager** shows you all images that are registered with VirtualBox, grouped in three tabs for the three supported formats. These are hard disk images, either in VirtualBox's own Virtual Disk Image (VDI) format or the widely supported **Virtual Machine DisK** (VMDK) format. CD and DVD images in standard ISO format are supported. There is support for floppy images in standard RAW format. As you can see in the figure below, for each image, the Virtual Disk Manager shows you the full path of the image file and other information, such as the virtual machine the image is currently attached to, if any.

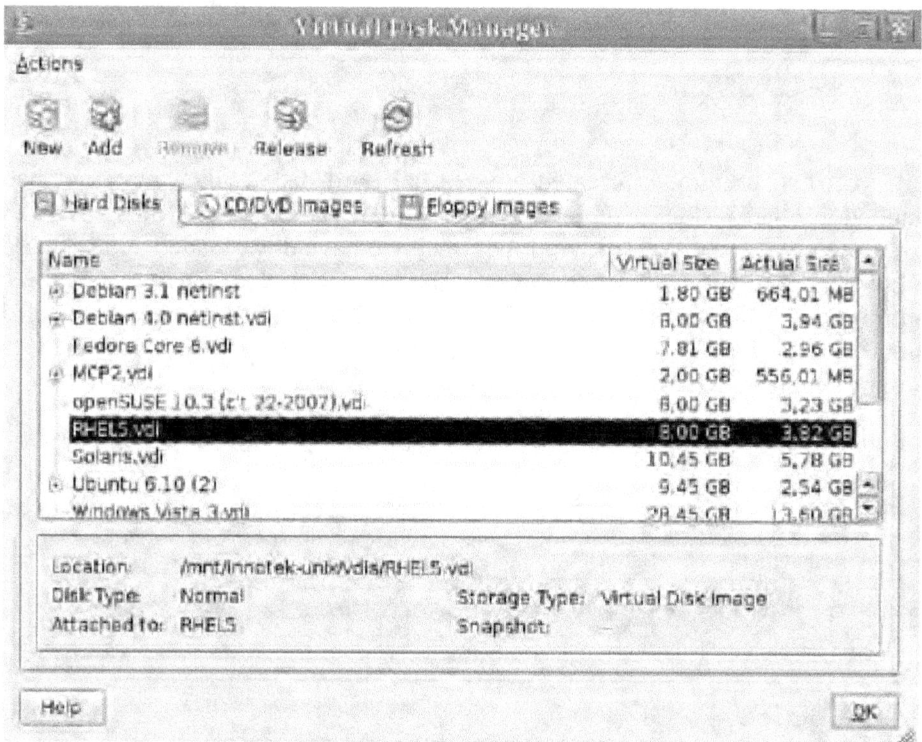

Clicking the **Add** button will bring you to the **Select a hard disk image file** dialog box, as shown below:

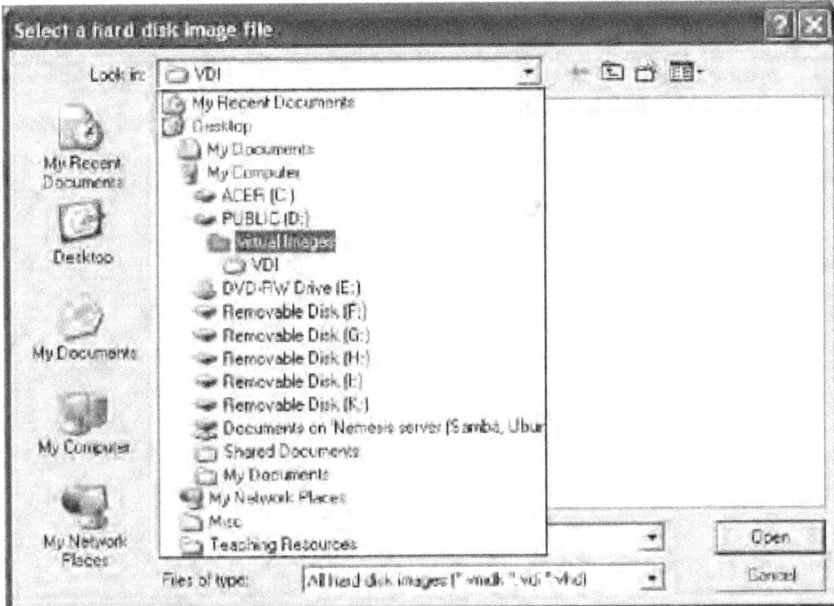

Using this file dialog, you must navigate to your VirtualGuests folder. In your VirtualGuests folder, open the **VDI** folder and highlight the **Free-DOS**. vdi file. Once you have it highlighted, simply click on the **Open** button. You are returned to the **Virtual Hard Disk** dialog box, where you earlier clicked the **Existing...** button:

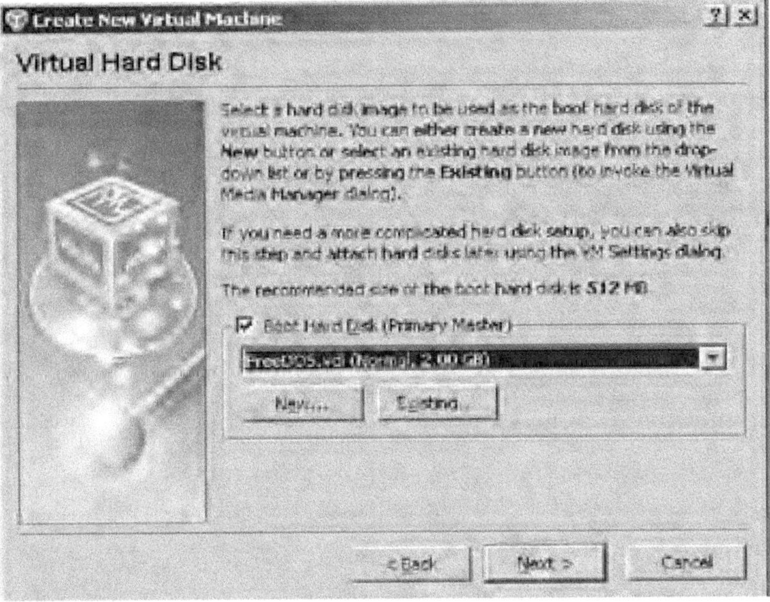

Click **Next >** to complete the addition of the FreeDOS virtual image. A summary screen, as shown below, will appear:

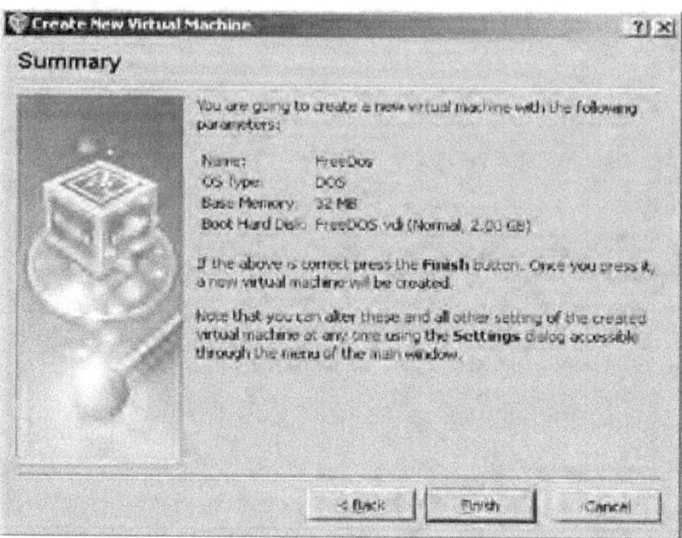

Here, simply click the **Finish** button and you will be returned to the Sun xVM VirtualBox main display. FreeDOS should be displayed in the left panel (it should be the only entry on your system) similar to the list shown in the following image:

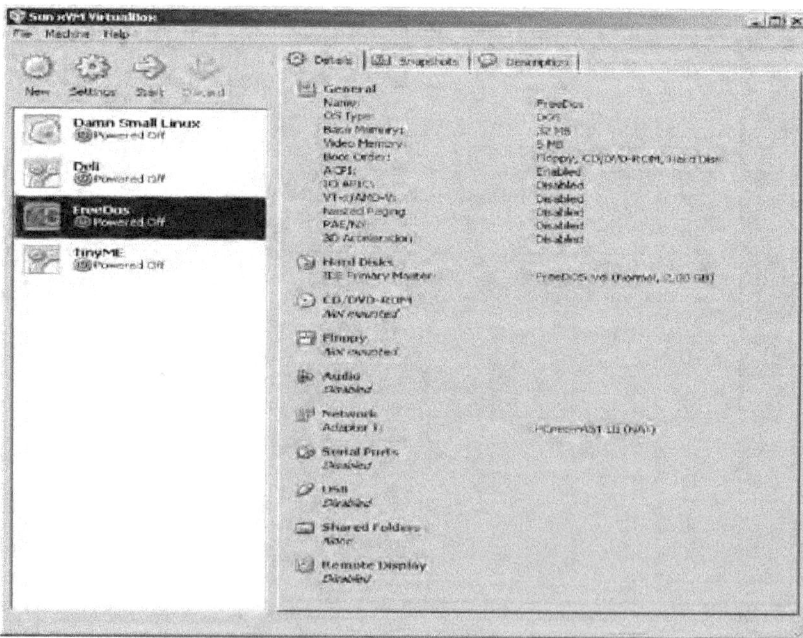

Before we explore the FreeDOS environment, it is a good idea to check the settings to ensure that the guest system will work the way you want. The **Settings** button (in the figure above, it looks like a gear) in the toolbar at the top of the VirtualBox main window brings up a detailed window where you can configure many of the properties of the VM that is currently selected:

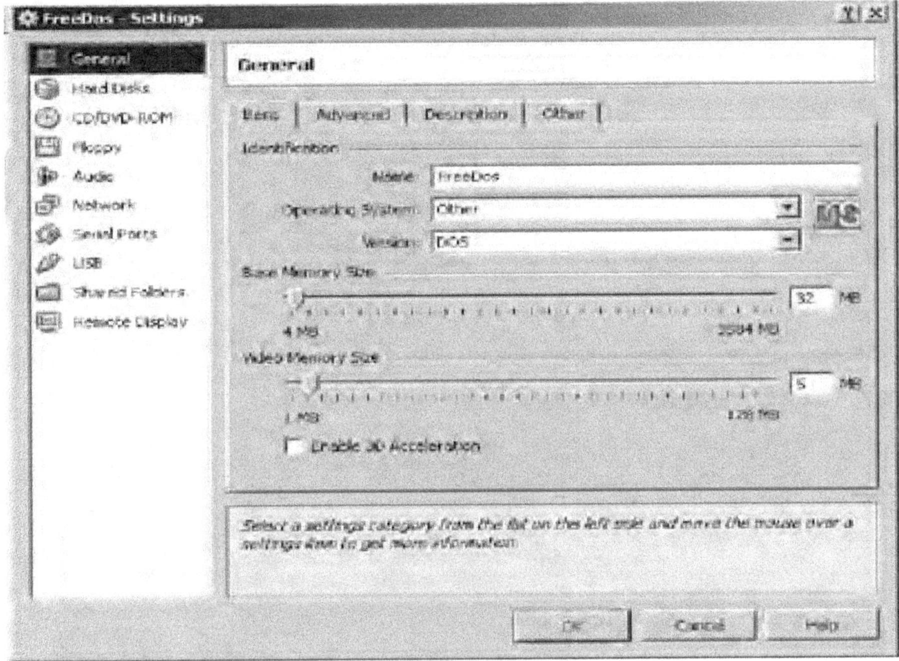

Click your desired settings—but be careful. Even though it is possible to change all VM settings after installing a guest operating system, certain changes after installation may prevent a guest operating system from functioning correctly.

Since you have just created an empty VM, you will probably be most interested in the settings in the **CD/DVD-ROM** section if you want to make a CD-ROM or a DVD-ROM available the first time you start Free-DOS, so that you can use it with your guest operating system. This will allow your VM to access the media in your host drive, and you can proceed to install from there. Check the box in the CD/DVD section if you want to use an optical device.

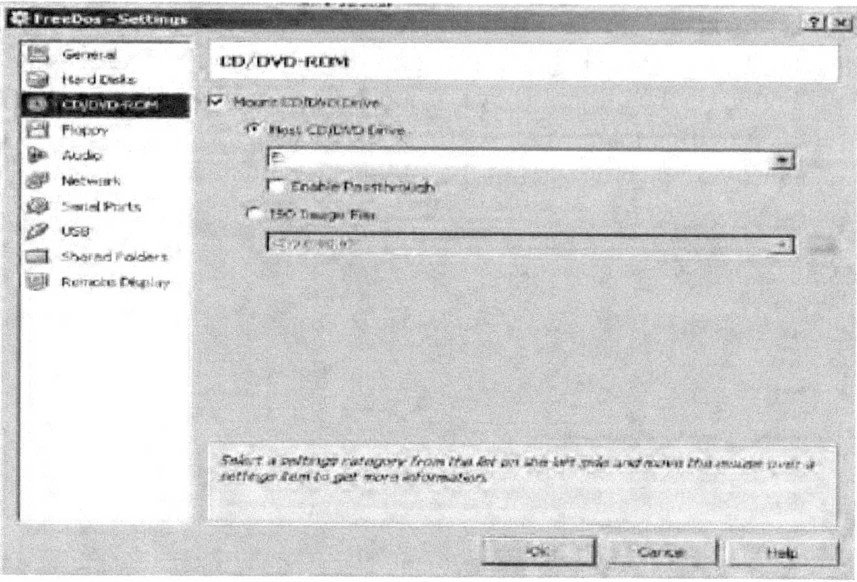

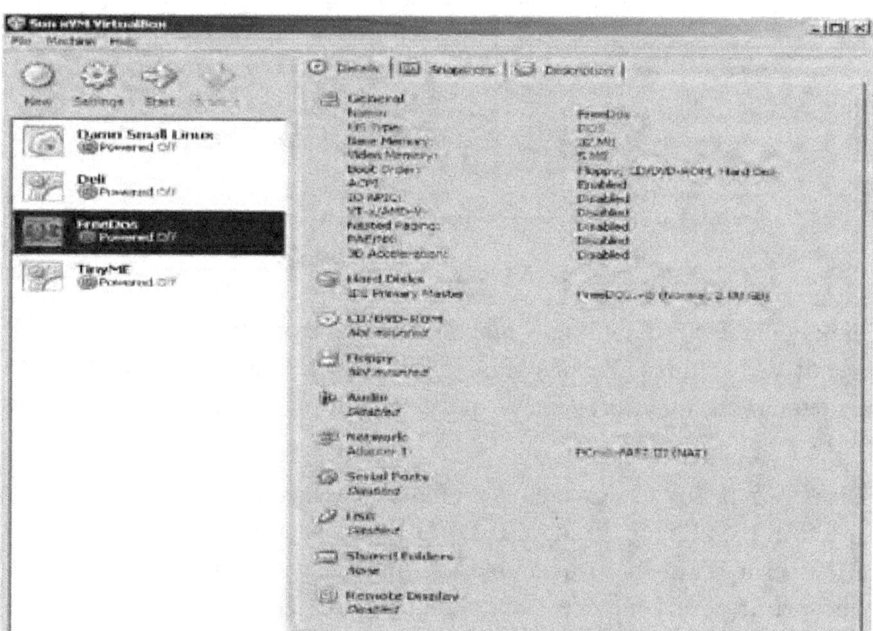

For now, that is all you need to do in Settings to prepare to run your virtual image. The next part of our practicum will take you inside the virtual guest system to use and see for yourself that it is a real, functioning environment. We will show you how to set up a graphical user interface within the DOS environment using an open source product called Open-GEM. OpenGEM was modeled after GEM, one of the earliest GUI environments widely available on the DOS platform.

To start FreeDOS, highlight **FreeDOS** in the selections panel and click the green **Start** arrow as shown below.

When you first start FreeDOS, you are presented with a "Load" menu, as shown below. Usually, the default selection best for your system is highlighted automatically. Choose the default option and press **Enter** (or just let the 5-second timer expire).

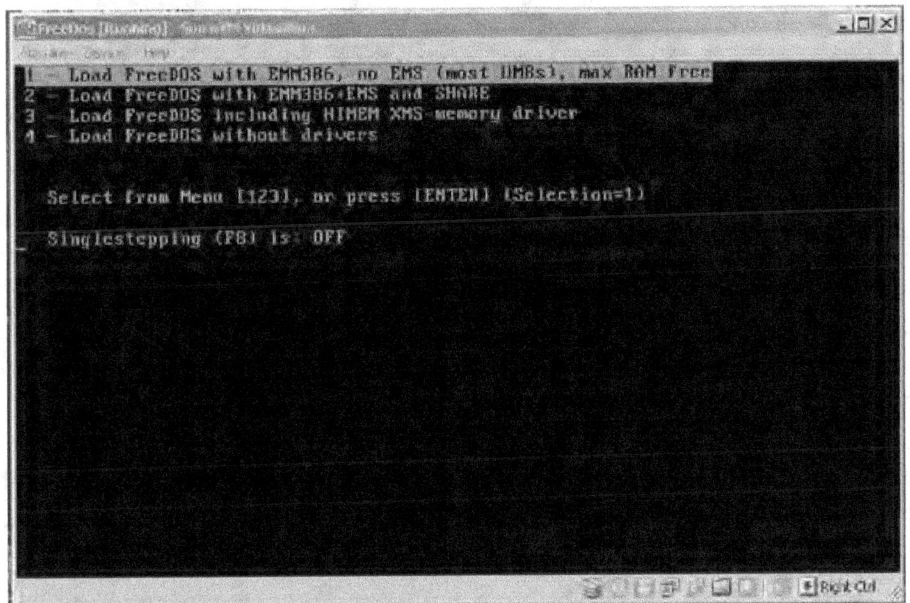

Since the operating system in the virtual machine does not "know" that it is not running on a real computer, it expects to have exclusive control over your keyboard and mouse. This is not so, however, since, unless you are running the VM in full-screen mode, your VM needs to share the keyboard and mouse with other applications and possibly other VMs on your host.

This becomes evident when you look at the figure below, showing Free-DOS running on a Windows XP installation.

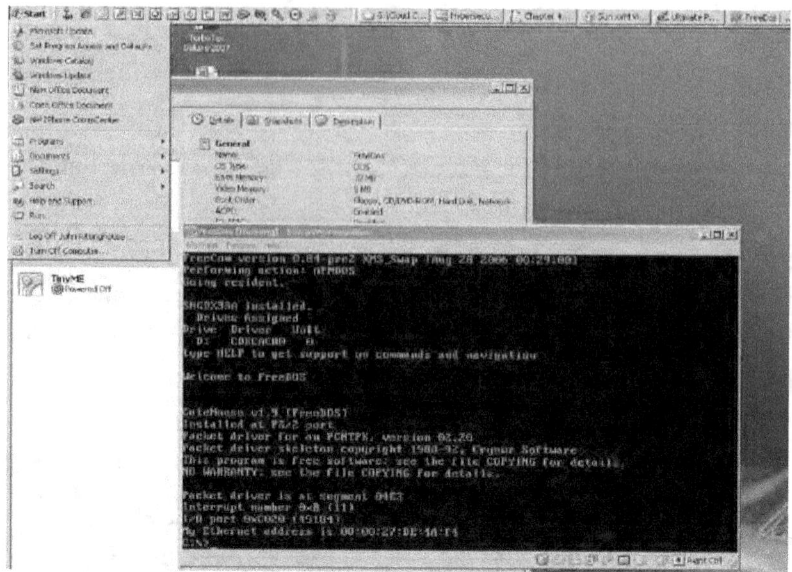

Only one of the two – either the VM or the host – can "own" the keyboard and the mouse at any one time. You will see a second mouse pointer, which will always be confined to   the limits of the VM window. Basically, you activate the VM by clicking inside it. To return ownership of the keyboard and mouse to your host operating system, VirtualBox reserves a special key on your keyboard, called the **Host key,** for itself. *By default, this is the Control (CTRL) key on the right lower part of your keyboard.* You can change this default in the VirtualBox Global Settings if you wish. In any case, the current setting for the Host key is always displayed at the bottom right of your VM window in case you may have forgotten which key to use. If needed, click the mouse in the virtualized window to gain focus in the guest system. Press the Host key to give focus back to the host.

FreeDOS comes with a graphical user interface (GUI) called Open-GEM that is ready to install. We are going to install OpenGEM in the Free-DOS environment to show you that it is a fully functioning virtualized platform. At the **c:\>** command prompt, type

FDOS\OPENGEM\INSTALL

and press **Enter.** The following screen appears when the GEM installer starts:

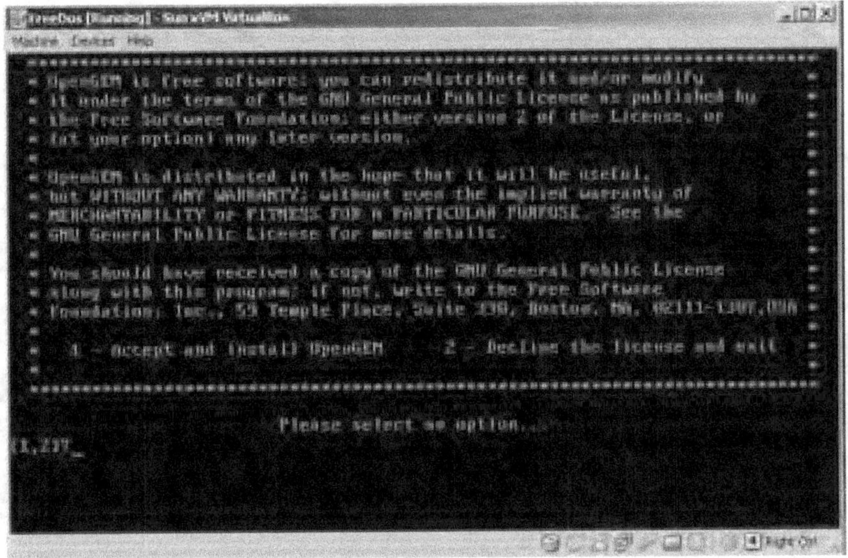

Choose option **1** from the menu and press **Enter.** The next screen to appear is the OpenGEM license agreement. Here, you must accept the license agreement by once again choosing option **1** (Accept and Install OpenGEM) and pressing **Enter** to continue the install process.

The installation will proceed and when it is completed, you will see the screen below:

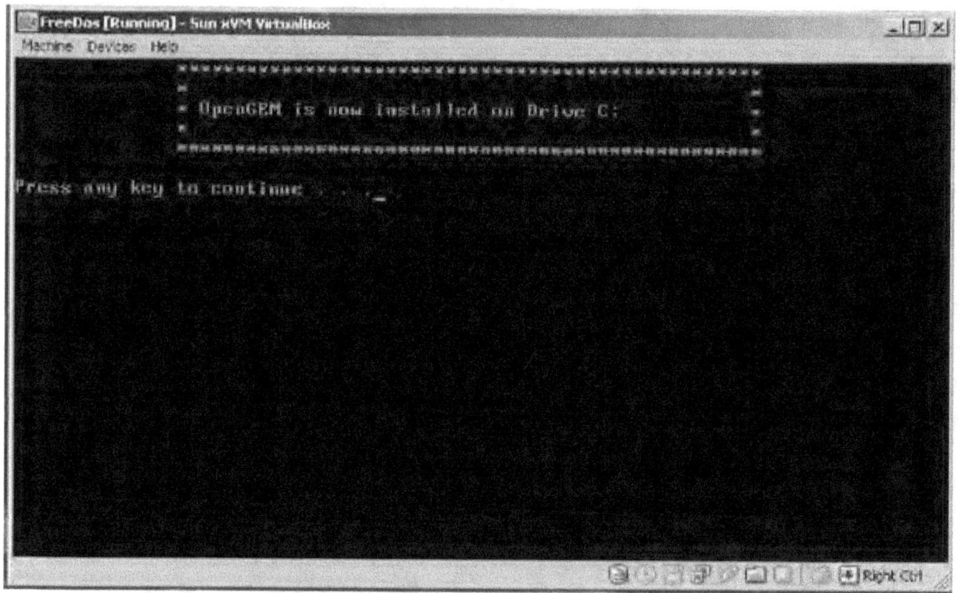

Press any key as instructed. You will then be shown an information screen and acknowledgment of your installation. Some basic information telling you how to start OpenGEM is displayed. Press any key again to continue.

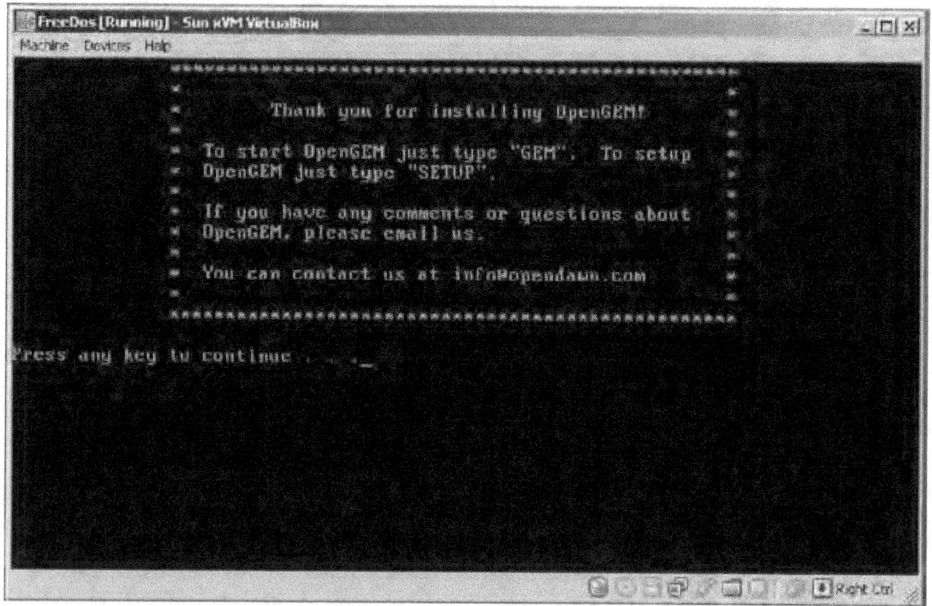

From the DOS command prompt c:\>, type **GEM** and press **Enter.** The GEM environment starts up and you should see something similar to the screen below.

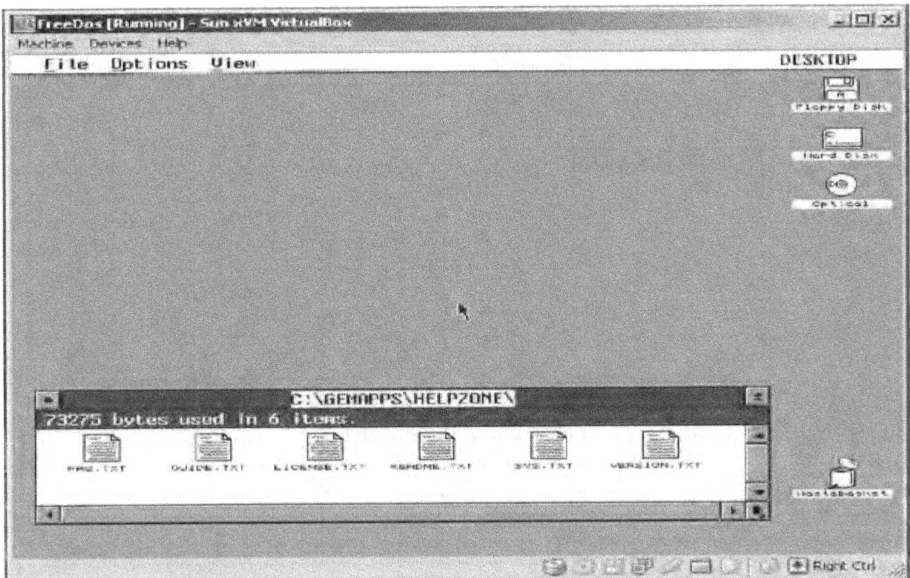

Play around with the environment and (for some of us) reminisce about the "good" old days. Once you are satisfied that everything works, you can exit GEM by using the **File |> Quit** option on the menu bar at the top. GEM will exit and show the following screen, where you are given the option to restart OpenGEM, return to DOS, reboot, or shut down.

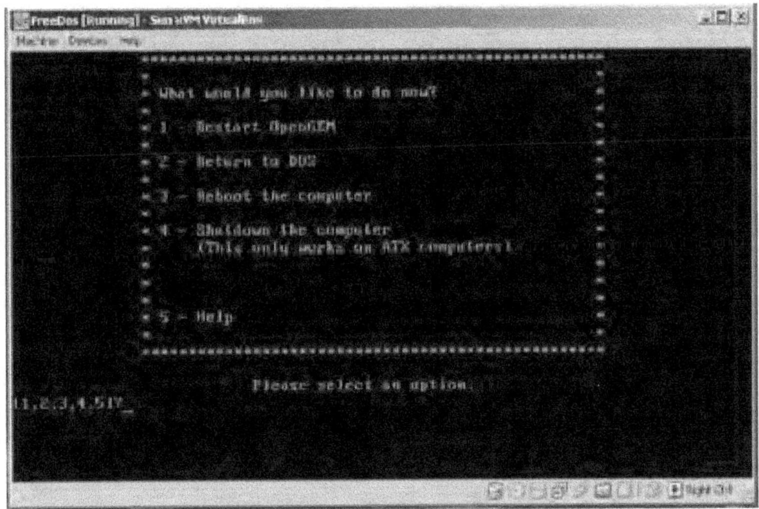

Choose option **4** and press **Enter.** You will be returned to the Sun xVM program. Note that FreeDOS is shown in a powered-off state.

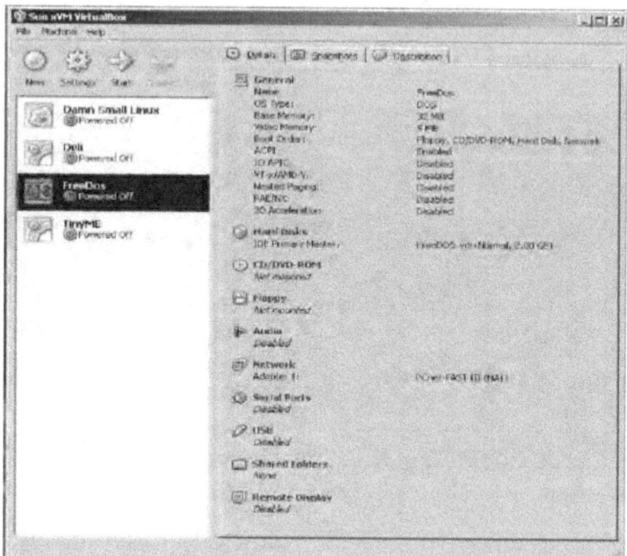

Bit Questions

1. ------------------means to create multiple, logical instances of software or hardware on a single physical hardware resource.

2. Between the VMs and the host platform, one needs to deploy a middleware layer called a----------------.

3. What is one significant advantage of Virtualization in datacenters
    (a) Can manage the Data center with Zero Manpower

    (b) Mirroring for Disaster Recovery

    (c) Eliminate the need of physical devices for the Data center

    (d) None of the above

4. XEN   [   ]

    (a) is a Para-Virtualized Interface

    (b) Can host Multiple and different Operating Systems

    (c) Supports Isolation

    (d) All the above

5.   The use of domain 0 is   [   ]
   (a)   Automatically started at boot time
   (b)   Automatically started at run time
   (c)   Automatically started at compile time
   (d)   all the above

Exercises

1.   What is virtualization? Enlist and explain some of the common pitfalls that come with virtualization.

2.   What is the fundamental differences between the virtual machine as perceived by a traditional operating system processes and a system VM?

3.   Discuss different Types of Virtualization.

4.   Write short notes on the following:
   (a)   VMware
   (b)   Xen
   (c)   Hyper-V

CHAPTER 6

SECURITY IN CLOUD

6.1 CHAPTER OVERVIEW

This chapter identifies current security concerns about cloud computing environments and describes the methodology for ensuring application and data security and compliance integrity for those resources that are moving from on-premises to public cloud environments. Security is one of the greatest challenge or issue of cloud computing. More important, this discussion focuses on why and how these resources should be protected in the Software-as-a-Service (SaaS), Platform-as-a-Service (PaaS), and Infrastructure-as-a-Service (IaaS) environments and offers security "best practices" for service providers and enterprises that are in or are contemplating moving into the cloud computing space.

6.2 INTRODUCTION

Cloud service providers (CSP) (e.g. Microsoft, Google, Amazon, Salesforce.com etc.) are leveraging virtualization technologies combined with self-service capabilities for computing resources via the Internet. In these service provider environments, virtual machines from multiple organizations have to be co-located on the same physical server in order to maximize the efficiencies of virtualization. Cloud service providers must learn from the managed service provider (MSP) model and ensure that their customer's applications and data are secure if they hope to retain their customer base and competitiveness. Today, enterprises are looking toward cloud computing horizons to expand their on-premises infrastructure, but most cannot afford the risk of compromising the security of their applications and data.

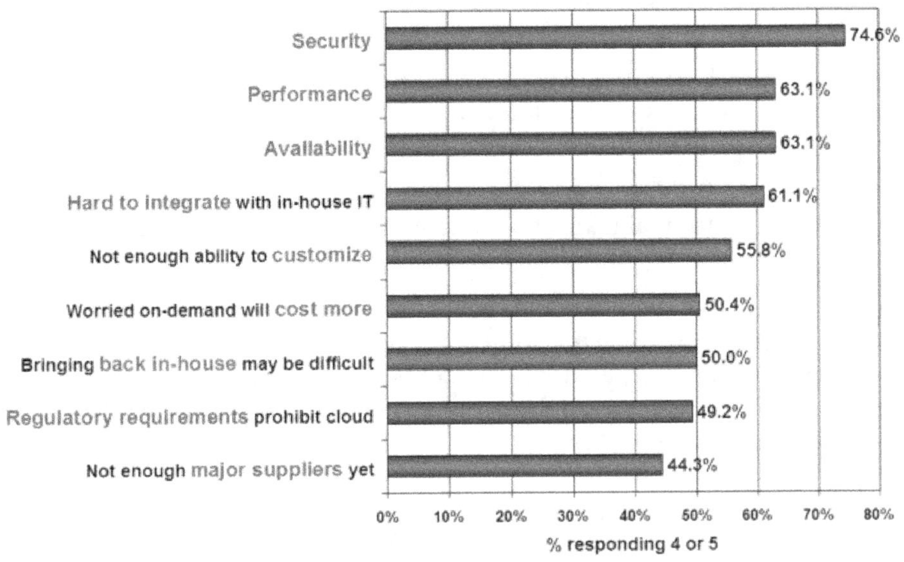

Figure 6.1 Results of IDC survey ranking security challenges

6.3   CLOUD SECURITY CHALLENGES

***Security Concern* 1:** With the cloud model control physical security is lost because of sharing computing resources with other companies. No knowledge or control of where the resources run.

***Security Concern* 2:** Company has violated the law (risk of data seizure by (foreign) government.

***Security Concern* 3:** Storage services provided by one cloud vendor may be incompatible with another vendor's services if user decides to move from one to the other (e.g. Microsoft cloud is incompatible with Google Cloud).

***Security Concern* 4:** Who controls the encryption/decryption keys? Logically it should be the customer.

***Security Concern* 5:** Ensuring integrity of the data (transfer, storage, or retrieval) really means that changes only in response to authorized transactions. A common standard to ensure data integrity does not yet exist.

***Security Concern* 6:** In case of Payment Card Industry Data Security Standard (PCI DSS) data logs must be provided to security managers and regulators.

***Security Concern* 7:** Users must keep up to date with application improvements to be sure they are protected.

***Security Concern* 8:** Some government regulations have strict limits on what data about its citizens can be stored and for how long, and some banking regulators require that customers financial data remain in their home country.

***Security Concern* 9:** The dynamic and fluid nature of virtual machines will make it difficult to maintain the consistency of security and ensure the auditability of records.

***Security Concern* 10:** Customers may be able to sue cloud service providers if their privacy rights are violated, and in any case the cloud service providers may face damage to their reputation. Concerns arise when it is not clear to individuals why their personal information is requested or how it will be used or passed on to other parties.

6.4   SOFTWARE-AS-A-SERVICE SECURITY

SaaS is the dominant cloud service model for the foreseeable future and the area where the most critical need for security practices and oversight will reside. Just as with a managed service provider, corporations or end users will need to research vendors policies on data security before using vendor services to avoid losing or not being able to access their data. The technology analyst and consulting firm Gartner lists seven security risks which one should discuss with a cloud-computing vendor:

1. **Privileged user access:** Get as much information as you can about the people who manage your data. Ask providers to supply specific information on the hiring and oversight of privileged administrators, and the controls over their access.

2. ***Regulatory compliance*:** Make sure that the vendor is willing to undergo external audits and/or security certifications.

3. ***Data location*:** When you use the cloud, you probably won't know exactly where your data is hosted. Infact, you might not even know what country it will be stored in. Ask providers if they will commit to storing and processing data in specific jurisdictions, and whether they will make a contractual commitment to obey local privacy requirements on behalf of their customers.

4. **Data segregation:** Make sure that encryption is available at all stages, and that these encryption schemes were designed and tested by experienced professionals.

5. ***Recovery*:** Even if you don't know where your data is, a cloud provider should tell you what will happen to your data and service in case of a

disaster. Any offering that does not replicate the data and application infrastructure across multiple sites is vulnerable to a total failure. Ask your provider if it has "the ability to do a complete restoration, and how long it will take".

6. ***Investigative support:*** Investigating in appropriate or illegal activity may be impossible in cloud computing. Cloud services are especially difficult to investigate, because logging and data   for multiple customers may be co-located and may also be spread across an ever- changing set of hosts and data centers. If you cannot get a contractual commitment to support specific forms of investigation, along with evidence that the vendor has already successfully supported such activities, then only safe assumption is that investigation and discovery requests will be impossible.

7. **Long-term viability:** Ideally, your cloud computing provider will never go broke or get acquired and swallowed up by a larger company. But you must be sure your data will remain available even after such an event. Ask potential providers how you would get your data back and if it would be in a format that you could import into a replacement application.

To address the security issues listed above, SaaS providers will need to incorporate and enhance security practices used by the managed service providers and develop new ones as the cloud computing environment evolves.

6.4.1   Security Management (People)

One of the most important actions for a security team is to develop a formal charter for the security organization and program. The charter should be aligned with the strategic plan of the organization or company the security team works for. Lack of clearly defined roles and responsibilities, and agreement on expectations, can result in a general feeling of loss and confusion among the security team about what is expected of them, how their skills and experienced can be leveraged, and meeting their performance goals.

6.4.2   Security Governance

A security steering committee should be developed whose objective is to focus on providing guidance about security initiatives and alignment with business and IT strategies. This committee must clearly define the roles and responsibilities of the security team and other groups involved in performing information security functions.

6.4.3   Risk Management

Risk management entails identification of technology assets; identification of data and its links to business processes, applications, and data stores; and assignment of ownership and custodial responsibilities. Actions should also include maintaining a repository of information assets. Owners have authority and accountability for information assets including protection requirements, and custodians implement confidentiality, integrity, availability, and privacy controls.

6.4.4   Risk Assessment

Security risk assessment is critical to helping the information security organization make informed decisions when balancing the dueling priorities of business utility and protection of assets. A formal information security risk management process should proactively assess information security risks as well as plan and manage them on a periodic or as-needed basis. More detailed and technical security risk assessments in the form of threat modeling should also be applied to applications and infrastructure.

6.4.5   Security Portfolio Management

Fundamental component of ensuring efficient and effective operation of any information security program and organization. Lack of portfolio and project management discipline can lead to projects never being completed or never realizing their expected return; unsustainable and unrealistic workloads and expectations because projects are not prioritized according to strategy, goals, and resource capacity; and degradation of the system or processes due to the lack of supporting maintenance and sustaining organization planning. For every new project that a security team undertakes, the team should ensure that a project plan and project manager with appropriate training and experience is in place so that the project can be seen through to completion. Portfolio and project management capabilities can be enhanced by developing methodology, tools, and processes to support the expected complexity of projects that include both traditional business practices and cloud computing practices.

6.4.6   Security Awareness

People are the weakest link for security. Knowledge and culture are among the few effective tools to manage risks related to people. Not providing proper awareness and training to the people who may need them can expose the company to a variety of security risks for which people, rather than system or application vulnerabilities, are the threats and points of entry. Social engineering attacks, lower reporting of and slower responses to potential security incidents, and inadvertent customer data leaks are all possible and probable risks that may be triggered by lack of an effective security awareness program.

6.4.7   Education and Training

Programs should be developed that provide a baseline for providing fundamental security and risk management skills and knowledge to the security team and their internal partners. This entails a formal process to assess and align skill sets to the needs of the security team and to provide adequate training and mentorship-providing a broad base of fundamental security, inclusive of data privacy, and risk management knowledge.

6.4.8   Policies, Standards, and Guidelines

Many resources and templates are available to aid in the development of information security policies and standards. A cloud computing security team should first identify the information security and business requirements unique to cloud computing, SaaS, and collaborative software application security. Policies should be developed, documented, and implemented, along with documentation for supporting standards and guidelines. To maintain relevancy, these policies, standards, and guidelines should be reviewed at regular intervals or when significant changes occur in the business or IT environment.

6.4.9   Secure Software Development Life Cycle (SecSDLC)

The SecSDLC must provide consistency, repeatability, and conformance. The SDLC consists of six phases, and there are steps unique to the SecSLDC in each of phases:

Phase 1: Investigation: Define project processes and goals, and document them in the program security policy.

Phase 2: Analysis: Analyze existing security policies and programs, analyze current threats and controls, examine legal issues, and perform risk analysis.

Phase 3: Logical design: Develop a security blueprint, plan incident response actions, plan business responses to disaster, and determine the feasibility of continuing and/or outsourcing the project.

Phase 4: Physical design: Select technologies to support the security blueprint, develop a definition of a successful solution, design physical security measures to support technological solutions, and review and approve plans.

Phase 5: Implementation: Buy or develop security solutions. At the end of this phase, present a tested package to management for approval.

Phase 6: Maintenance: Constantly monitor, test, modify, update, and repair to respond to changing threats.

6.4.10 Security Monitoring and Incident Response

Centralized security information management systems should be used to provide notification of security vulnerabilities and to monitor systems continuously through automated technologies to identify potential issues. They should be integrated with network and other systems monitoring processes (e.g., security information management, security event management, security information and event management, and security operations centers that use these systems for dedicated 24/7/365 monitoring). Management of periodic, independent third-party security testing should also be included.

6.4.11 Third-Party Risk Management

Lack of a third-party risk management program may result in damage to the provider's reputation, revenue losses, and legal actions should the provider be found not to have performed due diligence on its third-party vendors.

6.4.12 Requests for Information and Sales Support

The integrity of the provider's security business model, regulatory and certification compliance, and your company's reputation, competitiveness, and marketability all depend on the security team's ability to provide honest, clear, and concise answers to a customer request for information (RFI) or request for proposal (RFP). A structured process and a knowledge base of frequently requested information will result in considerable efficiency and the avoidance of ad-hoc, inefficient, or inconsistent support of the customer RFI/RFP process.

6.4.13 Business Continuity Plan

A business continuity plan should include planning for non-IT-related aspects such as key personnel, facilities, crisis communication, and reputation protection, and it should refer to the disaster recovery plan for IT-related infrastructure recovery/continuity.

The BC plan manual has five main phases:

- analysis
- solution design
- implementation
- Testing and
- organization acceptance and maintenance

Disaster recovery planning is a subset of a larger process known as Business continuity planning and should include planning for resumption of applications, data, hardware, communications (such as networking), and other IT infrastructure. Disaster recovery is the process, policies, and procedures related to preparing for recovery or continuation of technology infrastructure critical to an organization after a natural or human-induced disaster.

6.4.14 Forensics

Computer forensics is used to retrieve and analyze data. Computer forensics means responding to an event by gathering and preserving data, analyzing data to reconstruct events, and assessing the state of an event. Network forensics includes recording and analyzing network events to determine the nature and source of information abuse, security attacks, and other such incidents on your network. This is achieved by recording or capturing packets long-term from a key point or points in your infrastructure (the core or firewall) and then data mining for analysis and re-creating content.

6.4.15 Security Architecture Design

A security architecture framework should be established with consideration of processes (enterprise authentication and authorization, access control, confidentiality, integrity, non-repudiation, security management, etc.), operational procedures, technology specifications, people and organizational management, and security program compliance and reporting. A security architecture document should be developed that defines security and privacy principles to meet business objectives. Documentation is required for management controls and metrics specific to asset classification and control, physical security, system access controls, network and computer management, application development and maintenance, business continuity, and compliance. A design and implementation program should also be integrated with the formal system development life cycle to include a business case, requirements definition, design, and implementation plans.

Technology and design methods should be included, as well as the security processes necessary to provide the following services across all technology layers:

1. Authentication
2. Authorization
3. Availability
4. Confidentiality
5. Integrity
6. Accountability
7. Privacy

The creation of a secure architecture provides the engineers, data center operations personnel, and network operations personnel a common blueprint to design, build, and test the security of the applications and systems. Design reviews of new changes can be better assessed against this architecture to assure that they conform to the principles described in the architecture, allowing for more consistent and effective design reviews.

6.4.16 Vulnerability Assessment

Classifies network assets to more efficiently prioritize vulnerability-mitigation programs, such as patching and system upgrading. Measures the effectiveness of risk mitigation by setting goals of reduced vulnerability exposure and faster mitigation. Vulnerability management should be integrated with discovery, patch management, and upgrade management processes to close vulnerabilities before they can be exploited.

6.4.17 Password Assurance Testing

If the SaaS security team or its customers want to periodically test password strength by running password "crackers," they can use cloud computing to decrease crack time and pay only for what they use. Instead of using a distributed password cracker to spread the load across nonproduction machines, you can now put those agents in dedicated compute instances to alleviate mixing sensitive credentials with other workloads.

6.4.18 Logging for Compliance and Security Investigations

When your logs are in the cloud, you can leverage cloud computing to index those logs in real-time and get the benefit of instant search results. A true real-time view can be achieved, since the compute instances can be examined and scaled as needed based on the logging load. Due to concerns about performance degradation and log size, the use of extended logging through an operating system C2 audit trail is rarely enabled. If you are willing to pay for enhanced logging, cloud computing provides the option.

6.4.19 Security Images

Virtualization-based cloud computing provides the ability to create "Test image" VM secure builds and to clone multiple copies. Gold image VMs also provide the ability to keep security up to date and reduce exposure by patching offline. Offline VMs can be patched off-network, providing an easier, more cost-effective, and less production-threatening way to test the impact of security changes.

6.4.20 Data Privacy

A risk assessment and gap analysis of controls and procedures must be conducted. Based on this data, formal privacy processes and initiatives must be defined, managed, and sustained. As with security, privacy controls and protection must an element of the secure architecture design. Depending on the size of the organization and the scale of operations, either an individual or a team should be assigned and given responsibility for maintaining privacy.

A member of the security team who is responsible for privacy or a corporate security compliance team should collaborate with the company legal team to address data privacy issues and concerns. As with security, a privacy steering committee should also be created to help make decisions related to data privacy. Typically, the security compliance team, if one even exists, will not have formalized training on data privacy, which will limit the ability of the organization to address adequately the data privacy issues they currently face and will be continually challenged on in the future. The answer is to hire a consultant in this area, hire a privacy expert, or have one of your existing team members trained properly. This will ensure that your organization is prepared to meet the data privacy demands of its customers and regulators.

For example, customer contractual requirements/agreements for data privacy must be adhered to, accurate inventories of customer data, where it is stored, who can access it, and how it is used must be known, and, though often overlooked, RFI/RFP questions regarding privacy must answered accurately. This requires special skills, training, and experience that do not typically exist within a security team.

As companies move away from a service model under which they do not store customer data to one under which they do store customer data, the data privacy concerns of customers increase exponentially. This new service model pushes companies into the cloud computing space, where many companies do not have sufficient experience in dealing with customer privacy concerns, permanence of customer data throughout its globally distributed systems, cross-border data sharing, and compliance with regulatory or lawful intercept requirements.

6.4.21 Data Governance

This framework should describe who can take what actions with what information, and when, under what circumstances, and using what methods.

The data governance framework should include:

- Data inventory
- Data classification
- Data analysis (business intelligence)
- Data protection
- Data privacy
- Data retention/recovery/discovery
- Data destruction

6.4.22 Data Security

Security will need to move to the data level so that enterprises can be sure their data is protected wherever it goes. For example, with data-level security, the enterprise can specify that this data is not allowed to go outside of the European Union. It can also force encryption of certain types of data, and permit only specified users to access the data. It can provide compliance with the Payment Card Industry Data Security Standard (PCI DSS).

6.4.23 Application Security

This is where the security features and requirements are defined and application security test results are reviewed. Application security processes, secure coding guidelines, training, and testing scripts and tools are typically a collaborative effort between the security and the development teams. Although product engineering will likely focus on the application layer, the security design of the application itself, and the infrastructure layers interacting with the application, the security team should provide the security requirements for the product development engineers to implement.

6.4.24 Virtual Machine Security

In the cloud environment, physical servers are consolidated to multiple virtual machine instances on virtualized servers. Not only can data center security teams replicate typical security controls for the data center at large to secure the virtual machines, they can also advise their customers on how to prepare these.

6.4.25 Identity Access Management (IAM)

Identity and access management is a critical function for every organization, and a fundamental expectation of SaaS customers is that the "principle of least privilege" is granted to their data. The principle of least privilege states that only the minimum access necessary to perform an operation should be granted, and that access should be granted only for the minimum amount of time necessary.

6.4.26 Change Management

The security team can create security guidelines for standards and minor changes, to provide self-service capabilities for these changes and to prioritize the security team's time and resources on more complex and important changes to production.

6.4.27 Physical Security

Since customers lose control over physical assets, security model may need to be reevaluated. The concept of the cloud can be misleading at times, and people forget that everything is somewhere actually tied to a physical location. The massive investment required to build the level of security required for physical data centers is the prime reason that companies don't build their own data centers, and one of several reasons why they are moving to cloud services in the first place. Some samples of controls mechanisms:

- 24/7/365 onsite security.

- Biometric hand geometry readers.

- Security cameras should monitor activity throughout the facility.

- Heat, temperature, air flow, and humidity should all be kept within optimum ranges for the computer equipment.

- Policies, processes, and procedures are critical elements of successful physical security that can protect the equipment and data housed in the hosting center.

6.4.28 Business Continuity and Disaster Recovery

In the SaaS environment, customers rely heavily on 24/7/365 access to their services and any interruption in access can be catastrophic. Using the virtualization software virtual server can be copied, backed up, and moved just like a file (live migration).

Benefits are:

- Quickly reallocating computing resources without any downtime.

- Ability to deliver on service-level agreements and provide high-quality service.

6.4.29 The Business Continuity Plan

A business continuity plan should include planning for non-IT-related aspects such as key personnel, facilities, crisis communication, and reputation protection, and it should refer to the disaster recovery plan for ITrelated infrastructure recovery/continuity. The BC plan manual typically has five main phases: analysis, solution design, implementation, testing, and organization acceptance and maintenance. Disaster recovery planning is a subset of a larger process known as business continuity planning and should include planning for resumption of applications, data, hardware, communications (such as networking), and other IT infrastructure. Disaster recovery is the process, policies, and procedures related to preparing for recovery or continuation of technology infrastructure critical to an organization after a natural or human-induced disaster.

6.5   IS SECURITY-AS-A-SERVICE THE NEW MSSP?

Managed security service providers (MSSPs) were the key providers of security in the cloud that was created by Exodus Communications, Global Crossing, Digital Island, and others that dominated the outsourced hosting environments that were the norm for corporations from the mid-1990s to the early 2000's. The cloud is essentially the next evolution of that environment, and many of the security challenges and management requirements will be similar. An MSSP is essentially an Internet service provider (ISP) that provides an organization with some network security management and monitoring (e.g., security information management, security event management, and security information and event management, which may include virus blocking, spam blocking, intrusion detection, firewalls, and virtual private network [VPN] management and may also handle system changes, modifications, and upgrades. As a result of the .dot.com bust and the subsequent bankruptcies of many of the dominant hosting service providers, some MSSPs pulled the plug on their customers with short or no notice. With the increasing reluctance of organizations to give up complete control over the security of their systems, the MSSP market has dwindled over the last few years. The evolution to cloud computing has changed all this, and managed service providers that have survived are reinventing themselves along with a new concept of MSSP, which is now called Security-as-a-Service (SaaS)—not to be confused with Software-as-a-Service (SaaS), although it can be a component of the latter as well as other cloud services such as PaaS, IaaS, and MaaS.

Unlike MSSP, Security-as-a-Service does not require customers to give up complete control over their security posture. Customer system or security administrators have control over their security policies, system upgrades, device status and history, current and past patch levels, and outstanding support issues, on demand, through a web-based interface. Certain aspects of security are uniquely designed to be optimized for delivery as a web-based service, including:

- Offerings that require constant updating to combat new threats, such as antivirus and anti-spyware software for consumers

- Offerings that require a high level of expertise, often not found inhouse, and that can be conducted remotely. These include ongoing maintenance, scanning, patch management, and troubleshooting of security devices.

- Offerings that manage time- and resource-intensive tasks, which may be cheaper to outsource and offshore, delivering results and findings via a web-based solution. These include tasks such as log management, asset management, and authentication management.

Bit Questions

1. Which of the following are Cloud service providers?
   (a)   Microsoft   (b) Google
   (c)   Amazon   (d) all the above

2. The business impact analysis is usually performed after which other stage in creating the Business Continuity Plan?
   (a)   Sell the concept of the BCP
   (b)   None. It is never performed during the creation of the BCP
   (c)   Lower level departments understand the BCP
   (d)   Identify the scope of the BCP

3. The BCP usually contains several types of measures to reduce or eliminate security threats. Which types of measures are they?
   (a)   Preventive, Detective and Corrective measures
   (b)   Preventive and Corrective measures
   (c)   Corrective measures
   (d)   Preventive and Detective measures

Exercises

1. What are the Cloud Security Challenges?
2. What are the goals of data security in cloud? Explain.
3. What is the need of data security in cloud? Explain.
4. What are the advantages of data security in cloud? Explain.
5. Explain the security concepts in cloud.
6. Discuss about Software-as-a-Service Security

CHAPTER 7

COMMON STANDARDS IN CLOUD COMPUTING

7.1   CHAPTER OVERVIEW

In this chapter, we will discuss the Open Cloud Consortium (OCC) and the Distributed Management Task Force (DMTF) as examples of cloud-related working groups. We will also discuss the most common standards currently used in cloud environments.

7.2   THE OPEN CLOUD CONSORTIUM

The purpose of the Open Cloud Consortium (OCC) is to support the development of standards for cloud computing and to develop a framework for interoperability among various clouds. OCC manages a testing platform and a test-bed for cloud computing called the Open Cloud Test-bed.

The OCC is organized into several different working groups:

- **Working Group on Standards and Interoperability for Clouds**, which focuses on developing standards for interoperating clouds that provide on-demand computing capacity.

- **Working Group on Wide Area Clouds and the Impact of Network Protocols on Clouds**, which focuses on developing technology for wide area clouds, including creation of methodologies and benchmarks to be used for evaluating wide area clouds.

- **Working Group on Information Sharing, Security, and Clouds**, which has a primary focus on standards and standards-based architectures for sharing information between clouds.

- **Open Cloud Test-bed Working Group** that manages and operates the Open Cloud Test-bed. The Open Cloud Test-bed uses Cisco C-Wave and the UIC Teraflow Network for its network connections. C-Wave makes network resources available to researchers to conduct networking and applications research.

7.3   THE DISTRIBUTED MANAGEMENT TASK FORCE

It enables more effective management of millions of IT systems worldwide by bringing the IT industry together to collaborate on the development, validation and promotion of systems management standards. The group spans the industry with 160 member companies and organizations, and more than 4,000 active participants crossing 43 countries. The DMTF board of directors is led by 16 innovative, industry-leading technology companies. They include Advanced Micro Devices (AMD); Broadcom Corporation; CA, Inc.; Dell; EMC; Fujitsu; HP; Hitachi, Ltd.; IBM; Intel Corporation; Microsoft Corporation; Novell; Oracle; Sun Microsystems, Inc.; Symantec Corporation and VMware, Inc.

The DMTF started the Virtualization Management Initiative (VMAN). (See Fig. 7.1). VMAN enables IT managers to deploy preinstalled, preconfigured solutions across heterogeneous computing networks and to manage those applications through their entire life cycle.

DMTF builds on existing standards for server hardware, management tool vendors can easily provide holistic management capabilities to enable IT managers to manage their virtual environments in the context of the underlying hardware.

With the technologies available to IT managers through the VMAN Initiative, companies now have a standardized approach to:

- Deploy virtual computer systems
- Discover and take inventory of virtual computer systems
- Manage the life cycle of virtual computer systems
- Add/change/delete virtual resources
- Monitor virtual systems for health and performance

DMTF Initiatives

An initiative combines a management standard with activities designed to promote the standard in the industry and to help vendors develop interoperable solutions based on that standard.

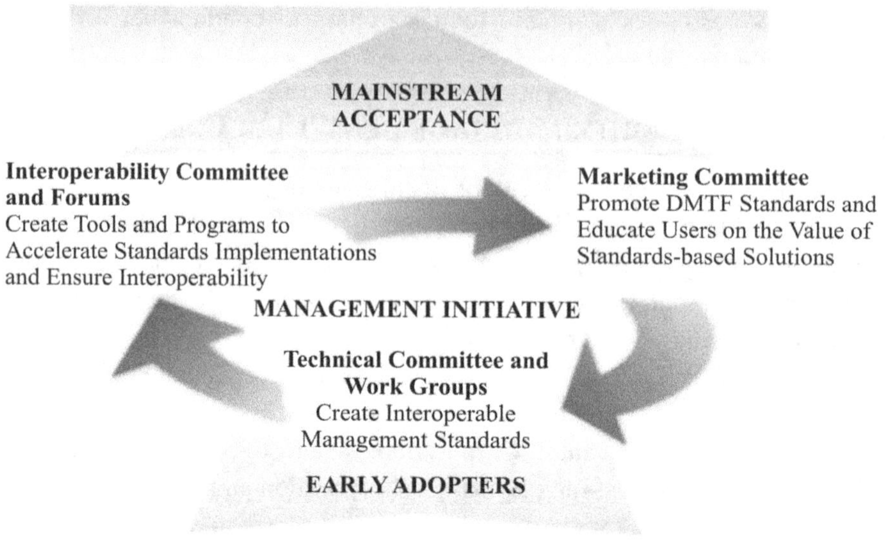

Figure 7.1 DMTF

The goal of each DMTF initiative is to accelerate the adoption of its associated standard into mainstream acceptance.

7.3.1   Open Virtualization Format

Benefits

- Improves your user experience with streamlined installations.
- Offers customers virtualization platform independence and flexibility.
- Creates complex pre-configured multi-tiered services more easily.
- Efficiently delivers enterprise software through portable virtual machines.
- Offers platform-specific enhancements and easier adoption of advances in virtualization through extensibility.

7.4   STANDARDS FOR APPLICATION DEVELOPERS

7.4.1 Browsers (Ajax)

Ajax, or its predecessor AJAX (Asynchronous JavaScript and XML), is a group of interrelated web development techniques used to create interactive web applications or rich Internet applications. Using Ajax, web applications can retrieve data from the server asynchronously, without interfering with the display and behaviour of the browser page currently being displayed to the user.

Using Ajax, a web application can request only the content that needs to be updated. This greatly reduces networking bandwidth usage and page load times.

An Ajax framework helps developers create web applications that use Ajax. The framework helps them to build dynamic web pages on the client side. Data is sent to or from the server using requests, usually written in JavaScript.

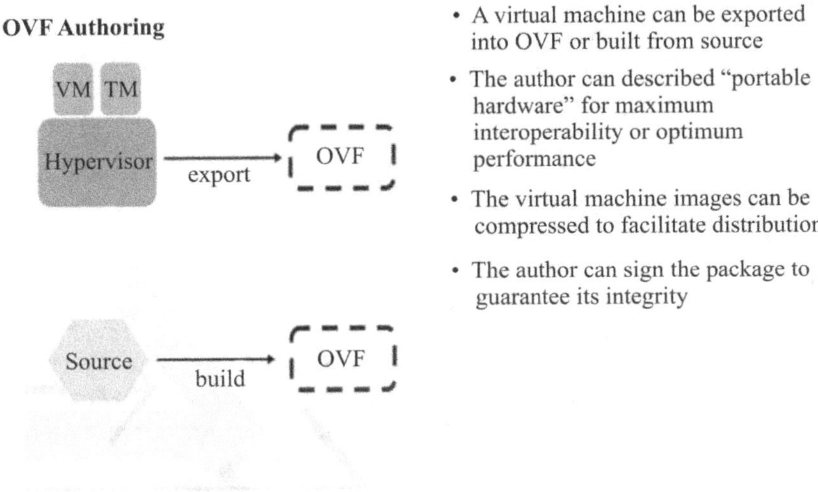

Figure 7.2 OVF Authoring

7.4.2   Data (XML, JSON)

Extensible Markup Language (XML) is a specification for creating custom markup languages. XML is often used to describe structured data and to serialize objects. An XML document has two correctness levels, *well formed* and *valid*. A well-formed document conforms to the XML syntax rules. A valid document is well formed and additionally conforms to semantic rules which can be user-defined or exist in an XML schema. JSON is a lightweight computer data interchange format. It is a text-based, human-readable format for representing simple data structures and associative arrays (called objects). The JSON format is often used for transmitting structured data over a network connection in a process called serialization.

7.4.3   Solution Stacks (LAMP and LAPP)

LAMP: LAMP is a popular open source solution commonly used to run dynamic web sites and servers. The acronym derives from the fact that it includes **Linux**, **Apache**, **MySQL**, and **PHP** (or Perl or Python) and is considered by many to be the platform of choice for development and deployment of high-performance web applications which require a solid and reliable foundation. LAMP combination has become popular because of its open source nature, low cost, and the wide distribution of its components. The combination of these technologies is used primarily to define a web server infrastructure or for creating a programming environment for developing software.

LAPP: The LAPP stack is an open source web platform that can be used to run dynamic web sites and servers. LAPP stands for Linux, Apache, PostgreSql, and PHP(or Pearl or Python). LAPP offers SSL, PHP, Python, and Perl support for Apache2 and PostgreSQL. There is an administration front-end for PostgreSQL as well as web-based administration modules for configuring Apache2 and PHP. PostgreSQL password encryption is enabled by default. The PostgreSQL user is trusted when connecting over local Unix sockets. The LAPP stack a more secure out-of-the-box solution than the LAMP stack.

7.5   STANDARDS FOR MESSAGING

Messaging means different things to different people. A *message* is a unit of information that is moved from one place to another. The term *standard* also is not always clearly defined. Different entities have differing interpretations of what a standard is, and we know there are open international standards, *de facto* standards, and proprietary standards. A true standard is usually characterized by certain traits, such as being managed by an international standards body or an industry consortium, and the standard is created jointly by a community of interested parties. The Internet Engineering Task Force (IETF) is perhaps the most open standards body on the planet, because it is open to everyone. Participants can contribute, and their work is available online for free (See Fig. 7.3).

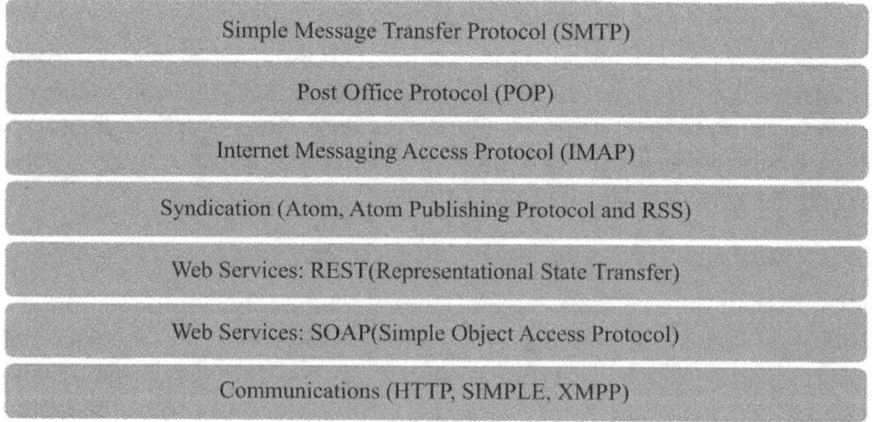

Figure 7.3 Standards Message

7.5.1   Simple Message Transfer Protocol (SMTP)

Simple Message Transfer Protocol is arguably the most important protocol in use today for basic messaging. Before SMTP was created, email messages were sent using File Transfer Protocol (FTP). A sender would compose a message and transmit it to the recipient as if it were a file. While this process worked, it had its shortcomings. The FTP protocol was designed to transmit files, not messages, so it did not provide any means for recipients to identify the sender or for the sender to designate an intended recipient. If a message showed up on an FTP server, it was up to the administrator to open or print it (and sometimes even deliver it) before anyone even knew who it was supposed to be receiving it.

SMTP was designed so that sender and recipient information could be transmitted with the message. SMTP was initially defined in 1973 by IETF RFC 561. It has evolved over the years and has been modified by RFCs 680, 724 and 733. The current RFCs applying to SMTP are RFC 821 and RFC 822. SMTP is a two-way protocol that usually operates using TCP (Transmission Control Protocol) port 25. Though many people don't realize it, SMTP can be used to both send and receive messages. Typically, though, workstations use POP (Post Office Protocol) rather than SMTP to receive messages. SMTP is usually used for either sending a message from a workstation to a mail server or for communications between mail servers.

7.5.2   Post Office Protocol (POP)

SMTP can be used both to send and receive messages, but using SMTP for this purpose is often impractical or impossible because a client must have a constant connection to the host to receive SMTP messages. The Post Office Protocol (POP) was introduced to circumvent this situation. POP is a lightweight protocol whose single purpose is to download messages from a server. This allows a server to store messages until a client connects and requests them. Once the client connects, POP servers begin to download the messages and subsequently delete them from the server (a default setting) in order to make room for more messages. Users respond to a message that was downloaded using SMTP. The POP protocol is defined by RFC1939 and usually functions on TCP port 110.

7.5.3   Internet Messaging Access Protocol (IMAP)

Once mail messages are downloaded with POP, they are automatically deleted from the server when the download process has finished. Thus POP users have to save their messages locally, which can present backup challenges when it is important to store or save messages. Many businesses have compulsory compliance guidelines that require saving messages. It also becomes a problem if users move from computer to computer or use mobile networking, since their messages do not automatically move where they go. To get around these problems, a standard called Internet Messaging Access Protocol was created. IMAP allows messages to be kept on the server but viewed and manipulated (usually via a browser) as though they were stored locally. IMAP is a part of the RFC 2060 specification, and functions over TCP port 143.

7.5.4   Syndication (Atom, Atom Publishing Protocol, and RSS)

Content syndication provides citizens convenient access to new content and headlines from government via RSS (Really Simple Syndication) and other online syndication standards. Governments are providing access to more and more information online. As web sites become more complex and difficult to sift through, new or timely content is often buried. Dynamically presenting "what's new" and the top of the web site is only the first step. Sharing headlines and content through syndication standards such as RSS (the little orange [XML] button, ATOM, and others) essentially allows a government to control a small window of content across web sites that choose to display the government's headlines. Headlines may also be aggregated and displayed through "newsreaders" by citizens through standalone applications or as part of their personal web page.

Portals can automatically aggregate and combine headlines and/or lengthier content from across multiple agency web sites. This allows the value of distributed effort to be shared, which is more sustainable. Press releases may be aggregated automatically from different systems, as long as they all are required to offer an RSS feed with content tagged with similar   metadata. Broader use of government information online, particularly time sensitive democratic information, justifies the effort of production and the accountability of those tasked to make it available.

Benefits

Ability to scan headlines from many sources, all in one place, through a newsreader. Time-saving awareness of new content from government, if the RSS feed or feeds are designed properly. Ability to monitor new content from across the council, as well as display feeds on their own web site. Awareness of new content position councilors as guides to government for citizens. Ability to aggregate new content or headlines from across multiple office locations and agencies. This allows a display of "joined-up" government despite structural realities. Journalists and other locally focused web sites will be among the primary feed users.

Limitations

Dissemination via syndication is a new concept to governments just getting used to the idea of remote online public access to information. Governments need to accept that while they control the content of the feed, the actual display of the headlines and content will vary. Popular RSS feeds can use significant amounts of bandwidth. Details on how often or when a feed is usually updated should be offered to those grabbing the code behind the orange [XML] button, so they "ping" it once a day instead of every hour. Automated syndication requires use of a content management system. Most viable content management systems have integrated RSS functions, but the sophistication, ease of use, and documentation of these tools vary. There are three variants of RSS, as well as the emerging ATOM standard. It is recommended that a site pick the standard most applicable to their content rather than confuse users with different feeds providing the same content.

RSS

RSS is a family of web feed formats used to publish frequently updated works such as blog entries, news headlines, audio, and video—in a standardized format. An RSS document includes full or summarized text, plus metadata such as publishing dates and authorship. Web feeds benefit publishers by letting them syndicate content automatically. They benefit readers who want to subscribe to timely updates from favored web sites or to aggregate feeds from many sites into one place. RSS feeds can be read using software called a reader that can be web-based, desktop-based, a mobile device, or any computerized Internet-connected device. Standardized XML file format allows the information to be published once and viewed by many different programs. The user subscribes to a feed by entering the feed's URI (often referred to informally as a URL, although technically, those two terms are not exactly synonymous) into the reader or by clicking an RSS icon in a browser that initiates the subscription process. The RSS reader checks the user's subscribed feeds regularly for new work, downloads any updates that it finds, and provides a user interface to monitor and read the feeds.

Atom and Atom Publishing Protocol (APP)

The name Atom applies to a pair of related standards. The Atom Syndication Format is an XML language used for web feeds, while the Atom Publishing Protocol (AtomPub or APP) is a simple HTTP-based protocol (HTTP is described later in this chapter) for creating and updating web resources, sometimes known as web feeds. Web feeds allow software programs to check for updates published on a web site. To provide a web feed, a site owner may use specialized software (such as a content management system) that publishes a list (or "feed") of recent articles or content in a standardized, machine-readable format. The feed can then be downloaded by web sites that syndicate content from the feed, or by feed reader programs that allow Internet users to subscribe to feeds and view their content. A feed contains entries, which may be headlines, full-text articles, excerpts, summaries, and/or links to content on a web site, along with various metadata.

The Atom format was developed as an alternative to RSS. Ben Trott, an advocate of the new format that became Atom, believed that RSS had limitations and flaws – such as lack of ongoing innovation and its necessity to remain backward compatible – and that there were advantages to a fresh design. Proponents of the new format formed the IETF Atom Publishing Format and Protocol Workgroup. The Atom syndication format was published as an IETF "proposed standard" in RFC 4287, and the Atom Publishing Protocol was published as RFC 5023.

Web feeds are used by the weblog community to share the latest entries headlines or their full text, and even attached multimedia files. These providers allow other web sites to incorporate the weblog's "syndicated" headline or headline-and-short-summary feeds under various usage agreements. Atom and other web syndication formats are now used for many purposes, including journalism, marketing, "bug" reports, or any other activity involving periodic updates or publications. Atom also provides a standardized way to export an entire blog, or parts of it, for backup or for importing into other blogging systems.

A program known as a feed reader or aggregator can check web pages on behalf of a user and display any updated articles that it finds. It is common to find web feeds on major web sites, as well as on many smaller ones. Some web sites let people choose between RSS or Atom-formatted web feeds; others offer only RSS or only Atom. In particular, many blog and wiki sites offer their web feeds in the Atom format.

Client-side readers and aggregators may be designed as standalone programs or as extensions to existing programs such as web browsers. Browsers are moving toward integrated feed reader functions. Such programs are available for various operating systems. Web-based feed readers and news aggregators require no software installation and make the user's feeds available on any computer with web access. Some aggregators syndicate web feeds into new feeds, e.g., taking all football-related items from several sports feeds and providing a new football feed. There are several search engines which provide search functionality over content published via these web feeds.

Web Services (REST)

REpresentational State Transfer (REST) is a style of software architecture for distributed hypermedia systems such as the World Wide Web. As such, it is not strictly a method for building "web services." The terms "representational state transfer" and "REST" were introduced in 2000 in the doctoral dissertation of Roy Fielding, one of the principal authors of the Hypertext Transfer Protocol (HTTP) specification.

REST refers to a collection of network architecture principles which outline how resources are defined and addressed. The term is often used in a looser sense to describe any simple interface which transmits domain-specific data over HTTP without an additional messaging layer such as SOAP or session tracking via HTTP cookies. These two meanings can conflict as well as overlap. It is possible to design a software system in accordance with Fielding's REST architectural style without using HTTP and without interacting with the World Wide Web. It is also possible to design simple XML+HTTP interfaces which do not conform to REST principles, but instead follow a model of remote procedure call. Systems which follow Fielding's REST principles are often referred to as "RESTful."

Proponents of REST argue that the web's scalability and growth are a direct result of a few key design principles. Application state and functionality are abstracted into resources. Every resource is uniquely addressable using a universal syntax for use in hypermedia links, and all resources share a uniform interface for the transfer of state between client and resource. This transfer state consists of a constrained set of well-defined operations and a constrained set of content types, optionally supporting code on demand. State transfer uses a protocol which is client-server based, stateless and cacheable, and layered. Fielding describes REST's effect on scalability thus:

REST's client-server separation of concerns simplifies component implementation, reduces the complexity of connector semantics, improves the effectiveness of performance tuning, and increases the scalability of pure server components. Layered system constraints allow intermediaries – proxies, gateways, and firewalls – to be introduced at various points in the communication without changing the interfaces between components, thus allowing them to assist in communication translation or improve performance via large-scale, shared caching. REST enables intermediate processing by constraining messages to be self-descriptive: interaction is stateless between requests, standard methods and media types are used to indicate semantics and exchange information, and responses explicitly indicate cacheability.

An important concept in REST is the existence of resources, each of which is referenced with a global identifier (e.g., a URI in HTTP). In order to manipulate these resources, components of the network (user agents and origin servers) communicate via a standardized interface (e.g., HTTP) and exchange representations of these resources (the actual documents conveying the information). For example, a resource which is a circle may accept and return a representation which specifies a center point and radius, formatted in SVG

(Scalable Vector Graphics), but may also accept and return a representation which specifies any three distinct points along the curve as a comma-separated list.

Any number of connectors (clients, servers, caches, tunnels, etc.) can mediate the request, but each does so without "seeing past" its own request (referred to as "layering," another constraint of REST and a common principle in many other parts of information and networking architecture). Thus an application can interact with a resource by knowing two things: the identifier of the resource, and the action required—it does not need to know whether there are caches, proxies, gateways, firewalls, tunnels, or anything else between it and the server actually holding the information. The application does, however, need to understand the format of the information (representation) returned, which is typically an   HTML, XML, or JSON document of some kind, although it may be an image, plain text, or any other content.

REST provides improved response time and reduced server load due to its support for the caching of representations. REST improves server scalability by reducing the need to maintain session state. This means that different servers can be used to handle different requests in a session. REST requires less client-side software to be written than other approaches, because a single browser can access any application and any resource. REST depends less on vendor software and mechanisms which layer additional messaging frameworks on top of HTTP. It provides equivalent functionality when compared to alternative approaches to communication, and it does not require a separate resource discovery mechanism, because of the use of hyperlinks in representations. REST also provides better long-term compatibility because of the capability of document types such as HTML to evolve without breaking backwards or forwards compatibility and the ability of resources to add support for new content types as they are defined without dropping or reducing support for older content types.

One benefit that should be obvious with regard to web-based applications is that a RESTful implementation allows a user to bookmark specific "queries" (or requests) and allows those to be conveyed to others across email, instant messages, or to be injected into wikis, etc. Thus this "representation" of a path or entry point into an application state becomes highly portable. A RESTful web service is a simple web service implemented using HTTP and the principles of REST. Such a web service can be thought of as a collection of resources comprising three aspects:

1. The URI for the web service

2. The MIME type of the data supported by the web service (often JSON, XML, or YAML, but can be anything)

3. The set of operations supported by the web service using HTTP methods, including but not limited to POST, GET, PUT, and DELETE

Members of the collection are addressed by ID using URIs of the form <baseURI>/<ID>.

The ID can be any unique identifier. For example, a RESTFul web service representing a collection of cars for sale might have the URI:

http://example.com/resources/cars

If the service uses the car registration number as the ID, then a particular car might be present in the collection as

http://example.com/resources/cars/yxz123

SOAP

SOAP, originally defined as Simple Object Access Protocol, is a protocol specification for exchanging structured information in the implementation of Web Services in computer networks. It relies on XML as its message format and usually relies on other application-layer protocols, most notably Remote Procedure Call (RPC) and HTTP for message negotiation and transmission. SOAP can form the foundation layer of a web services protocol stack, providing a basic messaging framework on which web services can be built.

As a simple example of how SOAP procedures can be used, a SOAP message can be sent to a web service-enabled web site – for example, a house price database – with the parameters needed for a search. The site returns an XML-formatted document with the resulting data (prices, location, features, etc). Because the data is returned in a standardized machine parseable format, it may be integrated directly into a third-party site.

The SOAP architecture consists of several layers of specifications for message format, message exchange patterns (MEPs), underlying transport protocol bindings, message processing models, and protocol extensibility. SOAP is the successor of XML-RPC. SOAP makes use of an Internet application layer protocol as a transport protocol. Critics have argued that this is an abuse of such protocols, as it is not their intended purpose and therefore not a role they fulfill well. Proponents of SOAP have drawn analogies to successful uses of protocols at various levels for tunneling other protocols.

Both SMTP and HTTP are valid application-layer protocols used as transport for SOAP, but HTTP has gained wider acceptance because it works well with today's Internet infrastructure; specifically, HTTP works well with network firewalls. SOAP may also be used over HTTPS (which is the same protocol as HTTP at the application level, but uses an encrypted transport protocol underneath) with either simple or mutual authentication; this is the advocated WS-I method to provide web service security as stated in the WS-I Basic Profile 1.1. This is a major advantage over other distributed protocols such as GIOP/IIOP or DCOM, which are normally filtered by firewalls. XML was chosen as the standard message format because of its widespread use by major corporations and open source development efforts. Additionally, a wide variety of freely available tools significantly eases the transition to a SOAP-based implementation.

Advantages of using SOAP over HTTP are that SOAP allows for easier communication through proxies and firewalls than previous remote execution technology. SOAP is versatile enough to allow for the use of different transport protocols. The standard stacks use HTTP as a transport protocol, but other protocols are also usable (e.g., SMTP). SOAP is platform-independent, language-independent, and it is simple and extensible.

Because of the verbose XML format, SOAP can be considerably slower than competing middleware technologies such as CORBA (Common Object Request Broker Architecture). This may not be an issue when only small messages are sent. To improve performance for the special case of XML with embedded binary objects, Message Transmission Optimization. Mechanism was introduced. When relying on HTTP as a transport protocol and not using WS-Addressing or an ESB, the roles of the interacting parties are fixed. Only one party (the client) can use the services of the other. Developers must use polling instead of notification in these common cases.

Most uses of HTTP as a transport protocol are made in ignorance of how the operation is accomplished. As a result, there is no way to know whether the method used is appropriate to the operation. The REST architecture has become a web service alternative that makes appropriate use of HTTP's defined methods.

7.5.5   Communications (HTTP, SIMPLE, and XMPP)

HTTP is a request/response communications standard based on a client/server model. A client is the end user, the server is the web site. The client making a HTTP request via a web browser or other tool sends the request to the server. The responding server is called the origin server. HTTP is not constrained to use TCP/IP and its supporting layers, although this is its most popular application on the Internet. SIMPLE, the Session Initiation Protocol for Instant Messaging and Presence Leveraging Extensions, is an instant messaging (IM) and presence protocol suite based on Session Initiation Protocol, and it is managed by the IETF. Like XMPP, SIMPLE is an open standard. Extensible Messaging and Presence Protocol (XMPP) is also an open, XML-based protocol originally aimed at near-real-time, extensible instant messaging and presence information (e.g., buddy lists) but now expanded into the broader realm of message-oriented middleware.

Hypertext Transfer Protocol (HTTP)

HTTP is an application-level protocol for distributed, collaborative, hypermedia information systems. Its use for retrieving linked resources led to the establishment of the World Wide Web. HTTP development was coordinated by the World Wide Web Consortium and the Internet Engineering Task Force, culminating in the publication of a series of Requests for Comments, most notably RFC 2616 (June 1999), which defines HTTP/1.1, the version of HTTP in common use today.

HTTP is a request/response standard between a client and a server. A client is the end-user, the server is the web site. The client making a HTTP request using a web browser, spider, or other end-user tool is referred to as the user agent. The responding server which stores or creates resources such as HTML files and images is called the origin server. In between the user agent and origin server may be several intermediaries, such as proxies, gateways, and tunnels. HTTP is not constrained to using TCP/IP and its supporting layers, although this is its most popular application on the Internet. In fact, HTTP can be implemented on top of any other protocol; all it requires is reliable transport, so any protocol, on the Internet or any other network, which provides reliable transport can be used.

Typically, an HTTP client initiates a request. It establishes a TCP connection to a particular port on a host (port 80 by default). An HTTP server listening on that port waits for the client to send a request message. Upon receiving the request, the server sends back a status line such as "HTTP/1.1 200 OK" and a message of its own, the body of which is perhaps the requested resource, an error message, or some other information. Resources to be accessed by HTTP are identified using Uniform Resource Identifiers (URIs or, more specifically, Uniform Resource Locators, URLs) using the http: or https URI schemes.

SIMPLE

Session Initiation Protocol for Instant Messaging and Presence Leveraging Extensions (SIMPLE) is an instant messaging (IM) and presence protocol suite based on the Session Initiation Protocol (SIP). Like XMPP, SIMPLE is an open standard. SIMPLE makes use of SIP for registering for presence information and receiving notifications when presence-related events occur. It is also used for sending short messages and managing a session of   real-time   messages between two or more participants. Implementations of the SIMPLE-based protocols can be found in SIP soft phones and also hard phones. The SIMPLE presence specifications can be broken up into core protocol methods, presence information, and the handling of privacy, policy and provisioning.

The core protocol methods provide SIP extensions for subscriptions, notifications, and publications. The methods used, **subscribe** and **notify,** are defined in RFC 3265. **Subscribe** allows a user to subscribe to an event on a server. **Notify** is the method used whenever the event arises and the server responds back to the subscriber. Another standard, RFC 3856, defines precisely how to use these methods to establish and maintain presence. Presence documents contain information encoded using XML. These documents are transported in the bodies of SIP messages.7 Privacy, policy, and provisioning information is needed by user agents to determine who may subscribe to presence information. A framework for authorization policies controlling access to application-specific data is defined in RFC 4745 and RFC 5025. SIP defines two modes of instant messaging, the Page mode and the Session mode. Page mode makes use of the SIP method MESSAGE, as defined in RFC 3428. This mode establishes no sessions, while the Session mode based on the Message Session Relay   Protocol (RFC 4975, RFC 4976) defines text-based protocol for exchanging arbitrarily sized content of any time between users.

XMPP

Extensible Messaging and Presence Protocol (XMPP) is an XML-based protocol used for near-real-time, extensible instant messaging and presence information. XMPP remains the core protocol of the Jabber Instant Messaging and Presence technology. Jabber provides a carrier-grade, best-inclass presence and messaging platform. According to a press release following its acquisition by Cisco Systems in November 2008, "Jabber's technology leverages open standards to provide a highly scalable architecture that supports the aggregation of presence information across different devices, users and applications. The technology also enables collaboration across many different presence systems such as Microsoft Office Communications Server, IBM Sametime, AOL AIM, Google and Yahoo!".

Built to be extensible, the XMPP protocol has grown to support features such as voice-over-IP and file transfer signaling. Unlike other instant messaging protocols, XMPP is an open standard. Like email, anyone who has a domain name and an Internet connection can run the Jabber server and chat with others. The Jabber project is open source software, available from Google at http://code.google.com/p/jabber-net.

XMPP-based software is deployed on thousands of servers across the Internet. The Internet Engineering Task Force has formalized XMPP as an approved instant messaging and presence technology under the name XMPP, and the XMPP specifications have been published as RFC 3920 and RFC 3921. Custom functionality can be built on top of XMPP, and common extensions are managed by the XMPP Software Foundation.

XMPP servers can be isolated from the public Jabber network, and robust security (via SASL and TLS) is built into the core XMPP specifications. Because the client uses HTTP, most firewalls allow users to fetch and post messages without hindrance. Thus, if the TCP port used by XMPP is blocked, a server can listen on the normal HTTP port and the traffic should pass without problems. Some web sites allow users to sign in to Jabber via their browser. Furthermore, there are open public servers, such as www.jabber80.com, which listen on standard http (port 80) and https (port 443) ports and allow connections from behind most   firewalls.

7.6   STANDARDS FOR SECURITY

Security standards define the processes, procedures, and practices necessary for implementing a security program. Basic philosophy of security is to have layers of defence, a concept known as *defence in depth. This means having overlapping systems designed to provide* security even if one system fails. No single security system is a solution by itself, so it is far better to secure all systems.

Today, with the advent of managed security services offered by cloud providers, additional security can be provided inside the cloud.

- Security Assertion Markup Language (SAML)
- Open Authentication (OAuth)
- Open ID
- Transport Layer Security/Secure Socket Layer (TLS/SSL)

7.6.1   Security (SAML OAuth, OpenID, SSL/TLS)

Security Assertion Markup Language (SAML)

SAML is an XML-based standard for communicating authentication, authorization, and attribute information among online partners. It allows businesses to securely send assertions between partner organizations regarding the identity and entitlements of a principal. The Organization for the Advancement of Structured Information Standards (OASIS) Security Services Technical Committee is in charge of defining, enhancing, and maintaining the SAML specifications. SAML is built on a number of existing standards, namely, SOAP, HTTP, and XML. SAML relies on HTTP as its communications protocol and specifies the use of SOAP (currently, version 1.1). Most SAML transactions are expressed in a standardized form of XML. SAML assertions and protocols are specified using XML schema.

Both SAML 1.1 and SAML 2.0 use digital signatures (based on the XML Signature standard) for authentication and message integrity. XML encryption is supported in SAML 2.0, though SAML 1.1 does not have encryption capabilities. SAML defines XML-based assertions and protocols, bindings, and profiles. The term SAML Core refers to the general syntax and semantics of SAML assertions as well as the protocol used to request and transmit those assertions from one system entity to another. SAML protocol refers to what is transmitted, not how it is transmitted. A SAML binding determines how SAML requests and responses map to standard messaging protocols. An important (synchronous) binding is the SAML SOAP binding.

SAML standardizes queries for, and responses that contain, user authentication, entitlements, and attribute information in an XML format. This format can then be used to request security information about a principal from a SAML authority. A SAML authority, sometimes called the asserting party, is a platform or application that can relay security information. The relying party (or assertion consumer or requesting party) is a partner site that receives the security information. The exchanged information deals with a subject's authentication status, access authorization, and attribute information. A subject is an entity in a particular domain. A person identified by an email address is a subject, as might be a printer.

SAML assertions are usually transferred from identity providers to service providers. Assertions contain statements that service providers use to make access control decisions. Three types of statements are provided by SAML: authentication statements, attribute statements, and authorization decision statements. SAML assertions contain a packet of security information in this form:

```
<saml:Assertion A...>

    <Authentication>

        ...

    </Authentication>

        <Attribute>

            ...

        </Attribute>

        <Authorization>

            ...

        </Authorization>

</saml:Assertion A>
```

The assertion shown above is interpreted as follows:

Assertion A, issued at time T by issuer I, regarding subject S, provided conditions C are valid.

Authentication statements assert to a service provider that the principal did indeed authenticate with an identity provider at a particular time using a particular method of authentication. Other information about the authenticated principal (called the authentication context) may be disclosed in an authentication statement. An attribute statement asserts that a subject is associated with certain attributes. An attribute is simply a name – value pair. Relying parties use attributes to make access control decisions. An authorization decision statement asserts that a subject is permitted to perform action A on resource R given evidence E. The expressiveness of authorization decision statements in SAML is intentionally limited.

A SAML protocol describes how certain SAML elements (including assertions) are packaged within SAML request and response elements. It provides processing rules that SAML entities must adhere to when using these elements. Generally, a SAML protocol is a simple request–response protocol. The most important type of SAML protocol request is a query. A service provider makes a query directly to an identity provider over a secure back channel. For this reason, query messages are typically bound to SOAP.

Corresponding to the three types of statements, there are three types of SAML queries: the authentication query, the attribute query, and the authorization decision query. Of these, the attribute query is perhaps most important. The result of an attribute query is a SAML response containing an assertion, which itself contains an attribute statement.

Open Authentication (OAuth)

OAuth is an open protocol, initiated by Blaine Cook and Chris Messina, to allow secure API authorization in a simple, standardized method for various types of web applications. Cook and Messina had concluded that there were no open standards for API access delegation. The OAuth discussion group was created in April 2007, for the small group of implementers to write the draft proposal for an open protocol. DeWitt Clinton of Google learned of the OAuth project and expressed interest in supporting the effort. In July 2007 the team drafted an initial specification, and it was released in October of the same year.

OAuth is a method for publishing and interacting with protected data. For developers, OAuth provides users access to their data while protecting account credentials. OAuth allows users to grant access to their information, which is shared by the service provider and consumers without sharing all of their identity. The Core designation is used to stress that this is the baseline, and other extensions and protocols can build on it.

By design, OAuth Core 1.0 does not provide many desired features (e.g., automated discovery of endpoints, language support, support for XML-RPC and SOAP, standard definition of resource access, OpenID integration, signing algorithms, etc.). This intentional lack of feature support is viewed by the authors as a significant benefit. The Core deals with fundamental aspects of the protocol, namely, to establish a mechanism for exchanging a user name and password for a token with defined rights and to provide tools to protect the token. It is important to understand that security and privacy are not guaranteed by the protocol. In fact, OAuth by itself *provides no privacy at all* and depends on other protocols such as SSL to accomplish that. OAuth can be implemented in a secure manner, however. In fact, the specification includes substantial security considerations that must be taken into account when working with sensitive data. With Oauth, sites use tokens coupled with shared secrets to access resources. Secrets, just like passwords, must be protected.

Open ID

Open ID is an open, decentralized standard for user authentication and access control that allows users to log onto many services using the same digital identity. It is a single-sign-on (SSO) method of access control. As such, it replaces the common log-in process (i.e., a log-in name and a password) by allowing users to log in once and gain access to resources across participating systems.

The original OpenID authentication protocol was developed in May 2005 by Brad Fitzpatrick, creator of the popular community web site Live Journal. In late June 2005, discussions began between OpenID developers and other developers from an enterprise software company named NetMesh. These discussions led to further collaboration on interoperability between OpenID and NetMesh's similar Light-Weight Identity (LID) protocol. The direct result of the collaboration was the Yadis discovery protocol, which was announced on October 24, 2005.

The Yadis specification provides a general-purpose identifier for a person and any other   entity, which can be used with a variety of services. It provides a syntax for a resource description document identifying services available using that identifier and an interpretation of the elements of that document. Yadis discovery protocol is used for obtaining a resource description document, given that identifier. Together these enable coexistence and interoperability of a rich variety of services using a single identifier. The identifier uses a standard syntax and a well-established namespace and requires no additional namespace administration infrastructure.

An OpenID is in the form of a unique URL and is authenticated by the entity hosting the OpenID URL. The OpenID protocol does not rely on a central authority to authenticate a user's identity. Neither the OpenID protocol nor any web sites requiring identification can mandate that a specific type of authentication be used; nonstandard forms of authentication such as smart cards, biometrics, or ordinary passwords are allowed. A typical scenario for using OpenID might be something like this: A user visits a web site that displays an OpenID log-in form somewhere on the page. Unlike a typical log-in form, which has fields for user name and password, the OpenID log-in form has only one field for the OpenID identifier (which is an OpenID URL). This form is connected to an implementation of an OpenID client library. A user will have previously registered an OpenID identifier with an OpenID identity provider. The user types this OpenID identifier into the OpenID log-in form.

The relying party then requests the web page located at that URL and reads an HTML link tag to discover the identity provider service URL. With OpenID 2.0, the client discovers the identity provider service URL by requesting the XRDS document (also called the Yadis document) with the content type **application/xrds+xml,** which may be available at the target URL but is always available for a target XRI. There are two modes by which the relying party can communicate with the identity provider: **checkid_immediate** and **checkid_setup.**

In **checkid_immediate,** the relying party requests that the provider not interact with the user. All communication is relayed through the user's browser without explicitly notifying the user. In **checkid_setup,** the user communicates with the provider server directly using the same web browser as is used to access the relying party site. The second option is more popular on the web.

To start a session, the relying party and the identity provider establish a shared secret referenced by an associate handle which the relying party then stores. Using **checked setup,** the relying party redirects the user's web browser to the identity provider so that the user can authenticate with the provider. The method of authentication varies, but typically, an OpenID identity provider prompts the user for a password, then asks whether the user trusts the relying party web site to receive his or her credentials and identity details. If the user declines the identity provider's request to trust the relying party web site, the browser is redirected to the relying party with a message indicating that authentication was rejected. The site in turn refuses to authenticate the user. If the user accepts the identity provider's request to trust the relying party web site, the browser is redirected to the designated return page on the relying party web site along with the user's credentials. That relying party must then confirm that the credentials really came from the identity provider. If they had previously established a shared secret, the relying party can validate the shared secret received with the credentials against the one previously stored. In this case, the relying party is considered to be stateful, because it stores the shared secret between sessions (a process sometimes referred to as persistence). In comparison, a stateless relying party must make background requests using the **check authentication** method to be sure that the data came from the identity provider.

After the OpenID identifier has been verified, OpenID authentication is considered successful and the user is considered logged in to the relying party web site. The web site typically then stores the OpenID identifier in the user's session. OpenID does not provide its own authentication methods, but if an identity provider uses strong authentication, OpenID can be used for secure transactions.

SSL/TLS

Transport Layer Security (TLS) and its predecessor, Secure Sockets Layer (SSL), are cryptographically secure protocols designed to provide security and data integrity for communications over TCP/IP. TLS and SSL encrypt the segments of network connections at the transport layer. Several versions of the protocols are in general use in web browsers, email, instant messaging, and voice-over-IP. TLS is an IETF standard protocol which was last updated in RFC 5246.

The TLS protocol allows client/server applications to communicate across a network in a way specifically designed to prevent eavesdropping, tampering, and message forgery. TLS provides endpoint authentication and data confidentiality by using cryptography. TLS authentication is oneway – the server is authenticated, because the client already knows the server's identity. In this case, the client remains unauthenticated. At the browser level, this means that the browser has validated the server's certificate – more specifically, it has checked the digital signatures of the server certificate's issuing chain of Certification Authorities (CAs).

Validation does not identify the server to the end user. For true identification, the end user must verify the identification information contained in the server's certificate (and, indeed, its whole issuing CA chain). This is the only way for the end user to know the "identity" of the server, and this is the only way identity can be securely established, verifying that the URL, name, or address that is being used is specified in the server's certificate. Malicious web sites cannot use the valid certificate of another web site because they have no means to encrypt the transmission in a way that it can be decrypted with the valid certificate. Since only a trusted CA can embed a URL in the certificate, this ensures that checking the apparent URL with the URL specified in the certificate is an acceptable way of identifying the site.

TLS also supports a more secure bilateral connection mode where by both ends of the connection can be assured that they are communicating with whom they believe they are connected. This is known as mutual (assured) authentication. Mutual authentication requires the TLS client side to also maintain a certificate. TLS involves three basic phases:

1. Peer negotiation for algorithm support

2. Key exchange and authentication

3. Symmetric cipher encryption and message authentication

During the first phase, the client and server negotiate cipher suites, which determine which ciphers are used; makes a decision on the key exchange and authentication algorithms to be used; and determines the message authentication codes. The key exchange and authentication algorithms are typically public key algorithms. The message authentication codes are made up from cryptographic hash functions. Once these decisions are made, data transfer may begin.

Bit Questions

1. --------------manages a testing platform and a test-bed for cloud computing called the Open Cloud Test-bed.

2. DMTF stands for----------------.

3. The benefits of Open Virtualization Format are -------------------.

4. AJAX stands for----------------.

5. ------------- is a lightweight computer data interchange format.

6. The ----------format is often used for transmitting structured data over a network connection in a process called---------------------.

7. LAMP stands for----------------.

8. LAPP stands for----------------.

9. ----------- is a request/response standard between a client and a server.

10. ----------- is an XML-based standard for communicating authentication, authorization, and attribute information among online partners.

11. -----------is a protocol specification for exchanging structured information in the implementation of Web Services in computer networks.

12. -----------helps enable systems management interoperability between IT products from different manufacturers or companies.

13. Open Virtualization Format key feature is virtual machine packaging ---------------.

14. OAuth is an-------------------   [   ]

    (a)   Open & authorization   (b)   Open & authentication

    (c)   Open & Access   (d)   None

15.   In LAMP, L stands for ------------------   [   ]

    (a)   Language   (b)   Limit

    (c)   Linux   (d)   None

16.   SAML stands   [   ]

    (a)   Security Assertion Markup Language

    (b)   Simple Assertion Markup Language

    (c)   Single Access Markup Language

    (d)   Sample Assertion Markup Language

17.   ----------------- is a single-sign-on (SSO) method of access control. [   ]

    (a)   Open ID   (b)   SAML

    (c)   O Auth   (d)   SSL/TLS

18.   --------- is a specification for creating custom markup language. [   ]

    (a)   XML   (b)   HTML

    (c)   DHTML   (d)   None

Exercises

1.   Describe Open Cloud Consortium (OCC).

2.   Discuss about Distributed Management Task Force.

3.   Explain the different Standards for Messaging.

4.   What are various Standards for Security? Explain.

CHAPTER 8

END USER ACCESS TO CLOUD COMPUTING

8.1 INTRODUCTION

Rishi Chandra, a Product Manager of Google Enterprise, cited consumer-driven innovation, the rise of power collaborators, changing economics, and a lowering of barriers to entry as the chief reasons why the cloud model is being so widely adopted.

Innovation behind the success of cloud services ultimately depends on the acceptance of the offering by the user community.

Acceptance of an offering by users changes the economics considerably.

As more users embrace such innovation, economies of scale for a product allow implementers to lower the costs, removing a barrier to entry and enabling even more widespread adoption of the innovation.

Some of the most popular Software-as-a-Service (SaaS) offerings for consumers are:

- Youtube
- Zimbra
- Facebook
- Zoho

8.2 YOUTUBE

YouTube is the leader in online video, and a premier destination to watch and share original videos worldwide across the Internet through web sites, mobile devices, blogs, and email. YouTube allows people to easily upload and share video clips on the YouTube web site.

On YouTube, people can view first-hand accounts of current events, find videos about their interests, and discover the quirky and unusual – all from videos shared by other subscribers. Founded in February 2005, YouTube received funding from Sequoia Capital and was officially launched in December 2005.

Chad Hurley and Steve Chen were the first members of the YouTube management team and currently serve as chief executive officer and chief technology officer, respectively. Within a year of its launch, in November 2006, YouTube was purchased by Google in one of the most talked-about acquisitions to date. YouTube has struck partnership deals with content providers such as CBS, the BBC, Universal Music Group, Sony Music Group, Warner Music Group, the NBA, and many more.

8.3   YOUTUBE: API OVERVIEW

The YouTube APIs and tools enable site developers to integrate YouTube's video content and functionality into their web site, software applications, or devices.

8.3.1   Widgets

Widgets are simple page elements that developers can embed in a web site to give it YouTube functionality. Widgets are JavaScript components that developers can place in a web page to enhance it with YouTube-based content

The Video Bar: The Video Bar is a simple way to integrate a strip of video thumbnails into your site. The Video Bar is implemented using the Google AJAX Search API.

Video Search Control: The Video Search Control also uses the Google AJAX Search API. It provides the ability to search through massive amounts of YouTube content.

8.3.2   YouTube: Player API

The Player APIs let us control the YouTube player using JavaScript or ActionScript. There is a basic embedded player (which is most often used), and there is also a "chromeless" player that lets you create your own player controls.

Embedded Player: The embedded player is the simplest way to place YouTube videos on a webpage. To customize the behaviour and color of the player, developers can use well-documented embedded player parameters. The code needed to display the embedded player and preconfigured parameters can be quickly generated using a wizard. This makes it possible to find a video by leveraging the Data API and subsequently displaying it using the embedded player.

Chromeless Player: Interface elements and controls (such as toolbars and buttons) placed around content are sometimes referred to as "chrome," so a chromeless player is, by definition, a YouTube video player without such controls. This makes it easy to customize a player used within a Flash or HTML environment. The chromeless player exposes the same JavaScript and ActionScript APIs as the embedded player.

8.3.3   YouTube: Data API

The YouTube Data API lets you incorporate YouTube functionality into your own application or web site. You can perform searches, upload videos, create playlists, and more.

A program can also authenticate as a user to upload videos, modify user playlists, and more. The Data API gives you programmatic access to the video and user information stored on YouTube. To make working with the API easier, there are a number of client libraries that abstract the API into a language-specific object model. These client libraries are open source and can be used and modified under Apache License 2.0. There are Developer's Guides for Java, .NET, PHP, and Python as well as sample code.

8.4   ZIMBRA

It is a messaging server with an innovative browser based email and calendar application. Alternative to Microsoft Outlook email.

Zimbra Goal

- To provide a better messaging experience for the administrators and end users.
- To become the leader in next generation messaging and collaboration.

Special Features

- E-mail, address book, calendars, contacts, documents.
- Yahoo Maps
- Phone & Skype
- RSS Feeds(Really Simple Syndication (RSS) is an XML-based format for content distribution)

Google Maps

Zimbra automatically recognizes patterns that conform to addresses then makes a web services call to the Yahoo Maps. The result is a map that can be displayed as a popup (See Fig. 8.1).

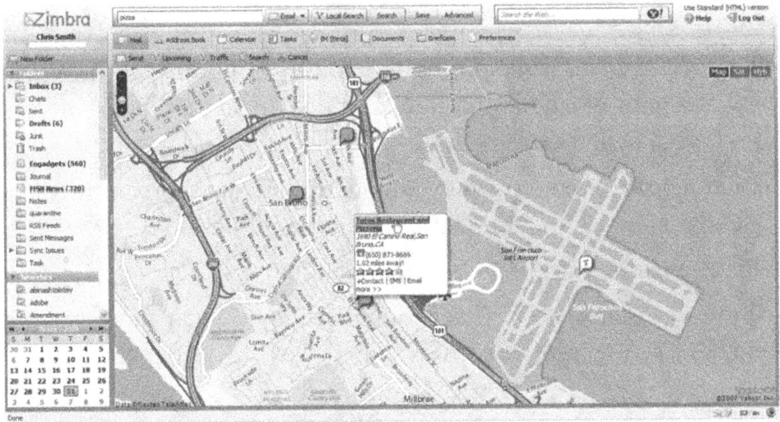

Figure 8.1 Google Map

Phone & Skype

You can program Zimbra to communicate with third party info systems. Recognizes your proprietary data such as shipping number, invoices, and purchase orders. To call the sender directly just clicks on the phone number in your e-mail. Zimbra uses the installed Skype application to initiate a domestic or international call.

RSS Feeds

Allows you to subscribe to RSS feeds and sends them to your inbox as e-mail type documents. Because they are e-mails, sharing information with friends or colleagues is easy! A new e-mail is sent each time the weblog/feed is updated. The Fig.8.2 shows the creation of a folder/RSS subscription.

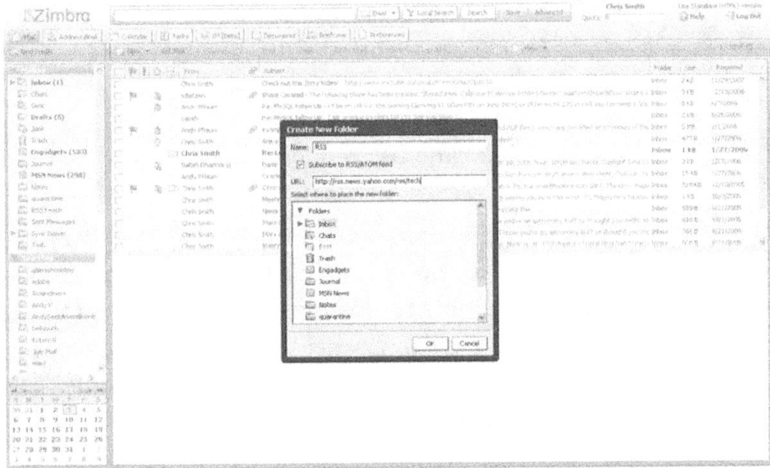

Figure 8.2 Creation of a folder/RSS subscription

Calendar & Inbox

- Zimbra connects calendar with email. You do not have to switch between your calendar and inbox. You can "date hover" in your e-mail to see your schedule.

- Zimbra will show you the day, date and any appointments as your calendar along with their status as shown in Fig.8.3.

- Share schedule information with all colleagues.

- Allows administrators to schedule meetings when there are a minimal number of scheduling conflicts.

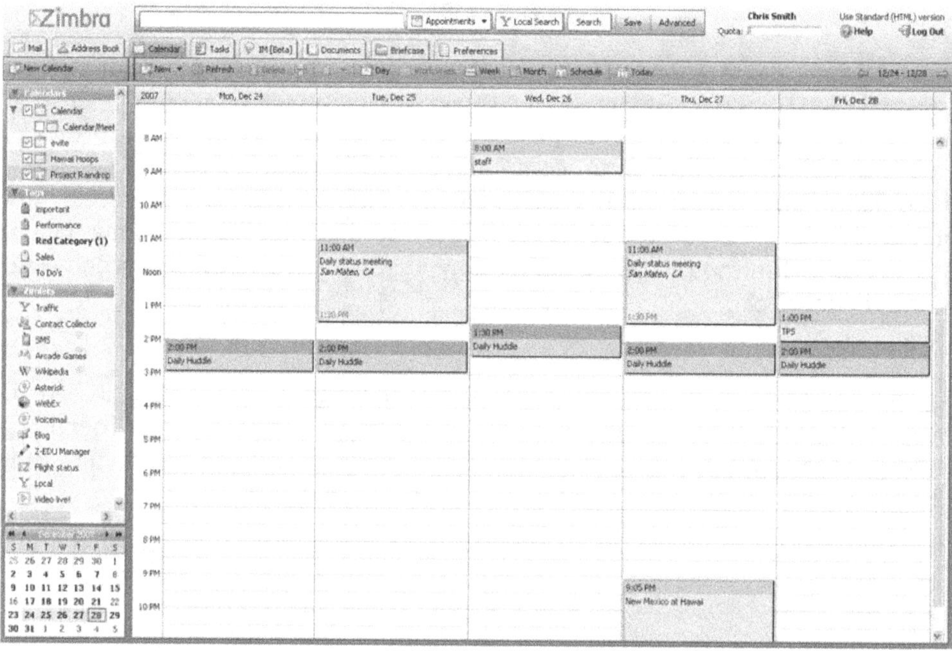

Figure 8.3 Zimbra *Calendar & Inbox*

ZIMBRA FOR EDUCATION

Rich, interactive web interface for complete functionality from campus, home, or any other PC location. Collaborative document authoring for efficient work on group projects and assignments. Comprehensive and flexible sharing model, enabling sharing of address books, calendars, documents, or other content by class list, study group, research team, faculty department, etc.

Figure 8.4 Zimbra for Education

ZIMBRA IN EDUCATION

Mykel Bates & Shawn Owens stand beside their newly configured Zimbra box.

- At the end of the 06-07 school year, the Mountain Pine EAST lab was searching for a E-mail server due to the restrictions of the Mountain School District Network. Eighth grade student administrator Shawn Owens decided to install Zimbra and attempt to configure the open source solution for the computer lab. The year ended with Zimbra that was running but configured improperly. In the 07-08 school year, eleventh grade student Mykel Bates decided to assist Shawn due to his lack of experience.

- After joining the Zimbra online community, the two students worked with professionals in the field and successfully configured the lab's new Zimbra network. Educators everywhere are encouraged to have students engage in this type of activity. The Zimbra community is more than helpful, and this project motivates students to engage in other high level Internet Technology projects.

Strengths and Advantages

- Allows for more rapid and efficient communication amongst teachers, administrators, and parents (Skype, Yahoo Maps, POs).

- Allows easy sharing of RSS feed/blog information.

- Makes administration and integration less time-consuming through calendar & scheduling applications.

- Encourages collaboration and communication.

8.5   FACEBOOK

What is Facebook?

- Facebook® is a "social networking website"

- Facebook® is a free service that allows you to create an online page to connect with friends, family, or make new friends with anyone anywhere.

- On your Facebook® page you can share pictures, personal information, messages, videos, join groups and add applications.

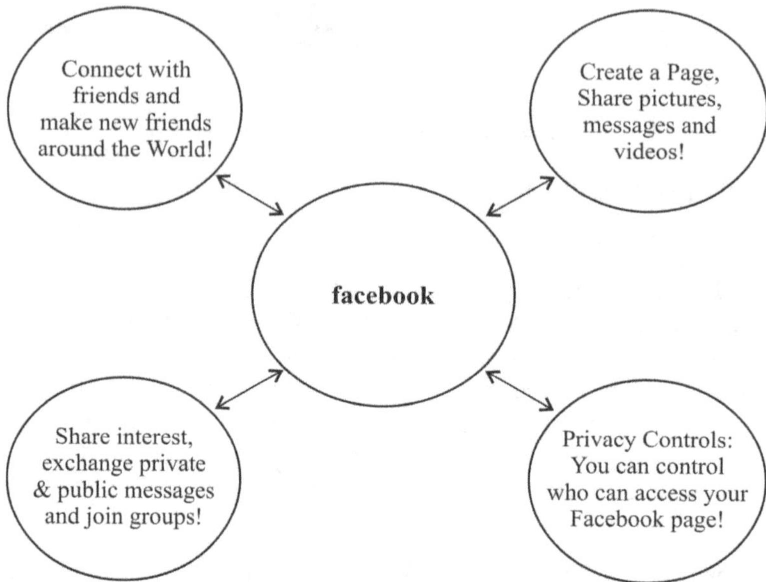

Figure 8.5 FaceBook Example

Figure 8.6 Facebook Founder

History

- Facebook® was founded in 2004 by Harvard student Mark E. Zuckerberg (Fig. 8.6) with help from his roommates Dustin Moskovitz and Chris Hughes.

- Facebook[®] was originally for Harvard students then expanded to other colleges then to anyone over the age of 18, and now currently to anyone 13 years of age or older.

Company Overview

"Facebook's mission is to give people the power to share and make the world more open and connected."Facebook® is a social networking website. You can access Facebook® by login into www.facebook.com and this is what you will see Fig.8.7.

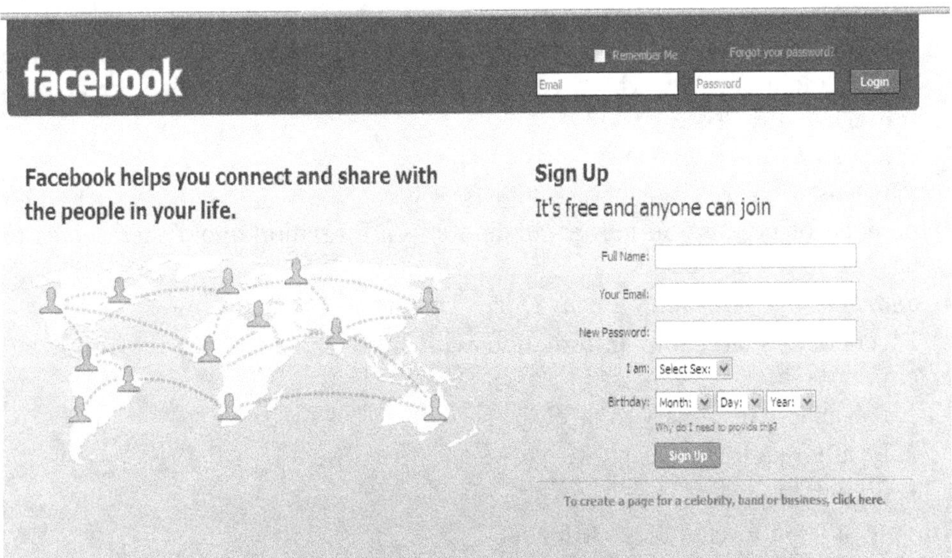

Figure 8.7 Facebook Login

What is Social Networking?

Social Networking is defined as:

- A phenomena defined by linking people to each other in some way - by topicguru.com

- A social network service focuses on building online communities of people who share interests and/or activities, or who are interested in exploring the interests and activities of others

--by wikipedia.com

- This is where people develop networks of friends and associates. It forges and creates links between different people. A social network can form a key element of collaborating and networking

--by edublog.org

Privacy Policy

Major points available on facebook.com:

1. *You should have control over your personal information.*

   Facebook® helps you share information with your friends and people around you. You choose what information you put in your profile, including contact and personal information, pictures, interests and groups you join. And you control the users with whom you share that information through the privacy settings on the Privacy page.

2. *Children between 13-18*

   Facebook® recommends that minors 13 years of age or older ask their parents for permission before sending any information about themselves to anyone over the Internet.

3. *Sharing Your Information with Third Parties*

   Facebook® share your information with third parties under the following circumstances:

   1. reasonably necessary to offer the service,

   2. legally required or,

   3. permitted by you.

Staying safe on Facebook®/ Internet

Available on www.facebook.com/safety/ :

Some important safety tips when using Facebook®:

- Keep the amount of private information you post to a minimum.

- Never post information like your address, birthday, telephone number, class schedule, or anything else that you would not want a stranger to know.

- Keep your password a secret

- Make sure to adjust your privacy setting so only people you want to review you page can

- Be cautious about posting and sharing personal information, especially information that could be used to identify you or locate you offline, such as your address or telephone number

- Block and report anyone that sends you unwanted or inappropriate communications

A Guide to Staying Safe on Facebook®/ Internet:

Major points available on www.facebook.com/safety/

- Facebook® strongly urges parents to talk to their children about the dangers they may encounter online, and to make sure their children are using Facebook® in a safe manner. Children must know that they should report any inappropriate or offensive Facebook® content to their parents and to Facebook® using the tools made available through the site.

- More information regarding Internet safety can be found on the following sites:

  - ✓ OnguardOnline.gov
  - ✓ WiredSafety.org
  - ✓ Commonsense.com
  - ✓ Ncmec.org
  - ✓ TRUSTe.org
  - ✓ ConnectSafely.org
  - ✓ NetSmartz.org
  - ✓ WebWiseKids.org

Advantages and Disadvantages of Facebook®

Advantages:

- It's a social network- It's a great way to keep in touch with friends and also make new friends. You can meet people with your same interest or hobbies, and even connect with people in your same field of study or job.

- Facebook® allows you to share information and photos, you can blog about a topic of interest, and you can also connect to other applications like, Twitter or Flickr.

- Facebook® allows people to connect, to learn from each other, to discuss issues, viewpoints and share advice. You can also join groups having similar likes and dislikes.

Disadvantages:

- Sharing too much private information could become a problem so share only what you are comfortable with sharing. Through your privacy settings you can control what you share.

Discussion

Are there anymore advantages and disadvantages you can think of?

Fun Facts

- Facebook® has over 200 million users
- Over 70% of Facebook® users are outside the United States
- The average person has 120 friends on Facebook®
- More than 3.5 billion minutes are spent on Facebook® each day
- The fastest growing demographic is those 35 years old and older
- Slogan "Facebook® helps you connect and share with the people in your life."

8.5.1 Facebook Development

- Facebook provides anyone the ability to create Facebook applications.
- A user can get a basic application up and running in minutes.
- To create a Facebook application, you should be well versed in PHP or some other coding language such as Ruby on Rails, JavaScript, or Python. It is preferable to know one that already has a client library for the Facebook API.
- You will need to have a basic understanding of the Internet, SSH, MySQL, and Unix.

8.6 ZOHO

- Zoho is an office productivity suite from AdventNet, Inc., which was founded in 1996. The Zoho product is supported by over 120 developers.
- To date, Zoho has launched 15 different applications, and more are in the works.
- Zoho Mail provides ample storage space. You can store and search through every email you have ever sent or received, and it offers offline support so you can take your mail with you.
- You can read and compose emails without an active Internet connection and send them out once you are connected.
- Zoho Mail supports both traditional folders as well as labels.
- A label is a type of folder that you can customize by both name and color.
- Zoho Mail offers advanced, self-learning algorithms that keep unwanted spam out of your inbox and deliver only legitimate emails.
- Using Zoho, you can have a personalized email address or create one using the zoho.com domain.
- Also, there is support for mobile users.

- Zoho Mail can be read from an iPhone, and support for other mobile phones is expected this year.

- Integrated instant messaging (IM) is available, so you can send instant messages from within Zoho Mail and, best of all, you don't need to download a separate client.

8.6.1 Zoho CloudSQL

CloudSQL is a technology that allows developers to interact with business data stored across Zoho Services using the familiar SQL language. Unlike other methods for accessing data in the cloud, CloudSQL encourages developers to leverage the years of experience they have with the SQL language. CloudSQL allows businesses to connect and integrate the data and applications they have in Zoho with the data and applications they have in-house, or even with other SaaS services. This leads to faster deployments and easier integration projects. CloudSQL is offered as an extension to the existing Zoho web API. It is meant to be used by developers, not end users. CloudSQL supports multiple database dialects (e.g., ANSI, Oracle,Microsoft SQL Server, IBM DB2, MySQL, PostgreSQL, and Informix). The main purpose of the SQL Interpreter component is to translate SQL statements that are executed by a third-party application into a neutral dialect that can be understood by any of the individual Zoho services. The federation layer understands and handles service-specific query delegation and result aggregation. The federation layer enables a query to span across multiple Zoho services to fetch data in an aggregated manner, thus virtualizing different Zoho services so they appear as a single service. Each of the specific Zoho services (i.e., Zoho CRM, Zoho Creator,Zoho Reports) comprises the last layer of the CloudSQL architecture. They collect, store, and mine business data consumed by Zoho users and developers.The services execute the query against their data store and pass the results back to the CloudSQL middleware. The services take care of authorizing each query to verify whether the user who is executing the query has permission to access or manipulate the data on which the query is executed.

8.6.2 DimDim Collaboration

Dimdim invested more than 15 person-years of engineering development into making a product to support complex web meetings. This free service lets anyone communicate using rich media in real time. Unlike competing web conference products, Dimdim does not require users to install software on their computers in order to attend a web meeting. Users can start or join meetings using only a few mouse clicks. Dimdim is available as open source software, and it already integrates with CRM and LMS software so it can be extended easily. It is extremely flexible, available in hosted and on-site configurations, and easily customizable. Dimdim Open Source Community Edition v4.5, code named "Liberty", is meant for developers and highly technical enthusiasts, and for use in noncritical environments. It has nearly all of the features touted by the commercial version of Dimdim (Enterprise) and is based on open source streaming and media components.

Dimdim Enterprise is based on commercial streaming and media components (Adobe Flash Server) and runs on top of their SynchroLive Communication Platform. The open source community supports the Open Source Community Edition. Dimdim has a simple user interface that is easy for presenters and attendees to learn. Meeting hosts and attendees do not have to install anything to broadcast audio or video, because all that is needed is a very tiny plug-in (which is required only if you want to share your desktop.) The free version is not a limited-feature trial product.

Dimdim Free boasts a powerful feature set that allows anyone to host meetings with up to 20 people simultaneously using diversified platforms such as Mac, Windows, and Linux. Online support for Dimdim includes a complete collection of tools designed specifically to improve the Dimdim experience. First, you can use Forums, where you can join the discussion group relevant to your topic and learn from others in the Dimdim community.

Dimdim employees also use the forums to gain better understanding of customer issues. There is an online knowledgebase that is connected to the support database. It is constantly updated and is a great place to get self-help.

Dimdim uses an issue tracker and keeps it updated so you can check the status of an issue or view issues for all users. Tools are available to help you check your system, bandwidth, and even test your webcam before you conduct meetings. You can also download any plug-ins if necessary.

Other support resources such as product and API documentation, videos, Dimdim support policies, supported platforms, and open source support links can also be found on the support site.

Bit Questions

1. -------------- is a messaging server with an innovative browser based email and calendar application.

2. --------------- is a social networking website.

3. The OASIS set of --------------- standards addresses message-level security concerns.

4. The Video Bar for YouTube is implemented using the ---------------- Search API.

5. ----------Services provides communities for team collaboration and makes it easy for users to work together on documents, tasks, events, and other information.

6. Who is founder of the social networking site Facebook   [   ]

    (a) Chris Hughes   (b) Dustin Moskovitz

    (b) Mark Zuckerberg   (d) All of the above

Exercises

1. Explain in detail about the following:

    (a) Youtube   (b) Zimbra

    (c) Facebook   (d) Zoho

CLOUD ARCHITECTURE DEFINING THE CLOUDS FOR THE ENTERPRISE

9.1 CLOUD COMPUTING COMPONENTS

Cloud computing has the following components:

1. Storage-as-a-service

2. Database-as-a-service

3. Information-as-a-service

4. Process-as-a-service

5. Application-as-a-service

6. Platform-as-a-service

7. Integration-as-a-service

8. Security-as-a-service

9. Management/governance-as-a-service

10. Testing-as-a-service

11. Infrastructure-as-a-service

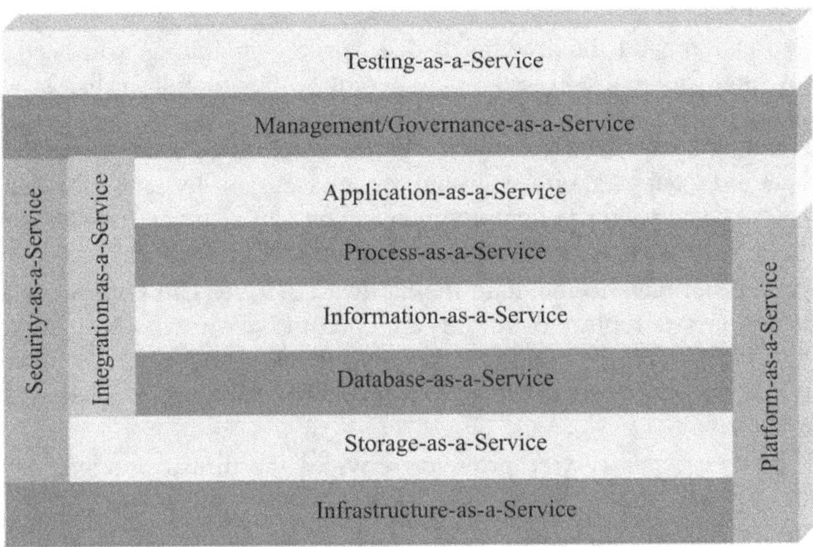

Figure 9.1 Components or categories of cloud computing

9.1.1   Storage-as-a-Service

Storage-as-a-service is the ability to leverage storage that physically exists remotely but is logically a local storage resource to any application that requires storage (see Figure 9.2). This is the most primitive component of cloud computing and is leveraged by most of the other cloud computing components.

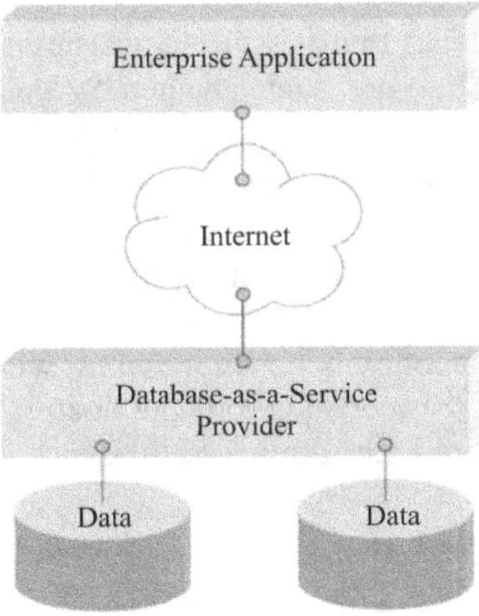

Figure 9.2 Storage-as-a-service allows you to store information on a remote disk drive as if it were local

Core benefits

1. You can expand the amount of disk space available as you need it and pay only for what you use. You can reduce the amount of disk space and thereby cost, as the need declines. This makes storage-as-a-service solutions cost effective only for larger volumes of data, typically more than 500 gigabytes, either through direct access or by using the disk as if it were local to your client computer. You can also use the storage-as-a-service provider as a redundant backup for critical files.

2. You do not have to maintain the hardware. Drives can go down and you do not have to replace them; it is all a part of the service. When compared with an on-premise solution where you have to physically repair the drive, storage-as-a-service removes you from having to deal with that issue.

3. The storage-as-a-service provider provides the disaster recovery system for you, and getting back deleted files or entire directories is part of the service. The provider backs up and restores the file system as you require. You do not have to pay someone to handle that task within the data center, and local staff will not have the responsibility of maintaining the storage systems properly.

Drawbacks to storage-as-a-service

First, you are dependent on the Internet as the mechanism to connect to your storage-as-a-service provider, and if the network goes down, you lose that connection. If a mission-critical need is compromised by a rare and temporary loss of access to your storage, then perhaps storage-as-a-service is not something that makes sense. In many instances, those who leverage storage-as-a-service are surprised to find that they cannot access their shared disk space when not connected to the Internet, such as when on a plane.

Second, performance can be an issue. When compared to on-premise storage, where the disks are physically located near the applications that leverage them, storage-as-a-service does not provide the same performance. Thus, if performance is a critical success factor, storage-as-a-service may not be the approach you want to leverage. Performance is usually about half the speed on a typical Internet connection when compared with a local network. Of course, you can use faster connections, but the cost of implementing a higher speed network connection quickly diminishes the cost savings of storage-as-a-service.

Finally, the cost of the storage-as-a-service provider can be prohibitive when compared with an on-premise solution. While SOA using cloud computing is cost effective in some instances, in many instances it is not. The cost effectiveness of cloud computing is enterprise and domain dependent. For instance, a shared disk in a storage-as-a-service solution would be of high value for a virtual business with a distributed employee base. It would save on hardware and maintenance and would provide easy sharing of disk space as well. However, if the employees or applications are in the same building, the benefits of storage-as-a-service versus on-premise storage solutions are not as compelling.

9.1.2 Database-as-a-Service

Database-as-a-service provides the ability to leverage the services of a remotely hosted database, sharing it with other users and having it logically function as if the database were local. You can self-provision a database, create the tables, load the data, and access the data using the interface provided, all on demand and via cloud computing (see Figure 9.3).

Like storage-as-a-service, database-as-a-service provides access to a resource that you neither own nor host and thus saves you the hardware, software, and maintenance costs. With the self-provisioning capabilities, you can think about a new database at 8:00 AM and have it running by noon, without buying hardware or software and without even leaving your office. This makes it incredibly easy to provision a database as needed.

Database services include everything that you can do with a local database, such as setting up the tables and the relations among them, adding data, extracting data, and deleting data. Database-as-a-service providers provide not only basic database functions but also brand-specific services such as Oracle, Sybase, and Microsoft, so you can leverage proprietary features if you need them.

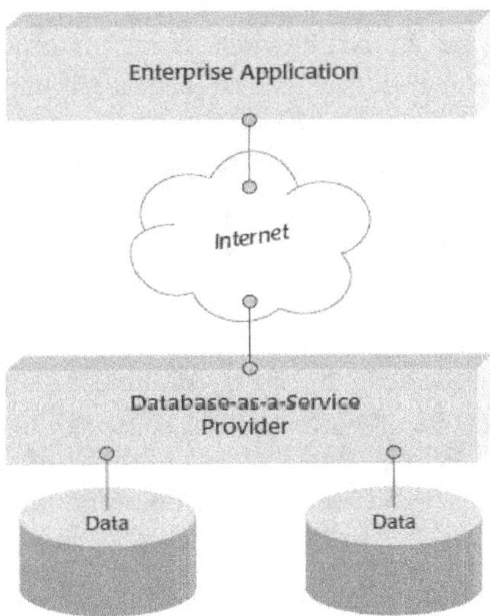

Figure 9.3 Database-as-a-service allows you to access enterprise-grade databases over the Internet

An effective database-as-a-service provider should be able to offer database services that appear local in terms of performance and functionality. However, as with the storage-as-a-service offerings, there is always trade-offs.

The benefits of database-as-a-service include, first, the ability to avoid hardware and software costs by leveraging a remote database that you use as you need it and just what you need to use. As many IT professionals already know, database licensing costs are a major part of the software budget, and avoiding those costs will go right to the bottom line.

Second, database maintenance, including backing up and restoring the database and managing users, can be avoided through the use of database-as-a-service. You do not have to focus on the maintenance activities required for a database; you can focus instead on its design and use.

Finally, you can avoid the task of doing upgrades and bug fixes to the database. Many a DBA (database administer) has spent a great deal of time applying patches and fixes to enterprise databases. Using database-as-a-service providers, that activity is handled for you and is transparent to you. You should always have the most current bug-free version of the database engine, since it is centrally updated on the cloud computing site and nothing needs to be distributed.

Database-as-a-service has a few drawbacks as well. First, there are legal, compliancy, and privacy issues around data, and in some instances, leveraging remote databases is illegal and/or not within compliance for some types of data. You must check before hosting data remotely, but in most cases, remote hosting is just fine and should meet your security requirements.

Second, security can be an issue when using database-as-a-service. When you require complete security, the use of remote databases that you do not control or secure may be contraindicated, depending on the type of data you place in those databases. However, there is no reason you cannot have your data exist securely on a database-as-a-service cloud offering if you leverage the right approach to security for your SOA and the right security technology. You need to work closely with your database-as-a-service provider and consider your own requirements to determine the best approach to secure your database.

Third, many of the interfaces offered by database-as-a-service providers are proprietary in nature and thus can be difficult to leverage from applications that need to access the data. While many cloud computing providers are moving toward standard interfaces, you need to understand and test their interfaces and/or APIs.

Finally, some database-as-a-service providers offer only a subset of the capabilities found in traditional on-premise enterprise databases. You may find that you are missing features and functions required by the enterprise applications. For example, stored procedures and triggers may not be supported in the same manner as in on-premise databases, or they may be proprietary, and thus difficult to port if you need to move off the database-as-a-service provider at some point in the future.

9.1.3   Information-as-a-Service

Information-as-a-service refers to the ability to consume any type of remotely hosted information – stock price information, address validation, credit reporting, for example – through a well-defined interface such as an API (see Figure 9.4). Over a thousand sources of information can be found these days, most of them listed at www.programmableweb.com. While they typically "serve up" information using standard Web Services APIs, some use proprietary interfaces. Therefore, as you must for database-as-a-service, you need to consider the interfaces offered by information-as-a-service providers.

Typically, APIs function like this:

GetSSNName(SSN_Number);

or

GetSSNName(333-33-3333);

with the return of

"John H. Smith"

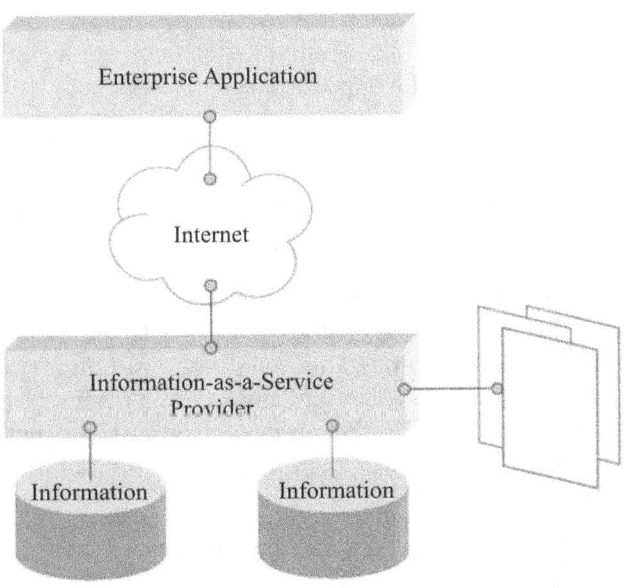

Figure 9.4 Information-as-a-service allows any application to access any type of information using an API

You can leverage a wide variety of Web APIs these days, including APIs for social networking sites like Twitter and Facebook, for business statistics, for stock quotes, and the list goes on. As far as cloud computing categories go, information-as-a-service is the most eclectic.

We use information through these APIs for several reasons, including the ability to mix and match a variety of information from many different sources through a single application or mashup. We can get stock quotes from one information-as-a-service provider, census data from another, and Dun & Bradstreet (D&B) information from a third. The idea is that it is much cheaper to leverage information that other people maintain and host than it is to host it yourself.

Those charged with creating an SOA using cloud computing must understand the value of Web APIs and must have the skills to produce a good-faith estimate as to what that value is. In essence, they must determine an approach to define the return on investment (ROI) and then determine the ROI itself. Let's explore these concepts, focusing on the costs, the benefits, and the business case in the context of leveraging information-as-a-service, or Web APIs.

The core value of leveraging Web APIs is that you do not have to incur the cost of creating or hosting the API or the information it abstracts. While most hang their value hat on that truth, there is indeed cost to leveraging an outside API:

- Cost of binding APIs into applications or processes, including abstracting an API to fit an application or process.
- Cost of inefficiencies brought about by the use of the API, such as downtime, or decreased speed.
- Cost of ongoing maintenance as APIs and applications change.
- Cost of the API service itself, typically per use.

Normally, the cost to bind an API to an application is not significant. However, in many instances, the API does not provide the exact function the application requires. Thus, some additional programming needs to be completed. And since you bind an application to a remote resource of a network, you have to account for the remote resource—the network—being down from time to time. Furthermore, there is always ongoing maintenance and the cost of the service itself. So,

Onetime cost = cost of binding and abstraction

Ongoing cost = cost of downtime + ongoing maintenance + cost of the
API service

As an example, consider a simple phone number verification service remotely hosted:

Onetime cost = $1,000

Ongoing cost (per month) = $100 + $200 + $100

The onetime cost is $1,000, and the ongoing cost is $400 per month. Together they equal the cost of leveraging an API. We use these figures when we look at benefits. So, while the costs are typically hidden and not significant, they do exist.

The larger issue around ROI and Web APIs is the value of leveraging versus creating a Web API and maintaining the back-end data yourself. We need to look at how much it would cost us if the API did not exist and we had to create it ourselves.

Again, functionality will vary greatly from API to API, but using our simple phone number verification service example, we can consider how much that API would cost were we to build it and host it ourselves. Generally speaking,

Onetime cost = cost of designing, building, and testing the API

Ongoing cost = cost of downtime + ongoing maintenance + cost of the
data subscription

Again, as an example, a simple phone number verification service remotely hosted might involve the following costs:

Onetime cost = $20,000

Ongoing cost (per month) = $200 + $1,000 + $500

The onetime cost is $20,000, and the ongoing is $1,700 per month, so for this particular case, we can look at the value of leveraging a Web API as follows:

	Onetime Cost	Ongoing Cost
Build and Host	$20,000	$1,700
Web API	$1,000	$400
Savings	$19,000	$1,300

On a yearly basis, that would be that would be $20,300 to the bottom line in the first year and $1,300 thereafter. Time-to-market costs are not considered here, but leveraging a prebuilt API will clearly provide better time-to-market.

Keep in mind that, typically, dozens of APIs are leveraged at the same time, thus multiplying the value. Also, keep in mind that each API has its own unique value to a particular business.

While the technology acquisition and maintenance costs are compelling, we must consider the larger and more difficult to determine "soft costs" of leveraging an API—or the value that the API brings to the business in terms of more sales, better customer satisfaction, and better employee morale.

Here is where we find the most value from leveraging a Web API. While there is indeed a cost savings in using a remotely hosted API versus supporting the same process on-premise, the service could be something that provides much more value.

For instance, the ability for the sales department to do a D&B lookup while on the phone with a particular customer provides critical customer information that will assist in closing a sale and prioritizing sales costs. The ability to do an instant credit check while completing a sale, without having to leverage a separate system and keep the customer waiting, benefits the salesperson, the customer, and thus the business.

9.1.4   Process-as-a-Service

Process-as-a-service refers to a remote resource that can bind many resources together, either hosted within the same cloud computing resource or remotely, to create business processes (see Figure 9.5). An example would be to create a business process that defines how to process an invoice on remote cloud-delivered systems and then have that process invoke any number of cloud-based or on-premise services to form the business process. The SOA gains the value of agility because processes are easier to change than applications.

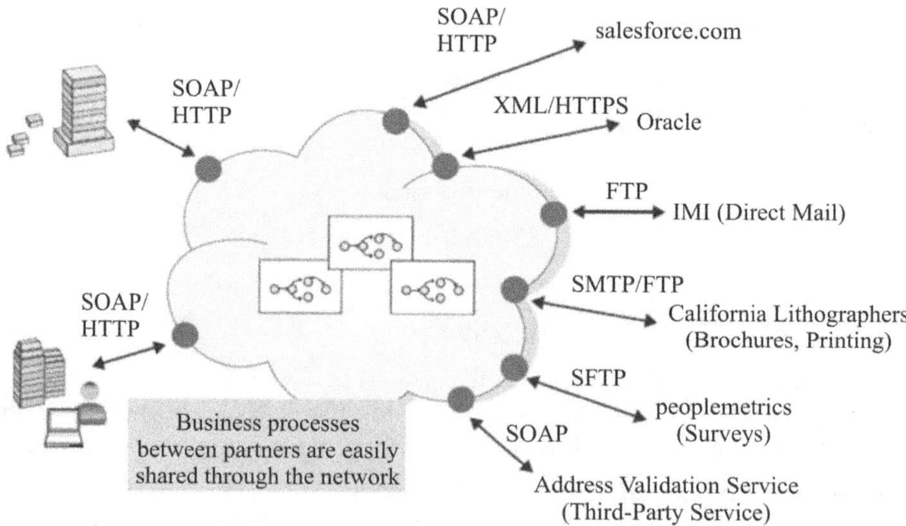

Figure 9.5 Process-as-a-service allows you to bind on-premise or cloud-delivered resources together to form business solutions

Process-as-a-service provides a mechanism to bind other resources together to form a solution. While your information and APIs may be hosted within a cloud provider, or perhaps on-premise, you would leverage this service to abstract and bind these resources together to form a business solution, such as processing a sale or shipping a product.

You can think of processes as a sequence of events that must occur in a certain order, leveraging any number of services and portions of data. For example,

Process "Ship Product"

1. Transmit order to warehouse.
2. Process shipping provider.
3. Price shipping.
4. Turn over to shipping provider.
5. Track shipment.
6. Report to customer.

Each step above includes services called by the process, but the services themselves are not processes. Processes provide control instructions about how to do something using many resources that can exist on-premise or in the clouds. Processes can span a single enterprise or, more often, many enterprises when dealing with process-as-a-service (see Figure 9.6).

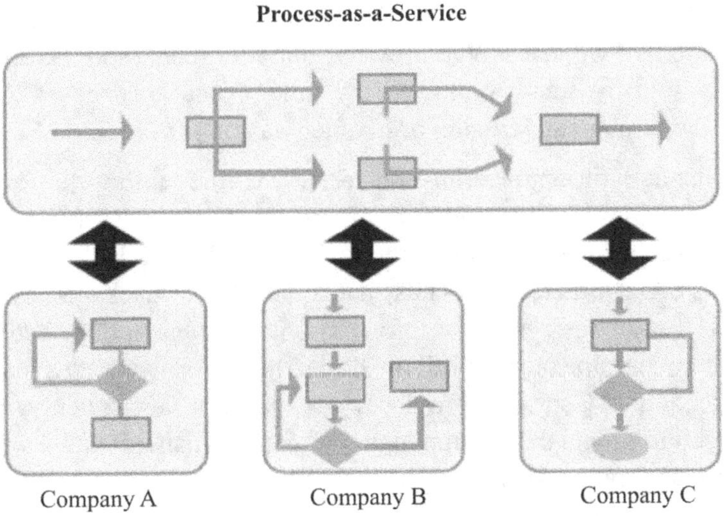

Figure 9.6 Process-as-a-service allows you to create common processes that span many companies, cloud services, and on-premise services

Process engines are really nothing new, although the existence of process engines on demand is. As we move forward with cloud computing, the use of process engines to leverage and manage any number of local and remote services to form them into business solutions will be an important component to cloud computing and to SOA using cloud computing.

9.1.5   Application-as-a-Service

Application-as-a-service, also known as software-as-a-service, is any application delivered over the platform of the Web to an end user, typically leveraging the application through a browser. While many associate application-as-a-service with enterprise applications, such as Salesforce SFA, office automation applications are indeed applications-as-a-service as well, including Google Docs, Gmail, and Google Calendar. They typically offer

- A user interface.
- Predefined application behavior.
- Predefined data.
- Support for any number of client platforms, since they run through the browser.

Application-as-a-service was really the first drive into modern cloud computing, but it is based on the more traditional time-sharing model from years past whereby many users shared one application and one computer. The differences are that we use a Web browser, not a terminal, and the applications are typically sold by subscription, not by time. Some are free of charge and obtain revenue through advertising or in other ways.

The advantage of application-as-a-service is the ability to leverage an enterprise-class application without having to buy and install enterprise software. Thus, business functionality typically only available to those who could afford SAP, Oracle Financials, and other larger packaged systems are available to any business user for a small subscription fee. Indeed, Salesforce.com became a multibillion dollar business using this model, and other application-as-a-service providers are catching up quickly, including many providing specialized applications for human resources, logistics management, and trade risk management, to name just a few.

In addition to the larger business application-as-a-service, there are also the office automation applications-as-a-service, including e-mail, document management, word processing, spreadsheets, and other productivity applications delivered through a browser. Google provides these applications for free, as do a few other providers. Some charge a small subscription fee.

The advantage of leveraging office automation applications-as-a-service are really around cost and convenience. Cost, because it is typically free. However, you can use Sun's Open Office open source office automation software on your desktop, which is also free, just to be fair. Convenience, since any computer with a browser can become your personal workspace with access to your documents and e-mail. So, you could be just as productive at an Internet cafe using a public computer as you would be at work.

9.1.6   Platform-as-a-Service

Platform-as-a-service is a complete platform, including application development, interface development, database development, storage, and testing, delivered through a remotely hosted platform to subscribers. Based on the traditional time-sharing model, modern platform-as-a-service providers offer the ability to create enterprise-class applications for use locally or on demand for a small subscription price or for free.

You can think of platform-as-a-service as one-stop shopping for those looking to build and deploy applications. Platform-as-a-service provides self-contained platforms with everything you need for application development and operational hosting. Platforms such as Google App Engine and Force.com (part of Salesforce.com) are popular ways to approach application development on the cloud.

Core to the platform-as-a-service notion are a few major components:

Design, development, deployment, integration, storage, and operations.

Design is the ability to design your application and user interfaces.

Development is the ability to design, develop, and test applications right out of the platform, on demand, using development tools that are delivered on demand. We have seen the Salesforce.com Apex language provide these services, with a few smaller players providing similar capabilities.

Deployment is the ability to test, bundle, and deliver the platform-as-a-service–created applications. This means hosting the applications, typically accessing them visually, through a browser, or as Web services.

Integration is the ability to integrate the applications developed on your platform-as-a-service provider with software-as-a-service applications or applications that may exist within your enterprise.

Storage, the ability to provide persistence for the application, means an on-demand database or on-demand file storage.

Finally, *operations* is the ability to run the application over a long period of time, dealing with backup, restore, exception handling, and other things that add value to operations.

Platform-as-a-service is going to deliver only a subset of the existing features and functions most of us look for in a platform, but it will deliver enough value to be interesting as a service. Platforms are costly, and the ability to create a platform through a subscription service is compelling. Many professionals in the Global 2000 companies see platform-as-a-service as a way to develop, deploy, and maintain critical applications on the cheap.

The advantage of platform-as-a-service is that you can access a complete enterprise-class development environment at a low cost and build complete enterprise applications, from the data to the user interface.

The disadvantage is that many of the platform-as-a-service vendors leverage proprietary programming languages and interfaces; thus, once your application is there, it may be difficult to move it to an on-premise server or another platform-as-a-service provider.

9.1.7   Integration-as-a-Service

Integration-as-a-service is the ability to deliver a complete integration stack from the cloud, including interfacing with applications, semantic mediation, flow control, and integration design. In essence, integration-as-a-service includes most of the features and functions found within traditional EAI (enterprise application integration) technology but delivered as a service.

Integration is a tough problem to solve, and integration on demand does not make that any easier. The core notion is that you link up to many information systems, either at the data or behavior level, and abstract information and/or behavior from those systems to be delivered with one or many systems, either within the same enterprise or within companies.

Basic functions:

- Transformation

- Routing
- Interface
- Logging

Transformation means that you can convert the information semantics from one system to the information semantics of another system, so the target system can receive information in a format it understands.

Routing means that information is routed to the correct systems on the basis of predefined logic (called intelligent routing).

Interface means that you can connect into the source or target systems using whatever interface they expose.

Logging means that you can log all integration activities, such as messages flowing in and out, as well as other events.

The advantage of integration-as-a-service is that you can access pretty pricy integration software functionality for the price of a rental agreement. Moreover, many of the integration-on-demand providers have very sophisticated software delivered through a browser that leverages the new rich Internet application technology such as AJAX.

9.1.8   Security-as-a-Service

Security-as-a-service, as you may have guessed, is the ability to deliver core security services remotely over the Internet. While the security services provided today are often rudimentary, more sophisticated services, such as identity management, are becoming available.

Security-as-a-service is a tough sell considering that security is typically a weak point of cloud computing. Providing security on demand seems like an unnatural act. However, there are times when security delivered out of the cloud makes sense, such as for securing a cluster of cloud resources you are leveraging within your enterprise or even between enterprises. Thus, you can enforce security hierarchies between physical organizations out of the cloud or perhaps have cloud-delivered on-demand encryption services or identity management solutions.

The downside is rather obvious, considering that most look at security as something that needs to be controlled and thus not outsourced. However, as time goes on and security on demand becomes more sophisticated, and as more corporate data and applications reside in the clouds, then there will be an uptake in security-as-a-service.

9.1.9   Management/Governance-as-a-Service

Management/governance-as-a-service is any on-demand service that provides the ability to manage one or more cloud services, typically simple things such topology, resource utilization, virtualization, and uptime management. Governance systems, such as the ability to enforce defined policies on data and services, are becoming available as well.

Much the same as with security on demand, this aspect of cloud computing is slow on the uptake. Most enterprises like to control management and governance. However, as more applications and data are outsourced, it may make sense to manage and govern those resources from the clouds as well.

9.1.10   Testing-as-a-Service

Testing-as-a-service is the ability to test local or cloud-delivered systems using remotely hosted testing software and services. It should be noted that while a cloud service requires testing unto itself, testing-as-a-service systems have the ability to test other cloud applications, Web sites, and internal enterprise systems, and they do not require a hardware or software footprint within the enterprise.

The advantages of testing-as-a-service include the ability to avoid purchasing test servers and testing software. Moreover, in many respects, testing, either on-premise or in the clouds, is better done through a testing service that connects to those applications over the Internet, since many real-life users will do the same thing. Thus, if you are looking to test a Web site or a Web-delivered application, testing-as-a-service is actually more logical than testing on-premise in many instances.

The downsides are the ones you might expect. Many of those who build and deploy applications like to control their testing environments and would not dream of leveraging testing servers and software that they do not own or host. Again, as more applications are rehosted in the cloud, testing-as-a-service will become more of an accepted paradigm.

9.1.11   Infrastructure-as-a-Service

Infrastructure-as-a-service is really data center-as-a-service, or the ability to access computing resources remotely. In essence, you lease a physical server that is yours to do with what you will and that for all practical purposes is your data center, or at least part of a data center. The difference with this approach versus more mainstream cloud computing is that instead of using an interface and a metered service, you get access to the entire machine and the software on that machine. In short, it is less packaged.

We defined database-as-a-service, storage-as-a-service, and so on, as separate categories of cloud computing. Infrastructure-as-a-service can provide all of them, including database, storage, governance, application development, application processing, security, and more. Anything that can be found in a traditional data center can be delivered as an infrastructure-as-a-service. The overlapping feature of infrastructure-as-a-service and the other cloud computing services can make this a bit confusing.

The advantage of infrastructure-as-a-service is that you can access very expensive data center resources through a rental arrangement and thus preserve capital for the business. Moreover, somebody is there to manage the physical machines for you, including replacement of downed disk drives and correction of any networking issues.

The disadvantage is that there is typically less granular on-demand expandability of the resource. With database-as-a-service and storage-as-a-service, you just purchase additional capability as you need it and as much as you need. However, many infrastructure-as-a-service providers require that you lease an entire server for a defined amount of time. Thus, the whole selling point of adjusting your cloud resources to meet your exact needs kind of goes out the door.

Bit Questions

1. Which cloud deployment model is operated solely for a single organization and its authorized users?   [   ]

    (a)   Private cloud   (b)   Hybrid cloud

    (c)   Public cloud   (d)   Community cloud

2. Which of these services is not Platform as a Service?   [   ]

    (a)   Force.com   (b)   Microsoft Azure

    (c)   Amazon EC2   (d)   Joyent

3. Amazon may be the most widely known   [   ]

    (a)   Cloud environment   (b)   Cloud technology

    (c)   Cloud vendor   (d)   Cloud infrastructure

4. Which of the following is an example of an IaaS? [   ]

   (a) Rackspace   (b) Amazon EC2

   (c) Windows Azure   (d) Force.com

5. Which is considered the most widely used cloud computing service? [   ]

   (a) IaaS

   (b) PaaS

   (c) Communication-as-a-Service (CaaS)

   (d) SaaS

6. Amazon is a [   ]

   (a) Private cloud   (c) Hybrid cloud

   (c) Public cloud   (d) Community cloud

7. ---------------- applications are designed for end-users, delivered over the web. [   ]

   (a) IaaS

   (b) PaaS

   (c) Communication-as-a-Service (CaaS)

   (d) SaaS

8. Which of the following is highly scalable [   ]

   (a) IaaS

   (b) PaaS

   (c) Communication-as-a-Service (CaaS)

   (d) SaaS

9. Which service model allows the customer to choose more layers in the computing architecture? [   ]

   (a) Infrastructure as a Service (IaaS)

   (b) Platform as a Service (PaaS)

   (c) Software as a Service (SaaS)

   (d) There is no difference between the service models.

10. AWS stands for ----------------

   (a) Amazon Web Service   (b) Alternate Web Service

   (c) Amazon Wide Service   (d) Amazon Web Suite

11. Iaas stands for ----------------
- (a) Integration-as-a-service
- (b) Information-as-a-service
- (c) Interface-as-a-service
- (d) Both A & B

Exercises

1. Explain in detail about the following:
- (a) Storage-as-a-service
- (b) Database-as-a-service
- (c) Information-as-a-service
- (d) Process-as-a-service
- (e) Application-as-a-service
- (f) Platform-as-a-service
- (g) Integration-as-a-service
- (h) Security-as-a-service
- (i) Testing-as-a-service
- (j) Infrastructure-as-a-service
- (k) Management/governance-as-a-service

CHAPTER 10

DISASTER RECOVERY AND SECURITY

10.1 DISASTER RECOVERY

Disaster recovery is the art of being able to resume normal systems operations when faced with a disaster scenario. What constitutes a disaster depends on your context. In general, I consider a disaster to be an anomalous event that causes the interruption of normal operations. In a traditional data center, for example, the loss of a hard drive is not a disaster scenario, because it is more or less an expected event. A fire in the data center, on the other hand, is an abnormal event likely to cause an interruption of normal operations.

The total and sudden loss of a complete server, which you might consider a disaster in a physical data center, happens – relatively speaking – all of the time in the cloud. Although such a frequency demotes such events from the realm of disaster recovery, you still need solid disaster recovery processes to deal with them. As a result, disaster recovery is not simply a good idea that you can keep putting off in favor of other priorities – it is a requirement.

What makes disaster recovery so problematic in a physical environment is the amount of manual labor required to prepare for and execute a disaster recovery plan. Furthermore, fully testing your processes and procedures is often very difficult. Too many organizations have a disaster recovery plan that has never actually been tested in an environment that sufficiently replicates real-world conditions to give them the confidence that the plan will work.

Disaster recovery in the cloud can be much more automatic. In fact, some cloud infrastructure management tools will even automatically execute a disaster recovery plan without human intervention.

What would happen if you lost your entire data center under a traditional IT infrastructure? Hopefully, you have a great off-site backup strategy that would enable you to get going in another data center in a few weeks. While we aren't quite there yet, the cloud will soon enable you to move an entire infrastructure from one cloud provider to another and even have that move occur automatically in response to a catastrophic event.

Another advantage for the cloud here is the cost associated with a response to a disaster of that level. Your recovery costs in the cloud are almost negligible beyond normal operations. With a traditional data center, you must shell out new capital costs for a new infrastructure and then make insurance claims. In addition, you can actually test out different disaster scenarios in the cloud in ways that are simply unimaginable in a traditional environment.

10.2 DISASTER RECOVERY PLANNING

Disaster recovery deals with catastrophic failures that are extremely unlikely to occur during the lifetime of a system. If they are reasonably expected failures, they fall under the auspices of traditional availability planning. Although each single disaster is unexpected over the lifetime of a system, the possibility of some disaster occurring over time is reasonably nonzero.

Through disaster recovery planning, you identify an acceptable recovery state and develop processes and procedures to achieve the recovery state in the event of a disaster. By "acceptable recovery state," I specifically mean how much data you are willing to lose in the event of a disaster.

Defining a disaster recovery plan involves two key metrics:

Recovery Point Objective (RPO)

The recovery point objective identifies how much data you are willing to lose in the event of a disaster. This value is typically specified in a number of hours or days of data. For example, if you determine that it is OK to lose 24 hours of data, you must make sure that the backups you'll use for your disaster recovery plan are never more than 24 hours old.

Recovery Time Objective (RTO)

The recovery time objective identifies how much downtime is acceptable in the event of a disaster. If your RTO is 24 hours, you are saying that up to 24 hours may elapse between the point when your system first goes offline and the point at which you are fully operational again.

In addition, the team putting together a disaster recovery plan should define the criteria that would trigger invocation of the plan. In general, invocation of any plan that results in accepting a loss of data should involve the heads of the business organization.

Everyone would love a disaster recovery scenario in which no downtime and no loss of data occur, no matter what the disaster. The nature of a disaster, however, generally requires you to accept some level of loss; anything else will come with a significant price tag. In a citywide disaster like Hurricane Katrina, the cost of surviving with zero downtime and zero data loss could have been having multiple data centers in different geographic locations that were constantly synchronized. In other words, you would need two distinct data centers from different infrastructure providers with dedicated, high-bandwidth connections between the two.

Accomplishing that level of redundancy is expensive. It would also come with a nontrivial performance penalty. The cold reality for most businesses is likely that the cost of losing 24 hours of data is less than the cost of maintaining a zero downtime/zero loss of data infrastructure.

Determining an appropriate RPO and RTO is ultimately a financial calculation: at what point does the cost of data loss and downtime exceed the cost of a backup strategy that will prevent that level of data loss and downtime? The right answer is radically different for different businesses. If you are in a senior IT management role in an organization, you should definitely know the right answer for your business.

The final element of disaster recovery planning understands the catastrophic scenario. There's ultimately some level of disaster your IT systems will not survive no matter how much planning and spending you do. A good disaster recovery plan can describe that scenario so that all stakeholders can understand and accept the risk.

The Recovery Point Objective

The Armageddon scenario results in total loss of all system data and the binaries of all applications required to run the system. Your RPO is somewhere between the application state when you first deployed it and the state at the time of the disaster. You may even define multiple disaster levels with different RPOs.

Any software system should be able to attain an RPO between 24 hours for a simple disaster to one week for a significant disaster without incurring absurd costs. Of course, losing 24 hours of banking transactions would never be acceptable, much less one week.

Your RPO is typically governed by the way in which you save and back up data:

- Weekly off-site backups will survive the loss of your data center with a week of data loss. Daily off-site backups are even better.

- Daily on-site backups will survive the loss of your production environment with a day of data loss plus replicating transactions during the recovery period after the loss of the system. Hourly on-site backups are even better.

- A NAS/SAN will survive the loss of any individual server, except for instances of data corruption with no data loss.

- A clustered database will survive the loss of any individual data storage device or database node with no data loss.

- A clustered database across multiple data centers will survive the loss of any individual data center with no data loss.

The Recovery Time Objective

Having up-to-the-second off-site backups does you no good if you have no environment to which you can restore them in the event of failure. The ability to assemble a replacement infrastructure for your disasters – including the data restore time – governs the RTO.

What would happen if your managed services provider closed its doors tomorrow? If you have a number of dedicated servers, it can be days or weeks before you are operational again unless you have an agreement in place for a replacement infrastructure.

In a traditional infrastructure, a rapid RTO is very expensive. As I already noted, you would have to have an agreement in place with another managed services provider to provide either a backup infrastructure or an SLA for setting up a replacement infrastructure in the event your provider goes out of business. Depending on the nature of that agreement, it can nearly double the costs of your IT infrastructure.

10.3 DISASTER MANAGEMENT

You are performing your backups and have an infrastructure in place with all of the appropriate redundancies. To complete the disaster recovery scenario, you need to recognize when a disaster has happened and have the tools and processes in place to execute your recovery plan.

One of the coolest things about the cloud is that all of this can be automated. You can recover from the loss of Amazon's U.S. data centers while you sleep.

Monitoring

Monitoring your cloud infrastructure is extremely important. You cannot replace a failing server or execute your disaster recovery plan if you don't know that there has been a failure. The trick, however, is that your monitoring systems cannot live in either your primary or secondary cloud provider's infrastructure. They must be independent of your clouds. If you want to enable automated disaster recovery, they also need the ability to manage your EC2 infrastructure from the monitoring site.

Your primary monitoring objective should be to figure out what is going to fail before it actually fails. The most common problem I have encountered in EC2 is servers that gradually decrease in local file I/O throughput until they become unusable. This problem is something you can easily watch for and fix before users even notice it. On the other hand, if you wait for your application to fail, chances are users have had to put up with poor performance for some period of time before it failed completely. It may also prove to be a precursor to a larger cloud failure event.

There are many other more mundane things that you should check on in a regular environment. In particular, you should be checking capacity issues such as disk usage, RAM, and CPU.

In the end, however, you will need to monitor for failure at three levels:

- Through the provisioning API (for Amazon, the EC2 web services API)
- Through your own instance state monitoring tools
- Through your application health monitoring tools

Your cloud provider's provisioning API will tell you about the health of your instances, any volumes they are mounting, and the data centers in which they are operating. When you detect a failure at this level, it likely means something has gone wrong with the cloud itself. Before engaging in any disaster recovery, you will need to determine whether the outage is limited to one server or affects indeterminate servers, impacting an entire availability zone or an entire region.

Monitoring is not simply about checking for disasters; mostly it is checking on the mundane. With enStratus, I put a Python service on each server that checks for a variety of server health indicators – mostly related to capacity management. The service will notify the monitoring system if there is a problem with the server or its configuration and allow the monitoring system to take appropriate action. It also checks for the health of the applications running on the instance.

Load Balancer Recovery

One of the reasons companies pay absurd amounts of money for physical load balancers is to greatly reduce the likelihood of load balancer failure. With cloud vendors such as GoGrid and in the future, Amazon you can realize the benefits of hardware load balancers without incurring the costs. Under the current AWS offering, you have to use less-reliable EC2 instances. Recovering a load balancer in the cloud, however, is lightning fast. As a result, the downside of a failure in your cloud-based load balancer is minor.

Recovering a load balancer is simply a matter of launching a new load balancer instance from the AMI and notifying it of the IP addresses of its application servers. You can further reduce any downtime by keeping a load balancer running in an alternative availability zone and then remapping your static IP address upon the failure of the main load balancer.

Application Server Recovery

If you are operating multiple application servers in multiple availability zones, your system as a whole will survive the failure of any one instance or even an entire availability zone. You will still need to recover that server so that future failures don't affect your infrastructure. The recovery of a failed application server is only slightly more complex than the recovery of a failed load balancer. Like the failed load balancer, you start up a new instance from the application server machine image. You then pass it configuration information, including where the database is. Once the server is operational, you must notify the load balancer of the existence of the new server (as well as deactivate its knowledge of the old one) so that the new server enters the load-balancing rotation.

Database Recovery

Database recovery is the hardest part of disaster recovery in the cloud. Your disaster recovery algorithm has to identify where an uncorrupted copy of the database exists. This process may involve promoting slaves into masters, rearranging your backup management, and reconfiguring application servers.

The best solution is a clustered database that can survive the loss of an individual database server without the need to execute a complex recovery procedure. Absent clustering, the best recovery plan is one that simply launches a new database instance and mounts the still functional EC2 volume formerly in use by the failed instance. When an instance goes down, however, any number of related issues may also have an impact on that strategy:

- The database could be irreparably corrupted by whatever caused the instance to crash.

- The volume could have gone down with the instance.

- The instance's availability zone (and thus the volume as well) could be unavailable.

- You could find yourself unable to launch new instances in the volume's availability zone.

On the face of it, it might seem that the likelihood of both things going wrong is small, but it happens. As a result, you need a fallback plan for your recovery plan. The following process will typically cover all levels of database failure:

1. Launch a replacement instance in the old instance's availability zone and mount its old volume.

2.   If the launch fails but the volume is still running, snapshot the volume and launch a new instance in any zone, and then create a volume in that zone based on the snapshot.

3.   If the volume from step 1 or the snapshot from step 2 are corrupt, you need to fall back to the replication slave and promote it to database master.

4.   If the database slave is not running or is somehow corrupted, the next step is to launch a replacement volume from the most recent database snapshot.

5.   If the snapshot is corrupt, go further back in time until you find a backup that is not corrupt.

Step 4 typically represents your worst-case scenario. If you get to 5, there is something wrong with the way you are doing backups.

10.4 WEB APPLICATION DESIGN

Figure 10.1 illustrates the generic application architecture that web applications share. You may move around or combine the boxes a bit, but you are certain to have some kind of (most often scripting) language that generates content from a combination of templates and data pulled from a model backed by a database. The system updates the model through actions that execute transactions against the model.

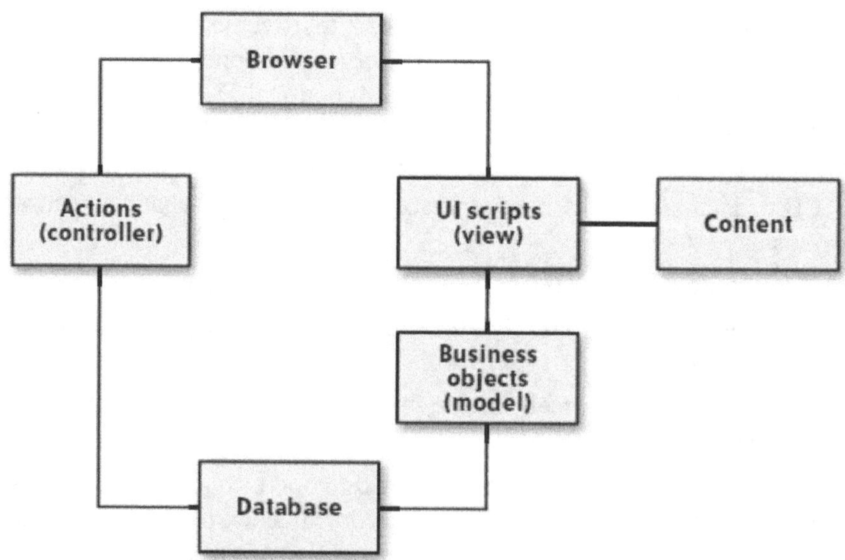

Figure 10.1 Most web applications share the same basic architecture

System State and Protecting Transactions

The defining issue in moving to the cloud is how your application manages its state. Let's look at the problem of booking a room in a hotel.

The architecture from Figure 10.1 suggests that you have represented the room and the hotel in a model. For the purposes of this discussion, it does not matter whether you have a tight separation between model, view, and data, or have mixed them to some degree. The key point is that there is some representation of the hotel and room data in your application space that mirrors their respective states in the database.

How does the application state in the application tier change between the time the user makes the request and the transaction is changed in the database?

The process might look something like this basic sequence:

1. Lock the data associated with the room.
2. Check the room to see whether it is currently available.
3. If currently available, mark it as "booked" and thus no longer available.
4. Release the lock.

The problem with memory locks

You can implement this logic in many different ways, not all of which will succeed in the cloud. A common Java approach that works well in a single-server environment but fails in a multiserver context might use the following code:

```java
public void book(Customer customer, Room room, Date [ ] days)

throws BookingException {

synchronized( room ) { // synchronized "locks" the room object

if( !room.isAvailable(days) ) {

throw new BookingException("Room unavailable.");

}

room.book(customer, days);

}

}
```

Because the code uses the Java locking keyword synchronized, no other threads in the current process can make changes to the room object. If you are on a single server, this code will work under any load supported by the server. Unfortunately, it will fail miserably in a multi-server context.

The problem with this example is the memory-based lock that the application grabs. If you had two clients making two separate booking requests against the same server, Java would allow only one of them to execute the synchronized block at a time. As a result, you would not end up with a double booking.

On the other hand, if you had each customer making a request against different servers (or even distinct processes on the same server), the synchronized blocks on each server could execute concurrently. As a result, the first customer to reach the room.book( ) call would lose his reservation because it would be overwritten by the second. Figure 10.2 illustrates the doublebooking problem.

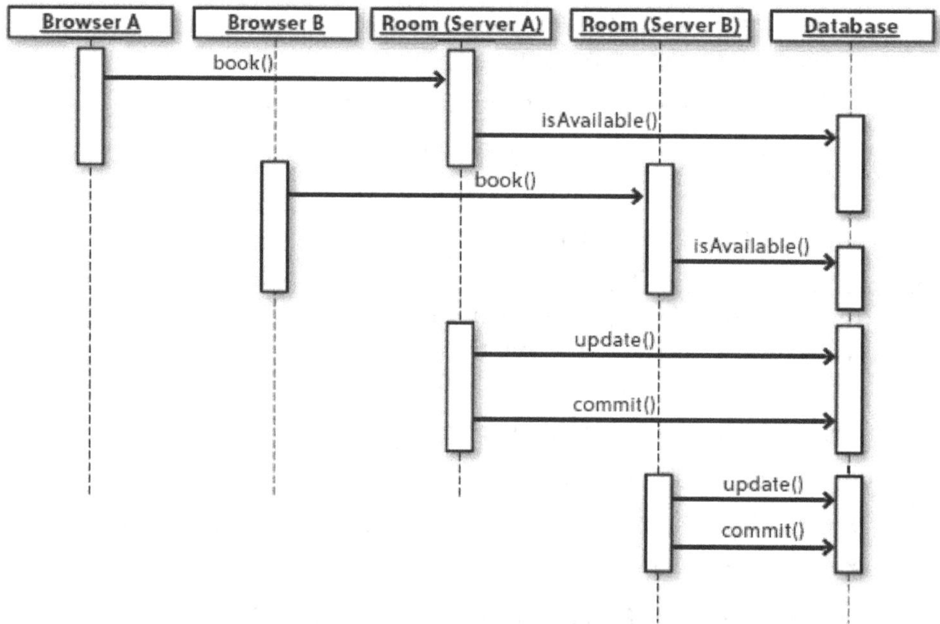

Figure 10.2 The second client overwrites the first, causing a double-booking

The non-Java way of expressing the problem is that if your transactional logic uses memory-based locking to protect the integrity of a transaction, that transaction will fail in a multi-server environment and thus it won't be able to take advantage of the cloud's ability to dynamically scale application processing.

One way around this problem is to use clustering technologies or cross-server shared memory systems. Another way to approach the problem is to treat the database as the authority on the state of your system.

Transactional integrity through stored procedures

A key benefit of stored procedures, however, is that they enable you to leverage the database to manage the integrity of your transactions. After all, data integrity is the main job of your database engine!

Instead of doing all of the booking logic in Java, you could leverage a MySQL stored procedure:

```
DELIMITER |
CREATE PROCEDURE book
(
IN customerId BIGINT,
IN roomId BIGINT,
IN startDate DATE,
IN endDate DATE,
OUT success CHAR(1)
)
BEGIN
DECLARE n DATE;
DECLARE cust BIGINT;
SET success = 'Y';
SET n = startDate;
bookingAttempt:
REPEAT
SELECT customer INTO cust FROM booking
WHERE room_id = roomId AND booking_date = n;
IF cust IS NOT NULL AND cust <> customerId
THEN
SET success = 'N';
LEAVE bookingAttempt;
END IF;
UPDATE booking SET customer = customerId
WHERE room_id = roomId AND booking_date = n;
```

```
SET n = DATE_ADD(n, INTERVAL 1 DAY);

UNTIL n > endDate

END REPEAT;

IF success = 'Y' THEN

COMMIT;

ELSE

ROLLBACK;

END IF;

END
```

This method goes through each row of the booking table in your MySQL database and marks it booked by the specified customer. If it encounters a date when the room is already booked, the transaction fails and rolls back.

An example using the stored procedure follows, using Python:

```python
def book(customerId, roomId, startDate, endDate):

conn = getConnection();

c = conn.cursor();

c.execute("CALL book(%s, %s, %s, %s, @success)", \

(customerId, roomId, startDate, endDate));

c.execute("SELECT @success");

row = c.fetchone();

success = row[0];

if success == "Y":

return 1

else:

report 0
```

Even if you have two different application servers running two different instances of your Python application, this transaction will fail, as desired, for the second customer, regardless of the point at which the second customer's transaction begins.

Two alternatives to stored procedures

They have the advantage of executing faster that the same logic in an application language. Furthermore, multi-server transaction management through stored procedures is very elegant.

It can have three key objections:

- Stored procedures are not portable from one database to another.

- They require an extended understanding of database programming – something that may not be available to all development teams.

- They don't completely solve the problem of scaling transactions across application servers under all scenarios. You still need to write your applications to use them wisely, and the result may, in fact, make your application more complicated.

In addition to these core objections, I personally strongly prefer a very strict separation of presentation, business modeling, business logic, and data.

The last objection is subjective and perhaps a nasty personal quirk. The first two objections, however, are real problems. After all, how many of you reading this book have found yourselves stuck with Oracle applications that could very easily work in MySQL if it weren't for all the stored procedures? You are paying a huge Oracle tax just because you used stored procedures to build your applications!

The second objection is a bit more esoteric. If you have the luxury of a large development staff with a diverse skill set, you don't see this problem. If you are in a small company that needs each person to wear multiple hats, it helps to have an application architecture that requires little or no database programming expertise.

To keep your logic at the application server level while still maintaining multi-server transactional integrity, you must either create protections against dirty writes or create a lock in the database.

The booking logic from the stored procedure essentially was an update to the booking table:

UPDATE booking SET customer = ? WHERE booking_id = ?;

If you add last_update_timestamp and last_update_user fields, that SQL would operate more effectively in a multi-server environment:

UPDATE booking

SET customer = ?, last_update_timestamp = ?, last_update_user = ?

WHERE booking_id = ? AND last_update_timestamp = ? AND last_update_user = ?;

In this situation, the first client will attempt to book the room for the specified date and succeed. The second client then attempts to update the row but gets no matches since the timestamp it reads – as well as the user ID of the user on the client – will not match the values updated by the first client. The second client realizes it has updated zero rows and subsequently displays an error message. No double booking!

This approach works well as long as you do not end up structuring transactions in a way that will create deadlocks. A deadlock occurs between two transactions when each transaction is waiting on the other to release a lock. Our reservations system example is an application in which a deadlock is certainly possible.

Because we are booking a range of dates in the same transaction, poorly structured application logic could cause two clients to wait on each other as one attempts to book a date already booked by the other, and vice versa. For example, if you and I are looking to book both Tuesday and Wednesday, but for whatever reason your client first tries Wednesday and my client first tries Tuesday, we will end up in a deadlock where I wait on you to commit your Wednesday booking and you wait on me to commit my Tuesday booking.

This somewhat contrived scenario is easy to address by making sure that you move sequentially through each day. Other application logic, however, may not have as obvious a solution. Another alternative is to create a field for managing your locks. The room table, for example, might have two extra columns for booking purposes: locked_by and locked_timestamp. Before starting the transaction that books the rooms, update the room table and commit the update.

Once your booking transaction completes, release the lock by nulling out those fields prior to committing that transaction.

Because this approach requires two different database transactions, you are no longer executing the booking as a single atomic transaction. Consequently, you risk leaving an open lock that prevents others from booking any rooms on any dates. You can eliminate this problem through two tricks:

- The room is considered unlocked not only when the fields are NULL, but also when the locked_timestamp has been held for a long period of time.

- When updating the lock at the end of your booking transaction, use the locked_by and locked_timestamp fields in the WHERE clause. Thus, if someone else steals a lock out from under you, you only end up rolling back your transaction.

Both of these approaches are admittedly more complex than taking advantage of stored procedures. Regardless of what approach you use, however, the important key for the cloud is simply making sure that you are not relying on memory locking to maintain your application state integrity.

When Servers Fail

The ultimate architectural objective for the cloud is to set up a running environment where the failure of any given application server ultimately doesn't matter. If you are running just one server, that failure will obviously matter at some level, but it will still matter less than losing a physical server.

One trick people sometimes use to get around the problems described in the previous section is data segmentation – also known as sharding. Figure 10.3 shows how you might use data segmentation to split processing across multiple application servers.

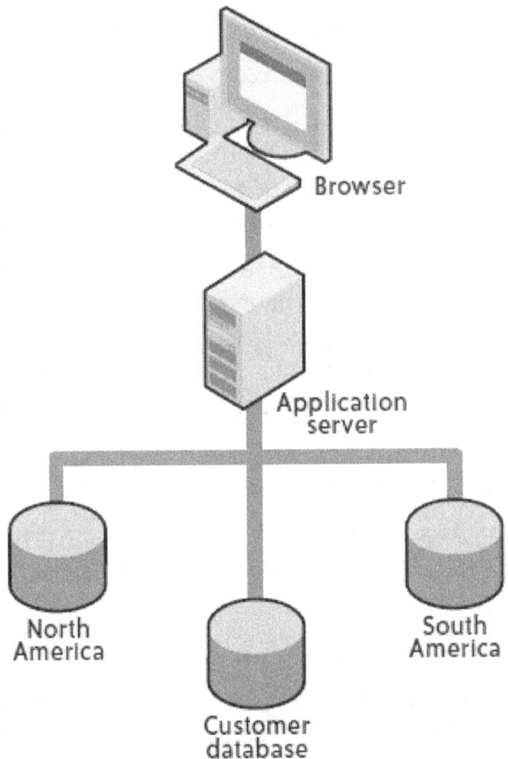

Figure 10.3 Supporting different hotels on different servers guarantees no double bookings

In other words, each application server manages a subset of data. As a result, there is never any risk that another server will overwrite the data. Although segmentation has its place in scaling applications, that place is not at the application server in a cloud cluster. A segmented application server cluster ultimately has a very low availability rating, as the failure of any individual server does matter.

The final corollary to all of this discussion of application state and server failure is that application servers in a cloud cannot store any state data beyond caching data. In other words, if you need to back up your application server, you have failed to create a solid application server architecture for the cloud. All state information, including binary data, belongs in the database, which must be on a persistent system.

10.5   MACHINE IMAGE DESIGN

Two indirect benefits of the cloud are:

- It forces discipline in deployment planning
- It forces discipline in disaster recovery

Thanks to the way virtualized servers launch from machine images, your first step in moving into any cloud infrastructure is to create a repeatable deployment process that handles all the issues that could come up as the system starts up. To ensure that it does, you need to do some deployment planning.

The machine image (in Amazon, the AMI) is a raw copy of your operating system and core software for a particular environment on a specific platform. When you start a virtual server, it copies its operating environment from the machine image and boots up. If your machine image contains your installed application, deployment is nothing more than the process of starting up a new virtual instance.

Amazon Machine Image Data Security

When you create an Amazon machine image, it is encrypted and stored in an Amazon S3 bundle. One of two keys can subsequently decrypt the AMI:

- Your Amazon key
- A key that Amazon holds

Only your user credentials have access to the AMI. Amazon needs the ability to decrypt the AMI so it can actually boot an instance from the AMI.

What Belongs in a Machine Image?

A machine image should include all of the software necessary for the runtime operation of a virtual instance based on that image and nothing more. The starting point is obviously the operating system, but the choice of components is absolutely critical. The full process of establishing a machine image consists of the following steps:

1. Create a component model that identifies what components and versions are required to run the service that the new machine image will support.
2. Separate out stateful data in the component model. You will need to keep it out of your machine image.
3. Identify the operating system on which you will deploy.
4. Search for an existing, trusted baseline public machine image for that operating system.
5. Harden your system using a tool such as Bastille.
6. Install all of the components in your component model.
7. Verify the functioning of a virtual instance using the machine image.
8. Build and save the machine image.

The starting point is to know exactly what components are necessary to run your service.

Figure 10.4 shows a sample model describing the runtime components for a MySQL database server. In this case, the stateful data exists in the MySQL directory, which is externally mounted as a block storage device. Consequently, you will need to make sure that your startup scripts mount your block storage device before starting MySQL.

The services you want to run on an instance generally dictate the operating system on which you will base the machine image. If you are deploying a .NET application, you probably will use one of the Amazon Windows images. A PHP application, on the other hand, probably will be targeting a Linux environment.

Hardening an operating system is the act of minimizing attack vectors into a server. Among other things, hardening involves the following activities:

- Removing unnecessary services.
- Removing unnecessary accounts.
- Running all services as a role account (not root) when possible.
- Running all services in a restricted jail when possible.
- Verifying proper permissions for necessary system services.

The best way to harden your Linux system is to use a proven hardening tool such as Bastille. Now that you have a secure base from which to operate, it is time to actually install the software that this system will support. In the case of the current example, it's time to install MySQL.

When installing your server-specific services, you may have to alter the way you think about the deployment thanks to the need to keep stateful data out of the machine image. For a MySQL server, you would probably keep stateful data on a block device and mount it at system startup. A web server, on the other hand, might store stateful media assets out in a cloud storage system such as Amazon S3 and pull it over into the runtime instance on startup.

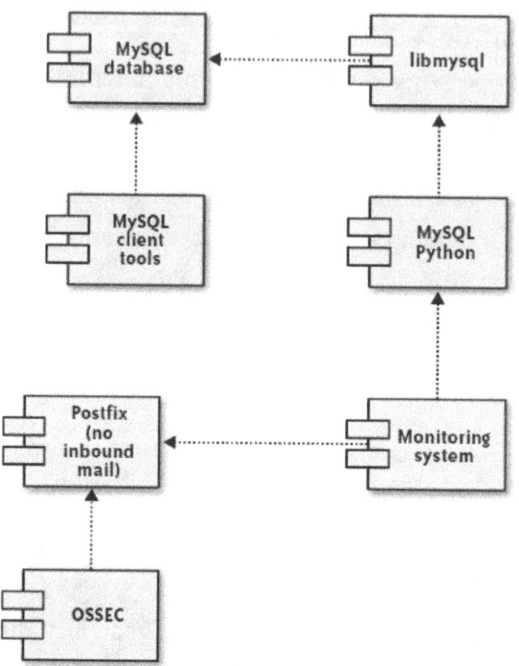

Figure 10.4 Software necessary to support a MySQL database server. Because the stateful data is assumed to be on a block storage device, this machine image is useful in starting any MySQL databases, not just a specific set of MySQL databases

Different applications will definitely require different approaches based on their unique requirements. Whatever the situation, you should structure your deployment so that the machine image has the intelligence to look for its stateful data upon startup and provide your machine image components with access to that data before they need it.

Once you have the deployment structured the right way, you will need to test it. That means testing the system from launch through shutdown and recovery. Therefore, you need to take the following steps:

1. Build a temporary image from your development instance.
2. Launch a new instance from the temporary image.
3. Verify that it functions as intended.
4. Fix any issues.
5. Repeat until the process is robust and reliable.

At some point, you will end up with a functioning instance from a well-structured machine image. You can then build a final instance and go have a beer (or coffee).

A Sample MySQL Machine Image

The trick to creating a machine image that supports database servers is knowing how your database engine of choice stores its data. In the case of MySQL, the database engine has a data directory for its stateful data. This data directory may actually be called any number of things (/usr/local/mysql/data, /var/lib/mysql, etc.), but it is the only thing other than the configuration file that must be separated from your machine image. In a typical custom build, the data directory is /usr/local/mysql/data.

Once you start an instance from a standard image and harden it, you need to create an elastic block storage volume and mount it. The standard Amazon approach is to mount the volume off of /mnt (e.g., /mnt/database). Where you mount it is technically unimportant, but it can help reduce confusion to keep the same directory for each image.

You can then install MySQL, making sure to install it within the instance's root filesystem (e.g., /usr/local/mysql). At that point, move the data over into the block device using the following steps:

1. Stop MySQL if the installation process automatically started it.

2. Move your data directory over into your mount and give it a name more suited to mounting on a separate device (e.g., /mnt/database/mysql).

3. Change your my.cnf file to point to the new data directory.

You now have a curious challenge on your hands: MySQL cannot start up until the block device has been mounted, but a block device under Amazon EC2 cannot be attached to an instance of a virtual machine until that instance is running. As a result, you cannot start MySQL through the normal boot-up procedures. However, you can end up where you want by enforcing the necessary order of events: boot the virtual machine, mount the device, and finally start MySQL.

You should therefore carefully alter your MySQL startup scripts so that the system will no longer start MySQL on startup, but will still shut the MySQL engine down on shutdown.

The best way to effect this change is to edit the MySQL startup script to wait for the presence of the MySQL data directory before starting the MySQL executable.

Amazon AMI Philosophies

In approaching AMI design, you can follow one of two core philosophies:

- A minimalist approach in which you build a few multipurpose machine images.

- A comprehensive approach in which you build numerous purpose-specific machine images.

The minimalist approach has the advantage of being easier for rolling out security patches and other operating-system-level changes. On the flip side, it takes a lot more planning and EC2 skills to structure a multipurpose AMI capable of determining its function after startup and self-configuring to support that function. If you are just getting started with EC2, it is probably best to take the comprehensive approach and use cloud management tools to eventually help you evolve into a library of minimalist machine images.

For a single application installation, you won't likely need many machine images, and thus the difference between a comprehensive approach and a minimalist approach is negligible.

SaaS applications especially ones that are not multitenant require a runtime deployment of application software.

Runtime deployment means uploading the application software such as the MySQL executable discussed in the previous section to a newly started virtual instance after it has started, instead of embedding it in the machine image. A runtime application deployment is more complex (and hence the need for cloud management tools) than simply including the application in the machine image, but it does have a number of major advantages:

You can deploy and remove applications from a virtual instance while it is running. As a result, in a multi application environment, you can easily move an application from one cluster to another.

You end up with automated application restoration. The application is generally deployed at runtime using the latest backup image. When you embed the application in an image, on the other hand, your application launch is only as good as the most recent image build.

You can avoid storing service-to-service authentication credentials in your machine image and instead move them into the encrypted backup from which the application is deployed.

10.6 PRIVACY DESIGN

It is important to consider how you approach an application architecture for systems that have a special segment of private data, notably e-commerce systems that store credit cards and health care systems with health data.

Privacy in the Cloud

The key to privacy in the cloud or any other environment is the strict separation of sensitive data from non-sensitive data followed by the encryption of sensitive elements. The simplest example is storing credit cards. You may have a complex e-commerce application storing many data relationships, but you need to separate out the credit card data from the rest of it to start building a secure e-commerce infrastructure.

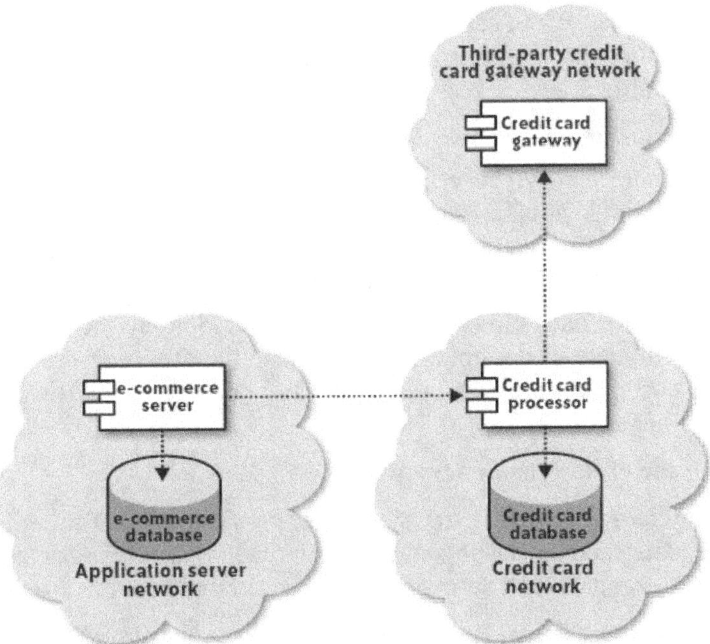

Figure 10.5 Host credit card data behind a web service that encrypts credit card data

Figure 10.5 provides an application architecture in which credit card data can be securely managed.

It's a pretty simple design that is very hard to compromise as long as you take the following precautions:

- The application server and credit card server sit in two different security zones with only web services traffic from the application server being allowed into the credit card processor zone.

- Credit card numbers are encrypted using a customer-specific encryption key.

- The credit card processor has no access to the encryption key, except for a short period of time (in memory) while it is processing a transaction on that card.

- The application server never has the ability to read the credit card number from the credit card server.

- No person has administrative access to both servers.

Under this architecture, a hacker has no use for the data on any individual server; he must hack both servers to gain access to credit card data. Of course, if your web application is poorly written, no amount of structure will protect you against that failing.

For now, I'll just list a couple rules of thumb:

- Make sure the two servers have different attack vectors. In other words, they should not be running the same software. By following this guideline, you guarantee that whatever exploit compromised the first server is not available to compromise the second server.

- Make sure that neither server contains credentials or other information that will make it possible to compromise the other server. In other words, don't use passwords for user logins and don't store any private SSH keys on either server.

Managing the credit card encryption

In order to charge a credit card, you must provide the credit card number, an expiration date, and a varying number of other data elements describing the owner of the credit card. You may also be required to provide a security code.

This architecture separates the basic capture of data from the actual charging of the credit card. When a person first enters her information, the system stores contact info and some basic credit card profile information with the e-commerce application and sends the credit card number over to the credit card processor for encryption and storage.

The first trick is to create a password on the e-commerce server and store it with the customer record. It's not a password that any user will ever see or use, so you should generate something complex using the strongest password guidelines. You should also create a credit card record on the e-commerce server that stores everything except the credit card number. Figure 10.6 shows a sample e-commerce data model.

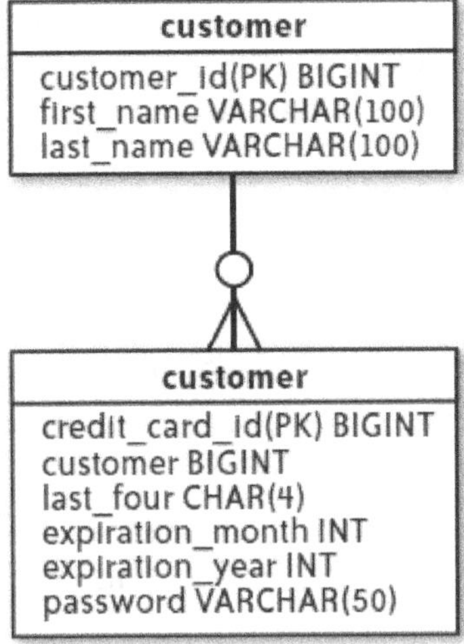

Figure 10.6 The e-commerce system stores everything but the credit card number and security code

With that data stored in the e-commerce system database, the system then submits the credit card number, credit card password, and unique credit card ID from the e-commerce system to the credit card processor.

The credit card processor does not store the password. Instead, it uses the password as salt to encrypt the credit card number, stores the encrypted credit card number, and associates it with the credit card ID. Figure 10.7 shows the credit card processor data model.

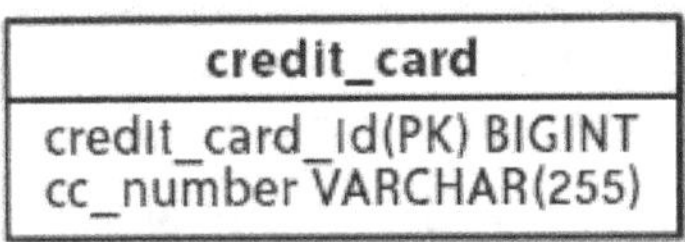

Figure 10.7 The credit card processor stores the encrypted credit card number and associates it with the e-commerce credit card *ID*

Neither system stores a customer's security code, because the credit card companies do not allow you to store this code.

Processing a credit card transaction

When it comes time to charge the credit card, the e-commerce service submits a request to the credit card processor to charge the card for a specific amount. The e-commerce system refers to the credit card on the credit card processor using the unique ID that was created when the credit card was first inserted. It passes over the credit card password, the security code, and the amount to be charged. The credit card processor then decrypts the credit card number for the specified credit card using the specified password. The unencrypted credit card number, security code, and amount are then passed to the bank to complete the transaction.

If the e-commerce application is compromised

If the e-commerce application is compromised, the attacker has access only to the non-sensitive customer contact info. There is no mechanism by which he can download that database and access credit card information or otherwise engage in identity theft. That would require compromising the credit card processor separately.

Having said all of that, if your e-commerce application is insecure, an attacker can still assume the identity of an existing user and place orders in their name with deliveries to their address.

In other words, you still need to worry about the design of each component of the system.

If the credit card processor is compromised

Compromising the credit card processor is even less useful than compromising the e-commerce application. If an attacker gains access to the credit card database, all he has are random unique IDs and strongly encrypted credit card numbers each encrypted with a unique encryption key. As a result, the attacker can take the database offline and attempt to brute-force decrypt the numbers, but each number will take a lot of time to crack and, ultimately, provide the hacker with a credit card number that has no individually identifying information to use in identity theft.

Another attack vector would be to figure out how to stick a Trojan application on the compromised server and listen for decryption passwords.

When the Amazon Cloud Fails to Meet Your Needs

The architecture I described in the previous section matches traditional non-cloud deployments fairly closely. You may run into challenges deploying in the Amazon cloud, however, because of a couple of critical issues involving the processing of sensitive data:

Some laws and specifications impose conditions on the political and legal jurisdictions where the data is stored. In particular, companies doing business in the EU may not store private data about EU citizens on servers in the U.S. (or any other nation falling short of EU privacy standards).

Some laws and specifications were not written with virtualization in mind. In other words, they specify physical servers in cases where virtual servers would do identically well, simply because a server meant a physical server at the time the law or standard was written.

The first problem has a pretty clear solution: if you are doing business in the EU and managing private data on EU citizens, that data must be handled on servers with a physical presence in the EU, stored on storage devices physically in the EU, and not pass through infrastructure managed outside the EU.

Amazon provides a presence in both the U.S. and EU. As a result, you can solve the first problem by carefully architecting your Amazon solution. It requires, however, that you associate the provisioning of instances and storage of data with your data management requirements.

The second issue is especially problematic for solutions such as Amazon that rely entirely on virtualization. In this case, however, it's for fairly stupid reasons. You can live up to the spirit of the law or specification, but because the concept of virtualization was not common at the time, you cannot live up to the letter of the law or specification. The workaround for this scenario is similar to the workaround for the first problem.

In solving these challenges, you want to do everything to realize as many of the benefits of the cloud as possible without running private data through the cloud and without making the overall complexity of the system so high that it just isn't worth it. Cloud providers such as Rackspace and GoGrid tend to make such solutions easier than attempting a hybrid solution with Amazon and something else.

To meet this challenge, you must route and store all private information outside the cloud, but execute as much application logic as possible inside the cloud. You can accomplish this goal by following the general approach I described for credit card processing and abstracting the concepts out into a privacy server and a web application server:

The privacy server sits outside the cloud and has the minimal support structures necessary to handle your private data.

The web application server sits inside the cloud and holds the bulk of your application logic.

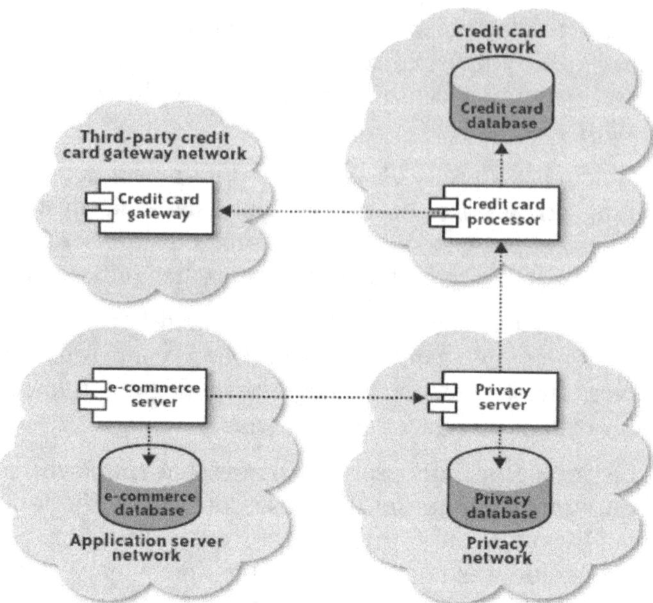

Figure 10.8 Pulling private data out of the cloud creates three different application components

Because the objective of a privacy server is simply to physically segment out private data, you do not necessarily need to encrypt everything on the privacy server. Figure 10.8 illustrates how the e-commerce system might evolve into a privacy architecture designed to store all private data outside of the cloud.

As with the cloud-based e-commerce system, you store credit card data on its own server in its own network segment. The only difference for the credit card processor is that this time it is outside of the cloud.

The new piece to this puzzle is the customer's personally identifying information. This data now exists on its own server outside of the cloud, but still separate from credit card data. When saving user profile information, those actions execute against the privacy server instead of the main web application. Under no circumstances does the main web application have any access to personally identifying information, unless that data is aggregated before being presented to the web application.

How useful this architecture is depends heavily on how much processing you are doing that has nothing to do with private data. If all of your transactions involve the reading and writing of private data, you gain nothing by adding this complexity. On the other hand, if the management of private data is just a tiny piece of the application, you can gain all of the advantages of the cloud for the other parts of the application while still respecting any requirements around physical data location.

10.7   DATABASE MANAGEMENT

The trickiest part of managing a cloud infrastructure is the management of your persistent data. Persistent data is essentially any data that needs to survive the destruction of your cloud environment. Because you can easily reconstruct your operating system, software, and simple configuration files, they do not qualify as persistent data. Only the data that cannot be reconstituted qualify. If you are following my recommendations, this data lives in your database engine.

The problem of maintaining database consistency is not unique to the cloud. The cloud simply brings a new challenge to an old problem of backing up your database, because your database server in the cloud will be much less reliable than your database server in a physical infrastructure. The virtual server running your database will fail completely and without warning. Count on it.

Whether physical or virtual, when a database server fails, there is the distinct possibility that the files that comprise the database state will get corrupted. The likelihood of that disaster depends on which database engine you are using, but it can happen with just about any engine out there.

Absent of corruption issues, dealing with a database server in the cloud is very simple. In fact, it is much easier to recover from the failure of a server in a virtualized environment than in the physical world: simply launch a new instance from your database machine image, mount the old block storage device, and you are up and running.

Clustering or Replication?

The most effective mechanism for avoiding corruption is leveraging the capabilities of a database engine that supports true clustering. In a clustered database environment, multiple database servers act together as a single logical database server. The mechanics of this process vary from database engine to database engine, but the result is that a transaction committed to the cluster will survive the failure of any one node and maintain full data consistency. In fact, clients of the database will never know that a node went down and will be able to continue operating.

Unfortunately, database clustering is very complicated and generally quite expensive.

- Unless you have a skilled DBA on hand, you should not even consider undertaking the deployment of a clustered database environment.

- A clustered database vendor often requires you to pay for the most expensive licenses to use the clustering capabilities in the database management system (DBMS). Even if you are using MySQL clustering, you will have to pay for five machine instances to effectively run that cluster.

- Clustering comes with significant performance problems. If you are trying to cluster across distinct physical infrastructures in other words, across availability zones you will pay a hefty network latency penalty.

The alternative to clustering is replication. A replication-based database infrastructure generally has a main server, referred to as the database master. Client applications execute write transactions against the database master. Successful transactions are then replicated to database slaves.

Replication has two key advantages over clustering:

- It is generally much simpler to implement.

- It does not require an excessive number of servers or expensive licenses.

Unfortunately, replication is not nearly as reliable as clustering. A database master can, in theory, fail after it has committed a transaction locally but before the database slave has received it. In that event, you would have a database slave that is missing data. In fact, when a database master is under a heavy load, the database slave can actually fall quite far behind the master. If the master is somehow corrupted, it can also begin replicating corrupted data.

Apart from reliability issues, a replicated environment does not failover as seamlessly as a clustered solution. When your database master fails, clients using that master for write transactions cannot function until the master is recovered. On the other hand, when a node in a cluster fails, the clients do not notice the failure because the cluster simply continues processing transactions.

Using database clustering in the cloud

The good news, in general, is that the cloud represents few specific challenges to database clustering. The bad news is that every single database engine has a different clustering mechanism (or even multiple approaches to clustering) and thus an in-depth coverage of cloud-based clustering is beyond the scope of this book. I can, however, provide a few guidelines:

A few cluster architectures exist purely for performance and not for availability. Under these architectures, single points of failure may still exist. In fact, the complexity of clustering may introduce additional points of failure.

Clusters designed for high availability are often slower at processing individual write transactions, but they can handle much higher loads than standalone databases. In particular, they can scale to meet your read volume requirements.

Some solutions such as MySQL may require a large number of servers to operate effectively. Even if the licensing costs for such a configuration are negligible, the cloud costs will add up.

The dynamic nature of IP address assignment within a cloud environment may add new challenges in terms of configuring clusters and their failover rules.

Using database replication in the cloud

For most non-mission-critical database applications, replication is a "good enough" solution that can save you a lot of money and potentially provide you with opportunities for performance optimization. In fact, a MySQL replication system in the cloud can provide you with a flawless backup and disaster recovery system as well as availability that can almost match that of a cluster. Because the use of replication in the cloud can have such a tremendous impact compared to replication in a traditional data center, we'll go into a bit more detail on using replication in the cloud than we did with clustering. Figure 10.9 shows a simple replication environment.

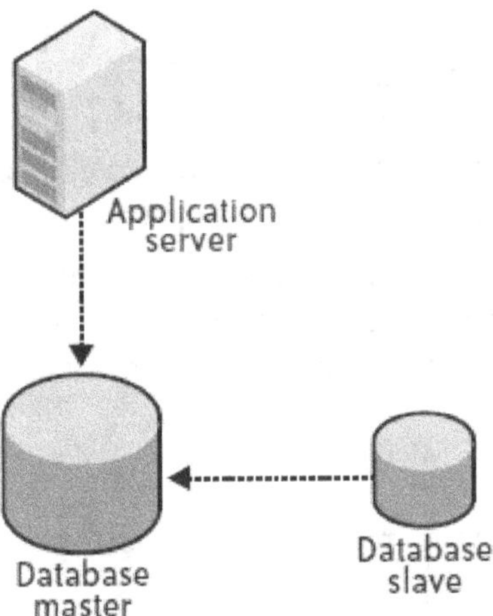

Figure 10.9 A simple replication (arrows show dependency)

In this structure, you have a single database server of record (the master) replicating to one or more copies (the slaves). In general, the process that performs the replication from the master to the slave is not atomic with respect to the original transaction. In other words, just because a transaction successfully commits on the master does not mean that it successfully replicated to any slaves. The transactions that do make it to the slaves are generally atomic, so although a slave may be out of sync, the database on the slave should always be in an internally consistent state (uncorrupted).

Under a simple setup, your web applications point to the database master. Consequently, your database slave can fail without impacting the web application. To recover, start up a new database slave and point it to the master.

Recovering from the failure of a database master is much more complicated. If your cloud provider is Amazon, it also comes with some extra hurdles you won't see in a standard replication setup.

Ideally, you will recover your database master by starting a new virtual server that uses your database machine image and then mounting the volume that was formerly mounted by the failed server. The failure of your master, however, may have resulted in the corruption of the files on that volume. At this point, you will turn to the database slave.

A database can recover using a slave in one of two ways:

- Promotion of a slave to database master (you will need to launch a replacement slave)

- Building a new database master and exporting the current state from a slave to a new Master

Promotion is the fastest mechanism for recovery and the approach you almost certainly want to take, unless you have a need for managing distinct database master and database slave machine images. If that's the case, you may need to take the more complex recovery approach.

As with other components in your web application architecture, putting your database in a replication architecture gives it the ability to rapidly recover from a node failure and, as a result, significantly increases overall system availability rating.

Replication for performance

Another reason to leverage replication is performance. Without segmenting your data, most database engines allow you to write against only the master, but you can read from the master or any of the slaves. An application heavy on read operations can therefore see significant performance benefits from spreading reads across slaves. Figure 10.9 illustrates the design of an application using replication for performance benefits.

The rewards of using replication for performance are huge, but there are also risks. The primary risk is that you might accidentally execute a write operation against one of the slaves. When you do that, replication falls apart and your master and slaves end up in inconsistent states.

Two approaches to solving this problem include:

- Clearly separating read logic from write logic in your code and centralizing the acquisition of database connections.

- Making your slave nodes read-only.

The second one is the most foolproof, but it complicates the process of promoting a slave to master because you must reconfigure the server out of read-only mode before promoting it.

Primary Key Management

With a web application operating behind a load balancer in which individual nodes within the web application do not share state information with each other, the problem of cross-database primary key generation becomes a challenge. The database engine's auto-increment functionality is specific to the database you are using and not very flexible; it often is guaranteed to be unique only for a single server.

How to generate globally unique primary keys

First, you could use standard UUIDs to serve as your primary key mechanism. They have the benefit of an almost nonexistent chance of generating conflicts, and most programming languages have built-in functions for generating them. You don't use them, however, for three reasons:

- They are 128-bit values and thus take more space and have longer lookup times than the 64-bit primary keys you prefer.
- Cleanly representing a 128-bit value in Java and some other programming languages is painful. In fact, the best way to represent such a value is through two separate values representing the 64 high bits and the 64 low bits, respectively.
- The possibility of collisions, although not realistic, does exist.

In order to generate identifiers at the application server level that are guaranteed to be unique in the target database, traditionally I rely on the database to manage key generation. You accomplish this through the creation of a sequencer table that hands out a key with a safe key space. The application server is then free to generate keys in that key space until the key space is exhausted.

The sequencer table looks like this:

```
CREATE TABLE sequencer (
name VARCHAR(20) NOT NULL,
next_key BIGINT UNSIGNED NOT NULL,
last_update BIGINT UNSIGNED NOT NULL,
spacing INT UNSIGNED NOT NULL;
PRIMARY KEY ( name, last_update ),
UNIQUE INDEX ( name )
);
```

The first thing of note here is that there is nothing specific to any database in this table structure and your keys are not tied to a particular table. If necessary, multiple tables can share the same primary key space. Similarly, you can generate unique identifiers that have nothing to do with a particular table in your database.

To generate a unique person_id for your person table:

1. Set up a next_key value in memory and initialize it to 0.

2. Grab the next spacing and last_update for the sequencer record with the name = 'person.person_id'.

3. Add 1 to the retrieved next_key and update the sequencer table with the name and retrieved last_update value in the WHERE clause.

4. If no rows are updated (because another server beat you to the punch), repeat steps 2 and 3.

5. Set the next person ID to next_key.

6. Increment the next_key value by 1.

7. The next time you need a unique person ID, simply execute steps 5 and 6 as long as next_key < next_key + spacing. Otherwise, set next_key to 0 and repeat the entire process.

Within the application server, this entire process must be locked against multithreaded access.

Support for globally unique random keys

The technique for unique key generation just described generates (more or less) sequential identifiers. In some cases, it is important to remove reasonable predictability from identifier generation. You therefore need to introduce some level of randomness into the equation.

To get a random identifier, you need to multiply your next_key value by some power of 10 and then add a random number generated through the random number generator of your language of choice. The larger the random number possibility, the smaller your overall key space is likely to be. On the other hand, the smaller the random number possibility, the easier your keys will be to guess.

The following Python example illustrates how to generate a pseudorandom unique person ID:

```
import thread

import random

next Key = −1;

spacing = 100;

lock = thread.allocate_lock();
```

```
def next():
try:
lock.acquire (); # make sure only one thread at a time can access
if next Key == −1 or next Key > spacing:
load Key();
next Id = (next Key * 100000);
next Key = next Key + 1;
finally:
lock .release ();
rnd = random. randint(0,99999);
next Id = next Id + rnd;
return next Id;
```

You can minimize the wasting of key space by tracking the allocation of random numbers and incrementing the next Key value only after the random space has been sufficiently exhausted.

The further down that road you go, however, the more likely you are to encounter the following challenges:

- The generation of unique keys will take longer.
- Your application will take up more memory.
- The randomness of your ID generation is reduced.

Database Backups

A good database backup strategy is hard, regardless of whether or not you are in the cloud. In the cloud, however, it is even more important to have a working database backup strategy.

Types of database backups

Most database engines provide multiple mechanisms for executing database backups. The rationale behind having different backup strategies is to provide a trade-off between the impact that executing a backup has on the production environment and the integrity of the data in the backup. Typically, your database engine will offer at least these backup options (in order of reliability):

- Database export/dump backup
- File system backup
- Transaction log backup

The most solid backup you can execute is the database export/dump. When you perform a database export, you dump the entire schema of the database and all of its data to one or more export files. You can then store the export files as the backup. During recovery, you can leverage the export files to restore into a pristine install of your database engine.

To execute a database export on SQL Server, for example, use the following command:

BACKUP DATABASE website to disk = 'D:\db\website.dump'

The result is an export file you can move from one SQL Server environment to another SQL Server environment.

The downside of the database export is that your database server must be locked against writes in order to get a complete export that is guaranteed to be in an internally consistent state.

Unfortunately, the export of a large database takes a long time to execute. As a result, full database exports against a production database generally are not practical.

Most databases provide the option to export parts of the database individually. For example, you could dump just your access_log table every night. In MySQL:

$ mysqldump website access_log > /backups/db/website.dump

If the table has any dependencies on other tables in the system, however, you can end up with inconsistent data when exporting on a table-by-table basis. Partial exports are therefore most useful on data from a data warehouse.

File system backups involve backing up all of the underlying files that support the database.

For some database engines, the database is stored in one big file. For others, the tables and their schemas are stored across multiple files. Either way, a backup simply requires copying the database files to backup media.

Though a file system backup requires you to lock the database against updates, the lock time is typically shorter. In fact, the snap shotting capabilities of block storage devices generally reduce the lock time to under a second, no matter how large the database is.

The following SQL will freeze MySQL and allow you to snapshot the file system on which the database is stored:

FLUSH TABLES WITH READ LOCK

With the database locked, take a snapshot of the volume, and then release the lock. The least disruptive kind of backup is the transaction log backup. As a database commits transactions, it writes those transactions to a transaction logfile. Because the transaction log contains only committed transactions, you can back up these transaction logfiles without locking the database or stopping. They are also smaller files and thus back up quickly. Using this strategy, you will create a full database backup on a nightly or weekly basis and then back up the transaction logs on a more regular basis.

Restoring from transaction logs involves restoring from the most recent full database backup and then applying the transaction logs. This approach is a more complex backup scheme than the other two because you have a number of files created at different times that must be managed together. Furthermore, restoring from transaction logs is the longest of the three restore options.

Applying a backup strategy for the cloud

The best backup strategy for the cloud is a file-based backup solution. You lock the database against writes, take a snapshot, and unlock it. It is elegant, quick, and reliable. The key cloud feature that makes this approach possible is the cloud's ability to take snapshots of your block storage volumes. Without snapshot capabilities, this backup strategy would simply take too long.

Your backup strategy cannot, however, end with a file-based backup. Snapshots work beautifully within a single cloud, but they cannot be leveraged outside your cloud provider. In other words, an Amazon EC2 elastic block volume snapshot cannot be leveraged in a cloud deployment. To make sure your application is portable between clouds, you need to execute full database exports regularly.

How regularly you perform your database exports depends on how much data you can use. The underlying question you need to ask is, "If my cloud provider suddenly goes down for an extended period of time, how much data can I afford to lose when launching in a new environment?"

For a content management system, it may be OK in such an extreme situation to lose a week of data. An e-commerce application, however, cannot really afford to lose any data – even under such extreme circumstances.

My approach is to regularly execute full database exports against a MySQL slave, as shown in Figure 10.11.

For the purposes of a backup, it does not matter if your database slave is a little bit behind the master. What matters is that the slave represents the consistent state of the entire database at a relatively reasonable point in time. You can therefore execute a very long backup against the slave and not worry about the impact on the performance of your production environment.

Because you can execute long backups, you can also execute numerous backups bounded mostly by your data storage appetite.

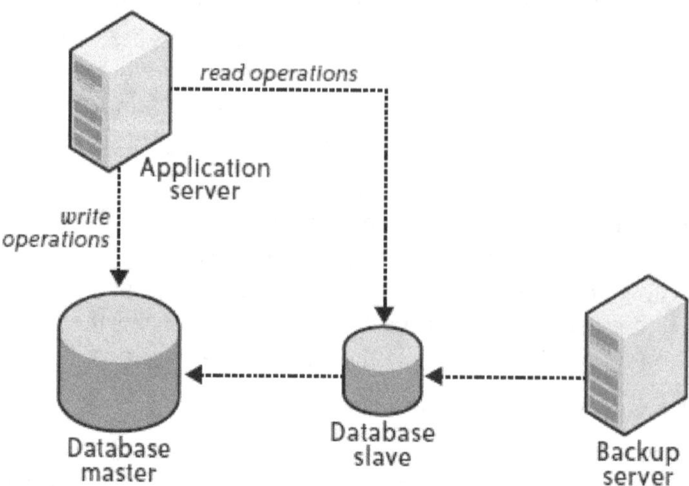

Figure 10.10 Execute regular full database exports against a replication slave

If your database backups truly take such a long time to execute that you risk having your slaves falling very far behind the master, it makes sense to configure multiple slaves and rotate backups among the slaves. This rotation policy will give a slave sufficient time to catch up with the master after it has executed a backup and before it needs to perform its next backup.

Once the backup is complete, you should move it over to S3 and regularly copy those backups out of S3 to another cloud provider or your own internal file server.

Your application architecture should now be well structured to operate not only in the Amazon cloud, but in other clouds as well.

10.8 DATA SECURITY

Physical security defines how you control physical access to the servers that support your infrastructure. The cloud still has physical security constraints. After all, there are actual servers running somewhere. When selecting a cloud provider, you should understand their physical security protocols and the things you need to do on your end to secure your systems against physical vulnerabilities.

Data Control

The big chasm between traditional data centers and the cloud is the location of your data on someone else's servers. Companies who have outsourced their data centers to a managed services provider may have crossed part of that chasm;

what cloud services add is the inability to see or touch the servers on which their data is hosted. The meaning of this change is a somewhat emotional matter, but it does present some real business challenges.

The main practical problem is that factors that have nothing to do with your business can compromise your operations and your data. For example, any of the following events could create trouble for your infrastructure:

- The cloud provider declares bankruptcy and its servers are seized or it ceases operations.

- A third party with no relationship to you (or, worse, a competitor) sues your cloud provider and obtains a blanket subpoena granting access to all servers owned by the cloud provider.

- Failure of your cloud provider to properly secure portions of its infrastructure especially in the maintenance of physical access controls results in the compromise of your systems.

The solution is to do two things you should be doing anyway, but likely are pretty lax about: encrypt everything and keep off-site backups.

- Encrypt sensitive data in your database and in memory. Decrypt it only in memory for the duration of the need for the data. Encrypt your backups and encrypt all network communications.

- Choose a second provider and use automated, regular backups (for which many open source and commercial solutions exist) to make sure any current and historical data can be recovered even if your cloud provider were to disappear from the face of the earth.

Let's examine how these measures deal with each scenario, one by one.

When the cloud provider goes down

This scenario has a number of variants: bankruptcy, deciding to take the business in another direction, or a widespread and extended outage. Whatever is going on, you risk losing access to your production systems due to the actions of another company. You also risk that the organization controlling your data might not protect it in accordance with the service levels to which they may have been previously committed.

When a subpoena compels your cloud provider to turn over your data

If the subpoena is directed at you, obviously you have to turn over the data to the courts, regardless of what precautions you take, but these legal requirements apply whether your data is in the cloud or on your own internal IT infrastructure. What we're dealing with here is a subpoena aimed at your cloud provider that results from court action that has nothing to do with you.

Technically, a subpoena should be narrow enough that it does not involve you. You cannot, however, be sure that a subpoena relating to cutting-edge technology will be properly narrow, nor even that you'll know the subpoena has been issued.

Encrypting your data will protect you against this scenario. The subpoena will compel your cloud provider to turn over your data and any access it might have to that data, but your cloud provider won't have your access or decryption keys. To get at the data, the court will have to come to you and subpoena you. As a result, you will end up with the same level of control you have in your private data center.

When your cloud provider fails to adequately protect their network

When you select a cloud provider, you absolutely must understand how they treat physical, network, and host security. Though it may sound counterintuitive, the most secure cloud provider is one in which you never know where the physical server behind your virtual instance is running. Chances are that if you cannot figure it out, a determined hacker who is specifically targeting your organization is going to have a much harder time breaching the physical environment in which your data is hosted.

Amazon publishes its security standards and processes at http://aws.amazon.com. Whatever cloud provider you use, you should understand their security standards and practices, and expect them to exceed anything you require.

Nothing guarantees that your cloud provider will, in fact, live up to the standards and processes they profess to support. If you follow everything else I recommend in this chapter, however, your data confidentiality will be strongly protected against even complete incompetence on the part of your cloud provider.

Encrypt Everything

In the cloud, your data is stored somewhere; you just don't know exactly where. However, you know some basic parameters:

Your data lies within a virtual machine guest operating system, and you control the mechanisms for access to that data.

Network traffic exchanging data between instances is not visible to other virtual hosts.

For most cloud storage services, access to data is private by default. Many, including Amazon S3, nevertheless allow you to make that data public.

Encrypt your network traffic

No matter how lax your current security practices, you probably have network traffic encrypted at least for the most part. A nice feature of the Amazon cloud is that virtual servers cannot sniff the traffic of other virtual servers. I still recommend against relying on this feature, since it may not be true of other providers. Furthermore, Amazon might roll out a future feature that renders this protection measure obsolete. You should therefore encrypt all network traffic, not just web traffic.

Encrypt your backups

When you bundle your data for backups, you should be encrypting it using some kind of strong cryptography, such as PGP. You can then safely store it in a moderately secure cloud storage environment like Amazon S3, or even in a completely insecure environment.

Encryption eats up CPU. As a result, I recommend first copying your files in plain text over to a temporary backup server whose job it is to perform encryption, and then uploading the backups into your cloud storage system. Not only does the use of a backup server avoid taxing your application server and database server CPUs, it also enables you to have a single higher security system holding your cloud storage access credentials rather than giving those credentials to every system that needs to perform a backup.

Encrypt your file systems

Each virtual server you manage will mount ephemeral storage devices (such as the /mnt partition on Unix EC2 instances) or block storage devices. The failure to encrypt ephemeral devices poses only a very moderate risk in an EC2 environment because the EC2 Xen system zeros out that storage when your instance terminates. Snapshots for block storage devices, however, sit in Amazon S3 unencrypted unless you take special action to encrypt them.

The most secure approach to both scenarios is to mount ephemeral and block storage devices using an encrypted file system. Managing the startup of a virtual server using encrypted file systems ultimately ends up being easier in the cloud and offers more security.

The challenge with encrypted file systems on servers lies in how you manage the decryption password. A given server needs your decryption password before it can mount any given encrypted file system. The most common approach to this problem is to store the password on an unencrypted root file system. Because the objective of file system encryption is to protect against physical access to the disk image, the storage of the password on a separate, unencrypted file system is not as problematic as it might appear on the face of it but it's still problematic.

In the cloud, you don't have to store the decryption password in the cloud. Instead, you can provide the decryption password to your new virtual instance when you start it up. The server can then grab the encryption key out of the server's startup parameters and subsequently mount any ephemeral or block devices using an encrypted file system.

You can add an extra layer of security into the mix by encrypting the password and storing the key for decrypting the password in the machine image. Figure 10-12 illustrates the process of starting up a virtual server that mounts an encrypted file system using an encrypted password.

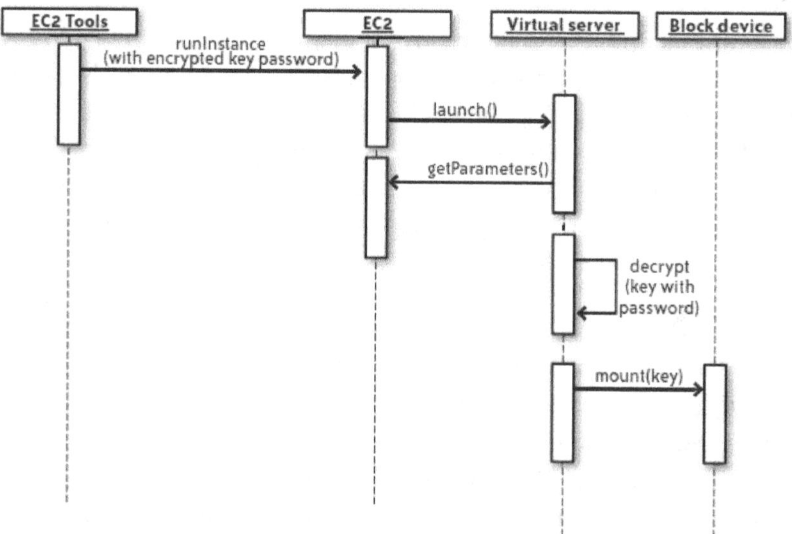

Figure. 10.11 The process of starting a virtual server with encrypted file systems

Regulatory and Standards Compliance

Most problems with regulatory and standards compliance lie not with the cloud, but in the fact that the regulations and standards written for Internet applications predate the acceptance of virtualization technologies. In other words, chances are you can meet the spirit of any particular specification, but you may not be able to meet the letter of the specification.

For example, if your target standard requires certain data to be stored on a different server than other system logic, can a virtualized server ever meet that requirement? I would certainly argue that it should be able to meet that requirement, but the interpretation as to whether it does may be left up to lawyers, judges, or other non-technologists who don't appreciate the nature of virtualization. It does not help that some regulations such as Sarbanes-Oxley (SOX) do not really provide any specific information security requirements, and seem to exist mostly for consultants to make a buck spreading fear among top-level management.

From a security perspective, you'll encounter three kinds of issues in standards and regulations:

"How" issues

These result from a standard such as PCI or regulations such as HIPAA or SOX, which govern how an application of a specific type should operate in order to protect certain concerns specific to its problem domain. For example, HIPAA defines how you should handle personally identifying health care data.

"Where" issues

These result from a directive such as Directive 95/46/EC that governs where you can store certain information. One key impact of this particular directive is that the private data on EU citizens may not be stored in the United States (or any other country that does not treat private data in the same way as the EU).

"What" issues

These result from standards prescribing very specific components to your infrastructure. For example, PCI prescribes the use of antivirus software on all servers processing credit card data.

The bottom line today is that a cloud-deployed system may or may not be able to meet the letter of the law for any given specification. For certain specifications, you may be able to meet the letter of the specification by implementing a mixed architecture that includes some physical elements and some virtual elements. Cloud infrastructures that specialize in hybrid solutions may ultimately be a better solution. Alternatively, it may make sense to look at vendors who provide as a service the part of your system that has specific regulatory needs. For example, you can use an e-commerce vendor to handle the e-commerce part of your website and manage the PCI compliance issues.

In a mixed environment, you don't host any sensitive data in the cloud. Instead, you offload processing onto privacy servers in a physical data center in which the hosts are entirely under your control. For example, you might have a credit card processing server at your managed services provider accepting requests from the cloud to save credit card numbers or charge specific cards.

With respect to "where" data is stored, Amazon provides S3 storage in the EU. Through the Amazon cloud and S3 data storage, you do have the ability to achieve Directive 95/46/EC compliance with respect to storing data in the EU without building out a data center located in the EU.

10.9   NETWORK SECURITY

Amazon's cloud has no perimeter. Instead, EC2 provides security groups that define firewall like traffic rules governing what traffic can reach virtual servers in that group. Although I often speak of security groups as if they were virtual network segments protected by a firewall, they most definitely are not virtual network segments, due to the following:

- Two servers in two different Amazon EC2 availability zones can operate in the same security group.

- A server may belong to more than one security group.

- Servers in the same security group may not be able to talk to each other at all.

- Servers in the same network segment may not share any IP characteristics they may even be in different class address spaces.

- No server in EC2 can see the network traffic bound for other servers (this is not necessarily true for other cloud systems). If you try placing your virtual Linux server in promiscuous mode, the only network traffic you will see is traffic originating from or destined for your server.

Firewall Rules

Typically, a firewall protects the perimeter of one or more network segments. Figure 10.13 illustrates how a firewall protects the perimeter.

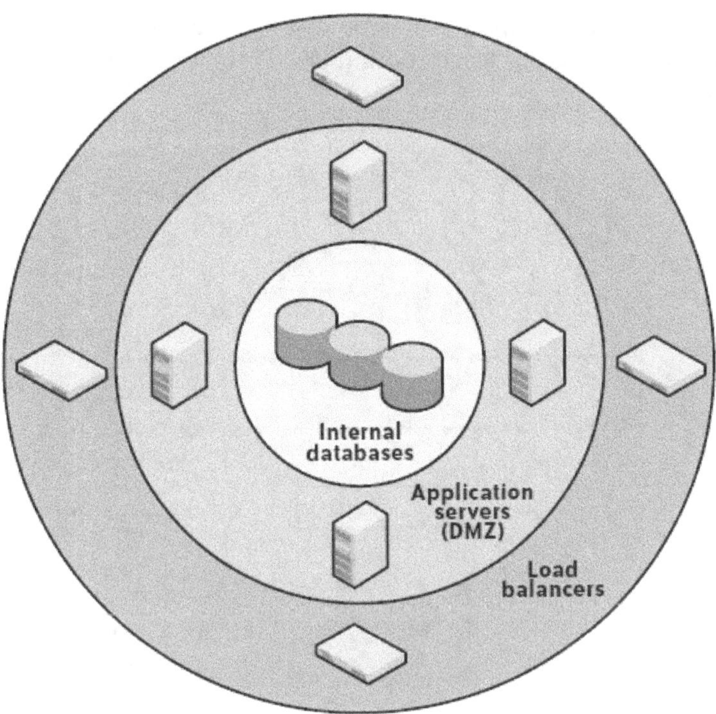

Figure 10.12 Firewalls are the primary tool in perimeter security

A main firewall protects the outermost perimeter, allowing in only HTTP, HTTPS, and (sometimes) FTP traffic. Within that network segment are border systems, such as load balancers, that route traffic into a DMZ protected by another firewall. Finally, within the DMZ are application servers that make database and other requests across a third firewall into protected systems on a highly sensitive internal network.

This structure requires you to move through several layers – or perimeters – of network protection in the form of firewalls to gain access to increasingly sensitive data. The perimeter architecture's chief advantage is that a poorly structured firewall rule on the inner perimeter does not accidentally expose the internal network to the Internet unless the DMZ is already compromised. In addition, outer layer services tend to be more hardened against Internet vulnerabilities, whereas interior services tend to be less Internet-aware. The weakness of this infrastructure is that a compromise of any individual server inside any given segment provides full access to all servers in that network segment.

Figure 10.14 provides a visual look at how the concept of a firewall rule in the Amazon cloud is different from that in a traditional data center.

Each virtual server occupies the same level in the network, with its traffic managed through a security group definition. There are no network segments, and there is no perimeter.

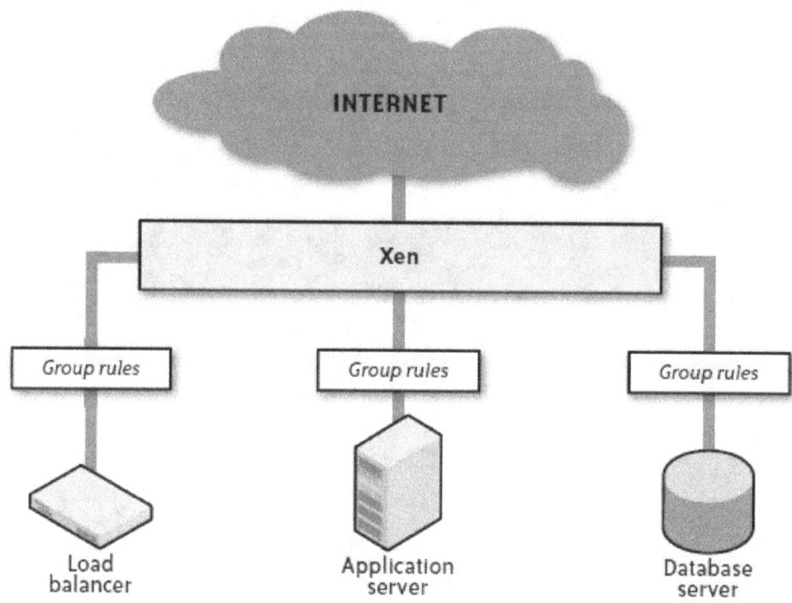

Figure 10.13 There are no network segments or perimeters in the cloud

Membership in the same group does not provide any privileged access to other servers in that security group, unless you define rules that provide privileged access. Finally, an individual server can be a member of multiple security groups. The rules for a given server are simply the union of the rules assigned to all groups of which the server is a member.

You can set up security groups to help you mimic traditional perimeter security. For example, you can create the following:

- A border security group that listens to all traffic on ports 80 and 443

- A DMZ security group that listens to traffic from the border group on ports 80 and 443

- An internal security group that listens to traffic on port 3306 from the DMZ security group

As with traditional perimeter security, access to the servers in your internal security group requires first compromising the outer group, then the DMZ, and then finally one of the internal servers. Unlike traditional perimeter security, there is the possibility for you to accidentally grant global access into the internal zone and thus expose the zone. However, an intruder who compromises a single server within any given zone gains no ability to reach any other server in that zone except through leveraging the original exploit. In other words, access to the zone itself does not necessarily provide access to the other servers in that zone.

The Amazon approach also enables functionality that used to be out of the question in a traditional infrastructure. For example, you can more easily provide for direct SSH access into each virtual server in your cloud infrastructure from your corporate IT network without relying on a VPN. You still have the security advantages of a traditional perimeter approach when it comes to the open Internet, but you can get quick access to your servers to manage them from critical locations.

Two other advantages of this security architecture are the following:

- Because you control your firewall rules remotely, an intruder does not have a single target to attack, as he does with a physical firewall.

- You don't have the opportunity to accidentally destroy your network rules and thus permanently remove everyone's access to a given network segment.

You recommend the approach of mimicking traditional perimeter security because it is a well understood approach to managing network traffic and it works. If you take that approach, it's important to understand that you are creating physical counterparts to the network segments of a traditional setup. You don't really have the layers of network security that come with a traditional configuration.

A few best practices for your network security include:

Run only one network service (plus necessary administrative services) on each virtual server

Every network service on a system presents an attack vector. When you stick multiple services on a server, you create multiple attack vectors for accessing the data on that server or leveraging that server's network access rights.

Do not open up direct access to your most sensitive data

If getting access to your customer database requires compromising a load balancer, an application server, and a database server (and you're running only one service per server), an attacker needs to exploit three different attack vectors before he can get to that data.

Open only the ports absolutely necessary to support a server's service and nothing more

Of course your server should be hardened so it is running only the one service you intend to run on it. But sometimes you inadvertently end up with services running that you did not intend, or there is a nonroot exploit in the service you are running that enables an attacker to start up another service with a root exploit. By blocking access to everything except your intended service, you prevent these kinds of exploits.

Limit access to your services to clients who need to access them

Your load balancers naturally need to open the web ports 80 and 443 to all traffic. Those two protocols and that particular server, however, are the only situations that require open access. For every other service, traffic should be limited to specific source addresses or security groups.

Even if you are not doing load balancing, use a reverse proxy

A reverse proxy is a web server such as Apache that proxies traffic from a client to a server. By using a proxy server, you make it much harder to attack your infrastructure. First of all, Apache and IIS are much more battle-hardened than any of the application server options you will be using. As a result, an exploit is both less likely and almost certain to be patched more quickly. Second, an exploit of a proxy provides an attacker with access to nothing at all. They must subsequently find an additional vulnerability in your application server itself.

Use the dynamic nature of the cloud to automate your security embarrassments

Admit it. You have opened up ports in your firewall to accomplish some critical business task even though you know better. Perhaps you opened an FTP port to a web server because some client absolutely had to use anonymous FTP for their batch file uploads. Instead of leaving that port open 24/7, you could open the port only for the batch window and then shut it down. You could even bring up a temporary server to act as the FTP server for the batch window, process the file, and then shut down the server.

The recommendations in the preceding list are not novel; they are standard security precautions. The cloud makes them relatively easy to implement, and they are important to your security there.

Network Intrusion Detection

Perimeter security often involves network intrusion detection systems (NIDS), such as Snort, which monitor local traffic for anything that looks irregular. Examples of irregular traffic include:

- Port scans

- Denial-of-service attacks
- Known vulnerability exploit attempts

You perform network intrusion detection either by routing all traffic through a system that analyzes it or by doing passive monitoring from one box on local traffic on your network. In the Amazon cloud, only the former is possible; the latter is meaningless since an EC2 instance can see only its own traffic.

The purpose of a network intrusion detection system

Network intrusion detection exists to alert you of attacks before they happen and, in some cases, foil attacks as they happen. Because of the way the Amazon cloud is set up, however, many of the things you look for in a NIDS are meaningless. For example, a NIDS typically alerts you to port scans as evidence of a precursor to a potential future attack. In the Amazon cloud, however, you are not likely to notice a port scan because your NIDS will be aware only of requests coming in on the ports allowed by your security group rules. All other traffic will be invisible to the NIDS and thus are not likely to be perceived as a port scan.

As with port scans, Amazon network intrusion systems are actively looking for denial-of-service attacks and would likely identify any such attempts long before your own intrusion detection software.

One place in which an additional network intrusion detection system is useful is its ability to detect malicious payloads coming into your network. When the NIDS sees traffic that contains malicious payload, it can either block the traffic or send out an alert that enables you to react.

Even if the payload is delivered and compromises a server, you should be able to respond quickly and contain the damage.

Implementing network intrusion detection in the cloud

As I mentioned in the previous section, you simply cannot implement a network intrusion detection system in the Amazon cloud (or any other cloud that does not expose LAN traffic) that passively listens to local network traffic. Instead, you must run the NIDS on your load balancer or on each server in your infrastructure. There are advantages and disadvantages to each approach, but I am not generally a fan of NIDS in the cloud unless required by a standard or regulation.

The simplest approach is to have a dedicated NIDS server in front of the network as a whole that watches all incoming traffic and acts accordingly. Figure 10.15 illustrates this architecture.

Because the only software running on the load balancer is the NIDS software and Apache, it maintains a very low attack profile. Compromising the NIDS server requires a vulnerability in the NIDS software or Apache – assuming the rest of the system is properly hardened and no actual services are listening to any other ports open to the Web as a whole.

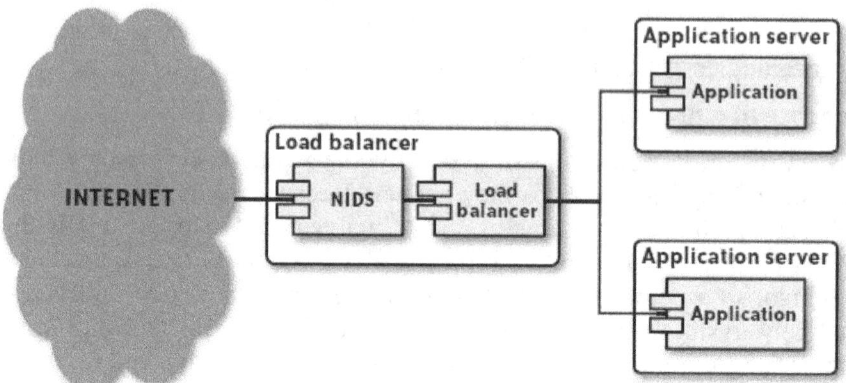

Figure 10.14 A network intrusion detection system listening on a load balancer

The load balancer approach creates a single point of failure for your network intrusion detection system because, in general, the load balancer is the most exposed component in your infrastructure. By finding a way to compromise your load balancer, the intruder not only takes control of the load balancer, but also has the ability to silence detection of further attacks against your cloud environment.

You can alternately implement intrusion detection on a server behind the load balancer that acts as an intermediate point between the load balancer and the rest of the system. This design is generally superior to the previously described design, except that it leaves the load balancer exposed (only traffic passed by the load balancer is examined) and reduces the overall availability of the system.

Another approach is to implement network intrusion detection on each server in the network. This approach creates a very slight increase in the attack profile of the system as a whole because you end up with common software on all servers. A vulnerability in your NIDS would result in a vulnerability on each server in your cloud architecture. On a positive note, you make it much more difficult for an intruder to hide his footprints.

Unlike a traditional infrastructure, there just is no meaningful way for a NIDS to serve its purpose. You simply cannot devise any NIDS architecture that will give your NIDS visibility to all traffic attempting to reach your instances. The best you can do is creating an implementation in which the NIDS is deployed on each server in your infrastructure with visibility to the traffic that

Amazon allows into the security group in which the instance is deployed. You would see minimally valid proactive alerting, and the main benefit would be protection against malicious payloads. But, if you are encrypting all your traffic, even that benefit is minimal. On the other hand, the presence of a NIDS will greatly reduce the performance of those servers and create a single attack vector for all hosts in your infrastructure.

10.10   HOST SECURITY

Host security describes how your server is set up for the following tasks:

- Preventing attacks.
- Minimizing the impact of a successful attack on the overall system.
- Responding to attacks when they occur.

It always helps to have software with no security holes. Good luck with that! In the real world, the best approach for preventing attacks is to assume your software has security holes. Each service you run on a host presents a distinct attack vector into the host. The more attack vectors, the more likely an attacker will find one with a security exploit. You must therefore minimize the different kinds of software running on a server.

Given the assumption that your services are vulnerable, your most significant tool in preventing attackers from exploiting a vulnerability once it becomes known is the rapid rollout of security patches. Here's where the dynamic nature of the cloud really alters what you can do from a security perspective. In a traditional data center, rolling out security patches across an entire infrastructure is time-consuming and risky. In the cloud, rolling out a patch across the infrastructure takes three simple steps:

- Patch your AMI with the new security fixes.
- Test the results.
- Relaunch your virtual servers.

Here a tool such as enStratus or RightScale for managing your infrastructure becomes absolutely critical. If you have to manually perform these three steps, the cloud can become a horrible maintenance headache. Management tools, however, can automatically roll out the security fixes and minimize human involvement, downtime, and the potential for human-error-induced downtime.

System Hardening

Prevention begins when you set up your machine image. As you get going, you will experiment with different configurations and constantly rebuild images. Once you have found a configuration that works for a particular service profile, you should harden the system before creating your image.

Server hardening is the process of disabling or removing unnecessary services and eliminating unimportant user accounts. Tools such as Bastille Linux can make the process of hardening your machine images much more efficient. Once you install Bastille Linux, you execute the interactive scripts that ask you questions about your server. It then proceeds to disable services and accounts. In particular, it makes sure that your hardened system meets the following criteria:

- No network services are running except those necessary to support the server's function.

- No user accounts are enabled on the server except those necessary to support the services running on the server or to provide access for users who need it.

- All configuration files for common server software are configured to the most secure settings.

- All necessary services run under a nonprivileged role user account (e.g., run MySQL as the mysql user, not root).

- When possible, run services in a restricted filesystem, such as a chroot jail.

Before bundling your machine image, you should remove all interactive user accounts and passwords stored in configuration files. Although the machine image will be stored in an encrypted format, Amazon holds the encryption keys and thus can be compelled to provide a third party with access through a court subpoena.

Antivirus Protection

Some regulations and standards require the implementation of an antivirus (AV) system on your servers. It's definitely a controversial issue, since an AV system with an exploit is itself an attack vector and, on some operating systems, the percentage of AV exploits to known viruses is relatively high.

Personally, I have mixed feelings about AV systems. They are definitely necessary in some circumstances, but a risk in others. For example, if you are accepting the upload of photos or other files that could be used to deliver viruses that are then served to the public, you have an obligation to use some kind of antivirus software in order to protect your site from becoming a mechanism for spreading the virus.

Unfortunately, not all AV systems are created equally. Some are written better than others, and some protect you much better than others. Finally, some servers simply don't have an operational profile that makes viruses, worms, and trojans viable attack vectors. I am therefore bothered by standards, regulations, and requirements that demand blanket AV coverage.

When looking at the AV question, you first should understand what your requirements are. If you are required to implement AV, then you should definitely do it. Look for two critical features in your AV software:

How wide is the protection it provides? In other words, what percentage of known exploits does it cover?

What is the median delta between the time when a virus is released into the wild and the time your AV product of choice provides protection against it?

Once you have selected an AV vendor and implemented it on your servers, you absolutely must keep your signatures up to date. You are probably better off with no AV system than one with outdated versions or protections.

Host Intrusion Detection

Whereas a network intrusion detection system monitors network traffic for suspicious activity, a host intrusion detection system (HIDS) such as OSSEC monitors the state of your server for anything unusual. An HIDS is in some ways similar to an AV system, except it examines the system for all signs of compromise and notifies you when any core operating system or service file changes.

In my Linux deployments, I use OSSEC (http://www.ossec.net) for host-based intrusion detection. OSSEC has two configuration profiles:

- Standalone, in which each server scans itself and sends you alerts.
- Centralized, in which you create a centralized HIDS server to which each of the other servers sends reports.

In the cloud, you should always opt for the centralized configuration. It centralizes your rules and analysis so that it is much easier to keep your HIDS infrastructure up to date. Furthermore, it enables you to craft a higher security profile for your HIDS processing than the individual services might allow for. Figure 10.16 illustrates a cloud network using centralized HIDS.

As with an AV solution, you must keep your HIDS servers up to date constantly, but you do not need to update your individual servers as often.

The downside of an HIDS is that it requires CPU power to operate, and thus can eat up resources on your server. By going with a centralized deployment model, however, you can push a lot of that processing onto a specialized intrusion detection server.

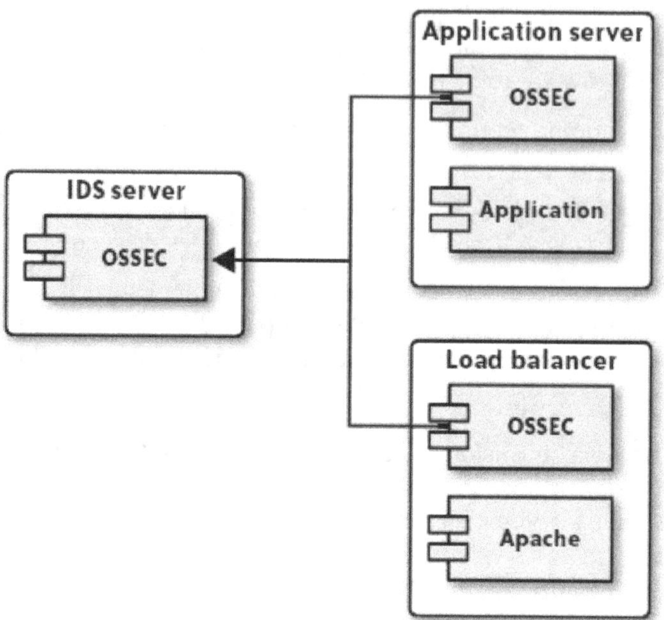

Figure 10.15 A HIDS infrastructure reporting to a centralized server

Data Segmentation

In addition to assuming that the services on your servers have security exploits, you should further assume that eventually one of them will be compromised. Obviously, you never want any server to be compromised. The best infrastructure, however, is tolerant of in fact, it assumes the compromise of any individual node. This tolerance is not meant to encourage lax security for individual servers, but is meant to minimize the impact of the compromise of specific nodes. Making this assumption provides you with a system that has the following advantages:

- Access to your most sensitive data requires a full system breach.

- The compromise of the entire system requires multiple attack vectors with potentially different skill sets.

- The downtime associated with the compromise of an individual node is negligible or nonexistent.

The segmentation of data based on differing levels of sensitivity is your first tool in minimizing the impact of a successful attack. For example, an attacker who accesses your customer database has found some important information, but that attacker still lacks access to the credit card data. To be able to access credit card data, decrypt it, and associate it with a specific individual, the attacker must compromise both the e-commerce application server and the credit card processor.

Here again the approach of one server/one service helps out. Because each type of server in the chain offers a different attack vector, an attacker will need to exploit multiple attack vectors to compromise the system as a whole.

Credential Management

Your machine images OSSEC profile should have no user accounts embedded in them. In fact, you should never allow password-based shell access to your virtual servers. The most secure approach to providing access to virtual servers is the dynamic delivery of public SSH keys to target servers. In other words, if someone needs access to a server, you should provide her credentials to the server when it starts up or via an administrative interface instead of embedding that information in the machine image.

Of course, it is perfectly secure to embed public SSH keys in a machine image, and it makes life a lot easier. Unfortunately, it makes it harder to build the general-purpose machine images I described in Chapter 4. Specifically, if you embed the public key credentials in a machine image, the user behind those credentials will have access to every machine built on that image.

To remove her access or add access for another individual, you subsequently have to build a new machine image reflecting the changed dynamics.

Therefore, you should keep things simple and maintainable by passing in user credentials as part of the process of launching your virtual server. At boot time, the virtual server has access to all of the parameters you pass in and can thus set up user accounts for each user you specify.

It's simple because it requires no tools other than those that Amazon already provides. On the other hand, adding and removing access after the system boots up becomes a manual task.

Another approach is to use existing cloud infrastructure management tools or build your own that enable you to store user credentials outside the cloud and dynamically add and remove users to your cloud servers at runtime. This approach, however, requires an administrative service running on each host and thus represents an extra attack vector against your server.

10.11 COMPROMISE RESPONSE

Because you should be running an intrusion detection system, you should know very quickly if and when an actual compromise occurs. If you respond rapidly, you can take advantage of the cloud to eliminate exploit-based downtime in your infrastructure.

When you detect a compromise on a physical server, the standard operating procedure is a painful, manual process:

- Remove intruder access to the system, typically by cutting the server off from the rest of the network.

- Identify the attack vector. You don't want to simply shut down and start over, because the vulnerability in question could be on any number of servers. Furthermore, the intruder very likely left a root-kit or other software to permit a renewed intrusion after you remove the original problem that let him in. It is therefore critical to identify how the intruder compromised the system, if that compromise gave him the ability to compromise other systems, and if other systems have the same vulnerability.

- Wipe the server clean and start over. This step includes patching the original vulnerability and rebuilding the system from the most recent uncompromised backup.

- Launch the server back into service and repeat the process for any server that has the same attack vector.

This process is very labor intensive and can take a long time. In the cloud, the response is much simpler.

First of all, the forensic element can happen after you are operating. You simply copy the root file system over to one of your block volumes, snapshot your block volumes, shut the server down, and bring up a replacement.

Once the replacement is up (still certainly suffering from the underlying vulnerability, but at least currently uncompromised), you can bring up a server in a dedicated security group that mounts the compromised volumes. Because this server has a different root file system and no services running on it, it is not compromised. You nevertheless have full access to the underlying compromised data, so you can identify the attack vector.

With the attack vector identified, you can apply patches to the machine images. Once the machine images are patched, simply relaunch all your instances. The end result is a quicker response to a vulnerability with little (if any) downtime.

Bit Questions

1. ------------------ Point in time to which applications data must be recovered to resume business transactions.

    (a)   Recovery Point Objective   (b)   Recovery Object Point

    (c)   Recovery Time Objective   (d)   all the above

2.   -------------- Maximum elapsed time allowed before lack of business function severely impacts an organization.

   (a)   Recovery Point Objective   (b)   Recovery Point Objective

   (c)   Recovery Time Objective   (d)   all the above

3.   The purpose of backup is:

   (a)   To restore a computer to an operational state following a disaster

   (b)   To restore small numbers of files after they have been accidentally deleted

   (c)   Is to free space in the primary storage

   (d)   None of the above

4.   Which of the following qualifies as best DR (Disaster Recovery) site?

   (a)   DR site in the same campus

   (b)   DR site in the same city

   (c)   DR site in the same country

   (d)   DR site in a different country

5.   To decide on a backup strategy for your organization, which of the following should you consider?

   (a)   RPO (Recovery Point Objective)

   (b)   RTO (Recovery Time Objective)

   (c)   Both RPO & RTO

   (d)   None of the above

6.   Which of the following can be used for reducing recovery time?

   (a)   Automatic failover

   (b)   By taking backup on a faster device

   (c)   Taking multiple backups – one in same location, another at different location

   (d)   All the above

7.   Which of the following is Backup software?

   (a)   Amanda   (b)   Bacula

   (c)   IBM Tivoli Storage Manager   (d)   All the above

8. A Hot Site is a term used in disaster recovery to describe a location that an organisation can move to after a disaster occurs. However, what does a Hot Site actually equate to?

    (a) A location that can resume some essential operations but obviously not all

    (b) None of these

    (c) A location that does not have the capacity to resume all operations but has the potential to give enough time

    (d) A location fully equipped to resume operations

9. Backing up data is a vital part of any disaster recovery plan. Which of the following is the best choice for storing the back media?

    (a) Store the data on-site but in a secure location

    (b) Store the data off-site

    (c) None of these

    (d) Store the data in any location, the tapes are encrypted

10. It is always hard to tell how your Disaster Recovery Plan will hold up in the event of disaster. This is especially true for newly created plans that have just been drawn up. Which of the following is a good step after creating your plan?

    (a) Set off a small fire in the office Load

    (b) Testing

    (c) Benchmarking

    (d) Simulation Testing

11. In the traditional data center, each application is tied to a

    (a) Logical server   (b) physical server

    (c) both A & B   (d) none of the above

12. The cloud center is used in -------------- delivery model.

    (a) Private   (b) public

    (c) On-demand   (d) all the above

13. -------------- is a component of a disaster recovery plan that involves maintaining copies of enterprise data in a cloud storage environment as a security measure.

    (a) Cloud disaster recovery   (b) Cloud Data center

    (c) Cloud center   (d) all the above

Exercises

1. What is Disaster Recovery? Explain different Disasters in the Cloud.

2. Explain about Disaster Recovery Planning.

3. Describe about Cloud Disaster Management.

4. Discuss about Web Application Design and Machine Image Design.

5. Discuss about Privacy Design and Compromise Response in cloud.

6. Describe Database Management in cloud

7. What is the need of data security in cloud? Explain.

8. Discuss about host security and network security in cloud.

ANSWERS

Chapter - 1

Bit Answers

1.	Distributed system	2.	Distributed computing
3.	Distributed computing	4.	Parallel computing
5.	Contention	6.	Multiprocessing
7.	Vectors	8.	Massive parallel processing
9.	Cluster	10.	Cluster
11.	High-performance	12.	Virtualization
13.	Platform virtualization.	14	(b)

Chapter - 2

Bit Answers

1.	Decentralizing	2.	User-centric, task-centric, programmable.
3.	Centralized	4.	Grid computing
5.	Cloud	6.	Utility computing
7.	(d) 8. (d)	9.	(c) 10. (a)
11.	(c) 12. (d)	13.	(d) 14. (c)
15.	(b) 16. (d)	17.	(c)

Chapter - 3

Bit Answers

1. Communication-as-a-Service
2. CaaS
3. Infrastructure-as-a-Service
4. Software-as-a-Service
5. Platforms-as-a-Service
6. Amazon Web Services
7. CaaS
8. Iaas
9. Amazon EC2
10. Pure virtualization
11. Cloud infrastructures
12. (a)
13. (d)
14. (a)
15. (d)

Chapter - 4

Bit Answers

1. Pay as you go
2. Free-standing, independent components, Combined by loose coupling
3. Security-as-a-Service
4. ping, power, and pipe
5. Remote network, desktop and security monitoring, incident response, patch management, and remote data backup
6. Data center virtualization
7. Message-level security, Security-as-a-Service, declarative and policy-based security
8. Security-as-a-Service

Chapter - 5

Bit Answers

1. Virtualization
2. Virtual machine monitor (VMM)
3. (b)
4.
5. (a)

Chapter - 6

Bit Answers

1. (d)   2. (d)   3. (a)

Chapter - 7

Bit Answers

1. OCC

2. Distributed Management Task Force

3. Improves your user experience with streamlined installations, Offers customers virtualization platform independence and flexibility, Creates complex pre-configured multi-tiered services more easily, efficiently delivers enterprise software through portable virtual machines.

4. Asynchronous JavaScript and XML

5. JSON

6. JSON, serialization

7. **Linux**, **Apache**, **MySQL**, and **PHP**

8. Linux, Apache, PostgreSql, and PHP

9. HTTP

10. SAML

11. SOAP

12. DMTF

13. Portability   14. (a)   15. (c)

16. (a)   17. (a)   18. (a)

Chapter - 8

Bit Answers

1. Zimbra   2. Facebook

3. WS-Security   4. Google AJAX

5. SharePoint   6. (d)

Chapter - 9

Bit Answers

1. (a)	2. (b)	3. (c)	4. (d)
5. (d)	6. (c)	7. (d)	8. (b)
9. (a)	10. (a)	11. (b)	

Chapter - 10

Bit Answers

1. (a)	2. (c)	3. (a) (b)	4. (d)
5. (c)	6. (d)	7. (d)	8. (d)
9. (b)	10. (d)	11. (b)	12. (c)
13. (a)			